CREATIVE

RHYTHMIC MOVEMENT

FOR CHILDREN

CREATIVE

RHYTHMIC MOVEMENT

FOR CHILDREN

Gladys Andrews, Ed.D.

Physical Education and Recreation
School of Education
New York University

PRENTICE-HALL, INC.
Englewood Cliffs

Library of Congress

Catalog Card No. : 54-8742

First printing .... May , 1954
Second printing............. August , 1955
Third printing............... June , 1956
Fourth printing .... October , 1958
Fifth printing............. January , 1961
Sixth printing .... September , 1961

19113-C

Foreword

This book adds new strength and vigor to understanding the origin and benefits of creativity. The author, a creative person, has concentrated upon one aspect of creative living—movement as a form of expression. She has skillfully and painstakingly shown that conditions necessary for experiencing creativity in this area are deeply similar to those conditions through which creativity in all areas of living advances. She recognizes that creative potentialities reside in all of us; that, in fact, to be human is to possess the possibility to live creatively.

How strikingly in contrast are the author's suggestions to those of an earlier day in education! Now the teacher plays a supportive and guiding role in helping children work toward a solution to their own problems. The children are encouraged to create, through patterns of movement and dance, their ways of doing, rather than to imitate set patterns. At all stages of the development of creative ideas, the author stresses ways of assisting children in thinking for themselves.

Both parents and teachers will benefit greatly by this book. The author has written it in full knowledge that optimum conditions for working do not always exist. She has in mind the hundreds, yes the thousands, of teachers—classroom, physical education, art, music, and other specialists—who have no spacious gymnasiums or rooms in which to work. Many of the interrelated activities (of movement with art, music, language) suggested here can be attempted, and have been attempted, in the limited space available in schools, homes, camps, and hospitals.

Throughout the book there is evidence that the procedures suggested are carefully related to the knowledge of human growth and development. A high level of integration between this body of knowledge and the practical curriculum suggestions is the result of actual experiences with boys and girls in many different kinds of situations. In addition, the material has been successfully applied with groups of children and adults in elementary and high schools, colleges, and other places.

I am glad to pay my tribute to a book that throws additional light upon the nature of creativity, and especially to one that offers practical help in better understanding children and the experiences that children and adults can explore together.

BEATRICE HURLEY
Elementary Education
School of Education
New York University

Preface

Creative Rhythmic Movement for Children is about children's and teachers' learning and sharing together through movement experiences. What children are like is the basis of this book. Because children are what they are, they need the kinds of experiences that are reported, analyzed, explored, and suggested herein.

The book has been written with the firm conviction that, though children differ, they are creative, and that for them movement is a natural and vital means of expression. It has been prepared for all those who are seeking better ways of understanding and working with children.

The author is grateful to the hundreds of children, in this and other countries, whose zest for movement and creative spirit and desire for expression have given purpose, direction, and substance to this work; and also to the children's teachers, who have contributed their time, suggestions, and enthusiasm.

Particular acknowledgment is made to Professors Beatrice Hurley and Leonard Larson and Dean Francis Rosecrance, School of Education, New York University, for their confidence, unselfish guidance, and criticism of the doctoral study upon which the major portion of this book is based; and also to Professors Isabel Crane, Western Michigan College of Education, and Margaret H'Doubler and Katherine Cronin, University of Wisconsin, for their inspiration in the formative stage and their assistance with the master's thesis that served as the original idea for this work.

Due recognition is extended to Marion Bozenhard Youngblood, for her cooperation and partnership as exemplified in writing the joint master's thesis; to Florence Burns, University of Wisconsin, Nina Coffing Cole, formerly of the University of Illinois, and Joyce Eldridge, New York University, for their assistance in adapting, composing, accompanying, and recording music as it spontaneously developed; to Meridan Richter Mies, formerly of the University of Illinois, for the appreciation of movement that she expressed in the sketches of children in action; and to the Summer Laboratory School of the University of Wisconsin, the Colonel Wolfe School, Champaign, Illinois, and the Bronxville Public School, Bronxville, New York, for the use of some photographs taken while classes were in progress.

The author also wishes to express sincere appreciation to Virginia Dennis, Jeannette Saurborn, and Jeanne Van Dusen, whose generous gift of their time, patience, circumspection, and encouragement was motivated by a happy combination of friendship and love of children; to Lloyd Appleton and Milton Gabrielson for their willingness to share their hobby of photography, and for their kindness and perseverence in trying to "catch" children in action while in regular class situations; and to Nancy Martin and Robert N. Harrington, of Prentice-Hall, Inc., for their artistic and editorial assistance.

For permission to reprint copyrighted material, acknowledgment is made to the following: Alfred A. Knopf, Inc.; The Macmillan Company; John Day Publishing Company; Brown & Williamson Tobacco Corporation; and Colgate-Palmolive Company.

G. A.

Table of Contents

CREATIVE

RHYTHMIC MOVEMENT

FOR CHILDREN

The nimble foot, the hankering hand,
The itching mind, the yearning heart,
The vibrant voice, the scintillating eye,
The creative spirit—*the child*

— Gladys Andrews

1. *The Child*

Educational emphasis today is centered about the child, and HIS world. Modern education has been increasingly concerned with his needs, personality, talents, powers of thinking and expression, and his desire to get along with himself and others. This concept is in rather sharp contrast with an earlier one, which regarded the child as a receptacle for knowledge and skills gathered from the past!

It is with this newer concept in mind that the writer presents this volume on Creative Rhythmic Movement—its place and function in the school program of today. Creative expression is a vital part of every child's life. The desire for expression through movement is especially strong in the child, to whom large, free movements are natural outlets for thinking and feeling. The inherent need of the child to *move*—to express himself through movement—demands the thoughtful attention and understanding of those concerned with elementary education. A stimulating environment, a wide variety of opportunities, and constant encouragement are essential requisites to the healthy and normal growth of every child.

Until quite recently there was little research in the field of child development. Before 1900 there were occasional studies concerned with measurements of growth; these were focused upon increments in size, primarily height and weight. Observations on the behavior of children were rare and were usually based on diary notes of infants.

The first studies of mental growth appeared in 1908. These early IQ (intelligence quotient) studies revealed little concerning the total development of children. In 1920 the relationships between physical and mental development of children began to be understood and applied to methods of education.

The White House Conference of 1932-1933 summarized the current knowledge and status of research in the area of child development and suggested the need for more searching studies. Since that time projects in various aspects of child development have flourished, and the literature has become voluminous.

The research in child development has come a long way from just thinking of the child in terms of the *physical*. Today, even though the emphasis in research may be primarily anatomical, physiological, and psychological in nature, it is evident that there is a great deal of overlapping in investigations, findings, collection of data, and reporting. Practical research workers, teachers and parents who have worked with children have come to realize the complexities, intricacies, and interrelatedness of various individual aspects of growth. The child cannot be studied in parts; modern emphasis is upon the child as a whole.

This book is an interpretation of what is known about children and how they develop, and comprises the basis for the creative rhythmic program which follows.

CHILDREN ARE PEOPLE

Competent teachers must know and understand children. They must know why they act the way they do, and why individual differences among children are so important in the educative process. There are many ways of thinking about children which are essential to understanding them as people. Children cannot be thought of as a number of separate entities; bodies to be nourished and kept in repair; minds with brains to be kept active and alert; or bundles of emotions to be kept from exploding. From the time he is born, the child has a body, mind, and emotions which are interrelated and interactive. Anything happening to one part affects the whole. Determination of childish reactions and how he is going to behave, develop, and make use of his potentialities is an intriguing problem. Impinging upon these endowed potentialities are the multitudinous factors of environment. A friendly, cooperative, and sympathetic environment will determine, to a large degree, how well the child makes use of his potentialities.

Arranging activities and sharing experiences with children require an understanding of how they get along with themselves and others. What are the known factors which will help teachers better understand children? Are there certain recognizable aspects of growth? Will an understanding of the meaning of growth, and how it is expressed by children, establish a happier and more effective relationship between adults and children? These are basic questions which will be discussed in this volume.

No two children are exactly alike; they differ in looks, in response to stimuli, and in their laughter. Despite these important individual differences, they are all children; they grow, talk, react, and progress through marked stages of development. All children follow a general basic growth pattern, but at their *own individual rates.* No two children are likely to arrive at the same growth stage, at the same time, or in identically the same way.[1] It is important, then, that teachers recognize these stages of growth, and realize

[1] In fact, variety (variation of maturation) can be witnessed within any given age group.

that one stage does not suddenly terminate, and the next begin. Children of any given chronological age will express varying levels of maturity and various stages of growth.

Children crave to belong to a social group. They constantly seek approval from others. They crave love and affection and a chance to display their feelings. They are eager to establish their worth through accomplishment. They are extremely curious about their surroundings. They have a desire to know how and why, and an urge to be active, to do something about a discovery. Childhood is characterized by an enormous zest for activity and phenomenal energy. *This knowledge, about children, is the basis for creative expression through rhythmic movement.*

Early childhood

EARLY CHILDHOOD—"I" PERIOD

Children in this group are generally in grades one through three. They range normally from age six through eight. This is the "I" period; an age in which the child generally thinks he is the center of the universe. It is commonly referred to as the "egotistical" period, and the most striking characteristics are exemplified by such outbursts as: "I did this." "See what I did." "Look at me." "When I grow up, I am going to be a. . . ." "I want to. . . ." It is an age of constant chatter and self-expression; an age which demands a stage and an audience for the star performer! It is likewise the time of the "toothless wonder"—the period during which permanent teeth make their appearance.

During early childhood, physical growth is relatively slow. Sometimes there is a marked lengthening of arms and legs. While all parts of the body continue to grow, the increment of change is slow. Essentially it is a period of slow, steady growth.

Healthy children of this age are in constant motion and find it almost impossible to stand or sit still. They bounce when they sit, run instead of walk, scuffle their feet, and jitter from one foot to the other. This zest for activity expresses itself not only in rhythms and games, but in all kinds of complex skills and random locomotor movements. They are constantly jumping puddles, climbing over and under everything, tugging, pushing, squeezing, hunching their shoulders, and slapping their heads. They love to move because it is fun. It is the time when motor abilities flourish.

No two children possess these aspects of growth in equal amount or reach any stage of development at exactly the same time. Variation of maturation is always evident in any given age group, in any classroom, and even in families.

Activity Is All Important. This period is in some respects unpredictable. The approach to activity is most frequently with abandon; at other times it is with serious determination. A child of this age requires boisterous, vigorous play; noise and boundless energy are co-existent. Strenuous play contributes best to growth if it is geared to the individual child. The child is the best guide of the amount and kind of activity he needs. When adults take the clue from the child, there is little danger of his overdoing. Rhythms and dance, directed by the child's activity needs, provide the opportunity for self regulation. Not all can "take" the same amount.

Doing—Learning

Early childhood is the time when large muscles are better developed than small ones. In general,
muscle development is uneven and incomplete, and the large muscle groups cry for action. Greatest concentration should be on the development of such gross locomotor movements as jumps, hops, and leaps and on such body movements as swings, twists and turns, bends, and stretches. These movements serve as the foundation for a program in creative rhythms. Childhood experiences in locomotor and body movements serve as a framework for the development of expression and understandings.

When children enter school, they have limited vocabularies. Increased ability to communicate with others develops from constant conversation about happenings of the moment, day, or week. Children often develop a language of their own. The latest radio or television program may influence their daily speech. They may use code language or "Pig Latin." Some children learn foreign languages readily at this age.

This is likewise the period in which children learn to read and acquire other new skills, such as writing, spelling, and telling time. It is the time when skills which require the use of the smaller muscles and eye-hand coordinations are attempted. Many skills can be developed if varied opportunities to learn and practice at this age are provided.

It is important that all children have the experience and chance to experiment; to use and master newly acquired skills at their own rate. Recognition of a child's readiness to learn a skill precludes a single standard of achievement or set pattern of action.

Children like to plan their daily programs in practical, realistic detail. They take delight in planning with the teacher what they will do from day to day. Creative rhythms provide ample and endless opportunities for planning by children and teachers. For example, a social studies unit can be reinforced and vitalized through creative rhythms. A group of seven-year-olds can be interested in going to the store, the firehouse, the post office, and other places that offer community services. They want to know where things come from. After they have visited a grocery store, the story of milk can take them on a visit to a farm where they can see how the cows were milked and the milk prepared for the dairy. They can follow the milk to the dairy and watch its processing to the point where it is ready for delivery to their home grocery store. All this they can demonstrate through movement in creative rhythms, even to the details of turning into milk cans rolled off the truck and delivered. Opportunities for planning can be provided as the children interpret their understanding of milk and its delivery.

Concepts

There is a steady increase in their ability to reason. Concepts concerning objects and human relationships develop gradually, change with repeated experiences, and, only very gradually, do they become logical and fully serviceable. Children's concepts of time, space, largeness, smallness, highness, lowness, heaviness, or lightness develop out of their own experiences. Such concepts cannot be acquired through mere verbal learning, so creative rhythmic movement is used as a medium of expression to help develop them. They are principally interested in "here" and "now" experiences; those which they can see, hear or feel, and which directly touch their lives. First-hand experiences are all-important. A child learns what he experiences, and often when he is forced into a situation for which he is not ready, he will protect himself by fighting back, arguing, sulking, or withdrawing.

Feelings

Children enter school with many emotional patterns fairly well established, bringing with them all their feelings of "having lived six years." Children of this age exhibit actions which can be described by such labels as being "fresh," "smart aleck," "demanding," "sensitive," "sulky," "withdrawn," "shy," "pensive," or "possessive." They can be very affectionate, although it is a period of showing off, of hitting, swearing, talking back, name-calling, and willingness to fight. It is an age of boasting; a time when children want to excel and to show others how much they know. The desire to win is clearly apparent and the bit-

terness of defeat ill-concealed in the familiar saying of children, "T'aint fair." Often they want their own way. It is the age when children begin to show in their eyes the "I dare you" look. They assert their authority and insist upon knowing who is boss. They frequently explore a situation to determine the lengths to which they will be permitted to go. There is a reason for being this way—the same reason for being six, seven, or eight years old. The child who is the "most" of all these things needs the most love and understanding. Actions of this sort must be accepted as right for six-, seven-, and eight-year-olds; there should be no penalties for being this way. Unless the expressions of the "I" drive are accepted as an important part of growth at this stage, they are apt to emerge later in much less desirable forms.

Strange new school experiences fill six-year-olds with uncertainties and apprehensions, until they learn what to expect and what to do about them. They ask adults for help and security by wanting to hold their hands and standing next to them. However, there are days when the entire group at the slightest provocation erupts like a volcano. During the early part of this period some difficulty may be encountered in adjusting to new and sudden changes. At first, a certain amount of routine and repetition is necessary, accounting for demands for the same story or skip over and over again. When change is thrust upon them, it should be gradual; if they can understand the reason for change, they accept it more readily.

The many intense inner feelings of children, their needs, frustrations, excitements, and pleasures make them feel and act as they do. Opportunities should be provided for children to talk, write, draw, sing, play, work, move, and dance out their feelings.

Children early become sensitive to praise and blame. They seek praise or approval and need opportunity to accomplish things in their own right. They begin to want adults to pay attention to them. As they mature, they increasingly desire prestige and individual distinction. They become particularly interested in activities in which they can excel.

They Like Tall Tales

Because children have vivid imaginations, they dramatize life around them. At times they may confuse imagination and memory. They particularly enjoy "here" and "now" things and places. Being curious about the physical world, they are constantly asking "What's this?" "What's that?" "What is it?" They often do not wait for answers but find out for themselves by poking or smelling or crawling over, under, or about the world around them. Time is of little consequence. Life takes on meaning for them with every new experience and association. For instance, in the city, children see busses every day. Busses do not become meaningful and important to children, however, until trips are planned and they have to be used as a means of transportation. As they learn more about transportation, visit bus terminals, and understand the contribution busses make to their life and the life of a city, the bus becomes something more than a vehicle whizzing by on the street.

Early in this period children are most interested in *their immediate environment and surroundings*. As they progress toward middle childhood, they become interested in more distant places and things, such as the neighborhood, city, and community. Toward the end of early childhood, they may become interested in the lives and adventures of early settlers, primitive people, and childhood days of their fathers, mothers, and grandparents.

This is the time when children relive experiences of other people; the things they did and how they did them. It is the adventures of people, and not the sequence of time events, which are important to children. It is their natural way of understanding and appreciating other people and their way of living. Here lie the basic ideas for creative dance experiences. How better relive them than through movement?

They like to dramatize, often carrying on long conversations with imaginary characters, or with their pets. Their sharp curiosities are evidenced in their playmaking. This is one way children find adventure; adventure of their own creation. It may take the form of exaggerating, bragging, or even tattling. These are only signs of a phase

Ann skipping

through which they are passing.

A well-conceived creative rhythms program can provide a multitude of experiences for all kinds of emotional outlets and dramatic interests. Children can have fun expressing their tall tales through movement. Transposing themselves into the heaviest, the lightest, the biggest, the bumpiest thing they can think of not only enhances their imagination but also expresses concepts. Transposing themselves into animals in the zoo, letters in the post office, or airplanes rising from the ground helps them to develop ideas of reality and relationships.

Collecting

Toward the end of this period children begin to develop a wider variety of interests of their own choosing. Some of these are lost overnight, but others develop into adulthood hobbies. These interests include movies, radio, comics, television, barter, and collecting. The collecting "mania" comprises everything from postage stamps, bottle tops, bird feathers, and playing cards to live animals. Turning an eight-year-old upside down will generally disclose a surprising array of collected articles, which may come tumbling out

Bobby and Wayne galloping

of his pockets. Coexistent with this desire to collect is the urge to barter. Quantity is much more important than quality, and children become involved in heated arguments about "the most." This is the period when they take tops off cereal boxes, save candy wrappers and cigar bands, and send away for advertised treasures.

Belonging

Children of this age are primarily interested in themselves as persons and secondarily in their relation to others. They experience tremulous beginnings as social beings, and need constant assurance of their positions in their social group. Learning to be one of a group, to enjoy organized play, to win friends, and to make a place for oneself outside of the home is a gradual process. This soon merges into readiness for organized group experiences. They want friends, best friends of their own choice, even though these friendships may or may not have lasting qualities. They begin to show a desire to play and work in small groups and to assume responsibilities and minor group leadership but this leadership is generally short-lived and changes frequently. Leadership is often based upon such possessions as footballs, baseballs, jacks, jump ropes, and play spaces. Transient, seasonal activities and ownership of equipment are seemingly of first importance in establishing both leadership of, and tenure for, such play groups. At this point chil-

dren begin to establish their own rules for games and to appreciate that all games must have rules. This may establish an awareness of "goodness" and "badness" in themselves and in others. It marks the beginning of recognition of individual differences and individual performances. As children approach their eighth year, they become conscious of family ideas and prejudices, begin to have some conception of cause and effect, understand how others feel and act, and show a certain curiosity about human relations.

Creative rhythmic experiences can substantially assist in the socialization process at this age by offering group and leadership opportunities. A group of forty third-graders were busy explaining, in movement, their ideas of different forms of transportation. They were boats, trains, airplanes, automobiles, horse-drawn carts, and rickshaws. Some were working alone, some with another child, and many were working in groups of three and four. Chip had the idea of a train, but he needed three other children. Susan could do her train alone. Billy wanted to be a rickshaw because his daddy told him when he was a little boy in China he used to go to school in one of those vehicles. He needed two other boys to be the rickshaw, while he was the rickshaw-boy. A compromise was made with Charlie and Vince; they would be a rickshaw if he would be part of their horse-drawn cart. All worked in the social group structure best suited to their way of working. They shared with others, they contributed to group action; even though a child worked alone, he was part of the larger group activity.

Movement, action, motion—these are synonymous with early childhood and the reasons and fun of being six, seven, and eight years old. Doing, going, exploring, collecting, feeling—these are the prominent characteristics of early childhood. Capitalizing upon all these should be the aim and the essence of creative rhythmic movement.

At no time are children ever typical six-, seven-, or eight-year-olds in all phases of their growth. At all times they represent what they were, what they are, and what they will be. Transition from six to seven and seven to eight is fairly complacent. Time, experiences, and having lived eight years give nine-year-olds a new quality and greater variance.

MIDDLE CHILDHOOD—"I AND WE" PERIOD

Children of middle childhood (roughly nine through eleven) are usually in grades four, five, and six. As a group they show an increasing tendency to leave behind "me" and "my" and adopt an "our" and "we" philosophy. Life begins to revolve around the "gang." They tend to think of themselves in terms of "our gang," "our crowd," "our bunch," or "our kids." This is the age when distinction is made between "our world" and "your world"; the world of boys and girls and the world of adults. Parents and teachers are generally regarded as "oldsters" or "has-beens." This is the age of unpredictable actions.

Middle childhood

Growing Up

This is definitely a growing up period. Children no longer want to be called children but demand to be recognized as older boys and girls. As previously stated, growth is continuous, each child having his own unique and distinctive pattern of growth. The tempo of growth and the patterns of acceleration and deceleration of social, mental, and physical development are highly individualistic. This age presents a notably wide range of individual differences and physical maturity. While the slow growers are trying to leave early childhood behind, the fast growers may be approaching preadolescence.

This is the period in which nicknames flourish. "Beanpole," "Fatso," "Shorty," "Slim," and "Pee Wee" seem to represent physical growth types. As boys and girls start their preadolescent growth spurt, they may exhibit tendencies of restlessness, laziness, or lack of initiative. When this is especially noticeable, growth may be taking place so rapidly that organic strength and vitality are at a low ebb, with tiredness and lack of ambition clearly apparent. The boy or girl whose growth spurt starts early may be easily fatigued and generally stands out in marked contrast to others of the same age group whose spurts have not yet begun. Caution must be taken with youngsters who have suddenly become heavy, tall, or lanky and who may consequently feel distressed or out of place. Excessive height or weight loom large in importance in the way children feel about themselves. Helping boys and girls understand and respect these differences in individual structures is essential. In rhythms and dance programs differences in size need not be emphasized. When boys and girls are square dancing, height makes no difference. The boy who has not yet started to "shoot up" will swing his tall partner with no concern about how tall she is, unless attention is called to it.

Doing—Learning

Children of this age exhibit increased manual dexterity, as shown by finer coordination, strength, and resistance to fatigue. Lively and active as boys and girls usually are, when they feel the need, they will stop and rest. There is apparently little danger of exhaustion during middle childhood. Watching a group at play, one observes that they are on the go most of the time, stopping only momentarily, and then, bounding off again as though their lives depended upon it. This is not only observable in a twenty-minute or half-hour period of activity each day, but during the entire day.

Development of the large muscle groups, together with increased motor coordination and endurance, makes participation in vigorous, rhythmic activities possible. During this period girls and boys apparently cannot get enough vigorous activity. This is the time when they want to develop and improve their skills. They will practice an activity of their own choosing for hours at a time. It is during this period that one often hears parents exclaim, "If only he would stop shooting that basketball and do something worth while." Too often, adults are apt to forget what is worth while, according to boy and girl standards. This is also the period when keen interest in "gang" games is first displayed. The game of the season becomes the game of the neighborhood, and it is often played from morning till night. At this age they are generally confident of their ability, engrossed with their own strength, and interested in making comparisons with others. Their play is noisy and boisterous; the larger the gang, the louder the noise. Neatness, cleanliness, and dressing up are looked upon as unnecessary evils which greatly inhibit the play opportunities of middle childhood.

As this period progresses, sex differences become more noticeable, especially in interests, play activities, and general behavior. Boys like and need rough and tumble play; girls like to engage in such activity, within their own group. Girls of this period are generally unconcerned by the term "tomboy," so fortified with their blue-jean garb, their desires and need for activity become more easily satisfied. Adult understanding and guidance, particularly in the planning of school programs, is vitally necessary.

This age cannot be better described than by the child who, when asked "What does it take to do a jump?" answered "Energy." This is the age of energy. Much of it can be used to advantage through creative rhythmic activities.

Learning Is Living

Usually children of the middle grades are avid and enthusiastic learners. They seek rich, varied, meaningful, "black and white," experiences, which afford them opportunity to see, hear, touch, taste, smell, and react. Because of the depth and range of their interests, their desire for information, and their concern with details they are ready and eager for varied learning experiences.

In this way they begin to acquire a realistic picture of themselves and the world about them. A capacity for more accurate thinking makes its appearance, which stems, in part, from their transfer from fantasy to reality and a growing ability to see causal relations.

Children of this age experiment with their environment, trying out things and people more intensively than in early childhood. They absorb information and accumulate ideas concerning the origin and function of sun, moon, earth, water, plants, animals, and mechanical and scientific devices. Their desire to know about the physical world in which they live and things and people around them offers a rich source of ideas for creative rhythmic experiences.

Language now becomes a tool for immediate use in reasoning and problem solving and for future exploration. When allowed to write about experiences of their own choosing, they do so vividly and in detail, although in somewhat less dramatic terms than in early childhood. Their writing is likely to be full of horror, fighting, humor, or desires. Animals frequently play leading roles in their writing. When they use factual material, they include much detail and action. Individually, or in a group, they write project reports, songs, music, stories, and dramatic skits. Poetry of this period seems to have lost some of the free, personal expression that was characteristic of early childhood. They are apt to spend long periods of time writing riddles, puns, and funny stories. This is the "note-passing" era.

It is the period when vocabularies expand and are vividly used to express ideas and feelings. When encouraged to write, it appears that boys and girls have a rich and extensive vocabulary.

Talking Is Important

Both boys and girls of this age enjoy carrying on conversations and using elaborate vocabularies. They like the sound of words, and at every opportunity dress up what they have to say by their choice of words. They develop an ability to use longer and more involved sentences, to stick to a point, and to develop topics logically, even though they include a variety of ideas. This is also the time when ten- and eleven-year-olds exhibit an interest in and an understanding of their own relationships to others, particularly evidenced in sharing group discussion. Four, five, or six boys and girls in a group allows each to take part. They are sensitive when a member of the group monopolizes the conversation, and they waste little time in such situations in making this an issue by the familiar, "Hey, let someone else talk for a change." Though they show a willingness to consider and weigh the points of view of others, pre-eminently they desire an opportunity to express their own thoughts. Often they are outspoken, which frequently makes them seem critical of adults. Opportunity is afforded, through creative rhythmic activity, to discuss and evaluate individual and group accomplishments.

Children of this age can talk about movement and the way they use it as a means of expression. They like to analyze movements and they reinforce their learnings when they can talk about what their bodies are doing.

The "Why," the "What," and the "How"

They want to know the "why" and the "what" of things and people. "Why does this work?" "Why does this go up or down?" "Why does the cowboy like to dance?" "What is this made of?" "What makes this so heavy?" "What is the Es-kimo like?" In the early part of this period they are most interested in how things started; in how and why things began; why some fathers are policemen and others businessmen; why some mothers work and others do not; why people are of different color; why some tunnels go under water while others go through mountains. They are curious about different parts of the world; what boys and girls are like in other countries, and about their holidays, modes of transportation, sports, and pets. During the later part of middle childhood, boys and girls go beyond "why" and "what"; they also want to know "how." For instance, How does the policeman do his work? What exactly is his job? How does he affect the lives of others? They want to know about American folk dancing; how "calls" came into existence; how they differ in various sections of the country and why; who made them up and how they can make up some of their "own" and "call" their own dances. Although they absorb some information from words, mere words are not enough. They still need many direct relationships and much first-hand information. Opportunities are needed to talk, write, dance, draw, sing, and act out these experiences.

A child of this age has difficulty with abstractions. He still needs to classify an object in terms of its function, and in terms of his relationship to that function. What makes a car run and a plane fly? Why does thunder precede lightning? Thinking about what is not observable has little meaning for him.

Intellectual curiosity is keen. They want to know about electricity, machinery, occupations, biography, history, mystery, and adventure. They like to make lists and inventories and can relate an amazing number of facts, figures, and percentages about football and baseball players. They want to know, and to gain understanding of, facts. As boys and girls concentrate on seeking realistic information, they tend to identify themselves with current interests and heroes—the adventurer, the explorer, the square-dance caller, the baseball player, the astronomer, the nurse or the doctor. They begin to contrast the present with the past. Though curious about these relationships, they are still not entirely clear about the past. Concepts of time are not yet very well developed.

The acquired skill of reading helps boys and girls in their search for information. Through reading they satisfy their urge to understand both their own world and the world beyond. Reading may be an avenue of vicarious experience, as well as a means of understanding causal relationships. It may serve as an escape from adult domination. To those who have acquired the skill, reading is a pleasurable pastime, and a source of enjoyment. To those who have failed to acquire reading skill, it can be the cause of discouragement, agony, and unhappiness. If children are forced to read before they are ready, serious emotional problems may result. Tensions may develop if pressure has been exerted by rigid production standards or by parents anxious to have them read too early. Children will read when they are ready.

Helping boys and girls to learn to use source material like dictionaries, encyclopedias, and maps aids them in their quest for information. They will devote hours to locating minute details, if those details are important to them. For the most part, they no longer rely on adults for answers; instead, they are confident of their own ability to observe, experiment, and learn. They are "self starters"; they can initiate projects and carry them to completion, if they are not interfered with by adult influence or an adult saying, "Let me show you."

During middle childhood there is a gain in performance of complex operations with increased speed. A large number of associations are brought to bear upon problems. Their attention span has increased, and if they are vitally interested in an activity, they may stay with it for hours on end. This becomes their work, and they soon learn to differentiate between work and play.

Growth in ability for reasoning and concrete thinking gradually follows. Displays of mental operations of boys and girls of this age are at times startling to adults. They seem to have a heightened curiosity about sex antagonisms, sex differences, and reproduction. They want information in simple, straightforward language. They frequently shock adults by the sex information and misinformation which they have acquired. Understanding and willingness on the part of parents and teachers to provide children of this age with basic facts appropriate to their maturity level is essential.

Boys and Girls Have Their Own Values

At all stages of their lives boys and girls are learning "values," and applying the concept of "right" and "wrong" to themselves and to others. Their frank expressions of honesty may at times seem cruel. They are quick to classify others as fair, honest, cheater, "chicken," and so forth. Intensive arguments may ensue over these concepts and judgments. They weigh pros and cons carefully before coming to a decision. They want to participate actively in making their own plans, rules, and regulations. They realize why games have rules, and when given opportunity, can help adapt game rules for their particular group and situation. Team play and cooperation become understandable concepts. When planning a unit, field trip, or creative rhythm project, they want to know specifically what the plan offers them. Original plans may be side-tracked by alternate suggestions. Many opportunities need to be provided by adults to facilitate explorations, experimentations, fact finding, problem solving, idea expression, and decision making. The classroom teacher, consultant, and special teachers can utilize these experiences to help make the curriculum come alive.

For the most part, middle childhood is the time when boys and girls are recognizing, expressing, and trying out their power as individuals. They are unpredictable in feelings and actions. At times they appear to be aggressive, inconsiderate, inattentive, careless, disobedient, and overly critical. They always seem to be in a hurry, breathlessly tearing from one activity to another. When they slow down to a walk, it is usually because they are deep in conversation about something important to them. At times they seem hard to live with; they are often sassy, silly, and incessant gigglers. They roughhouse, poke, trip, push, and punch one another. Some are practical jokers; others strut about as proud as peacocks, wanting people to know they are no longer babies. In contrast to this overt behavior, they may daydream, become shy, retreat from their friends, and otherwise act as though they have been deeply hurt. This is the age of head-tossing and shoulder-shrugging when one hears the common belligerent words: "I don't care," "Make me," "When you were my age, I'll bet your mother didn't . . . ," or "Gee, whiz, the kids will call me a panty-waist." Girls get together in a gossipy way to chat about others in the school and the neighborhood.

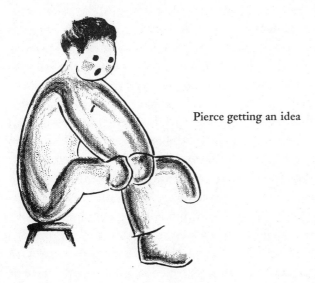

Pierce getting an idea

By contrast, and as if in contradiction, they can be enthusiastic, effervescent, loving, and courteous. When one least expects it, they may be serious, conscientious, cooperative, and responsible. Though possessed of deep feelings of kindness and loyalty, at times they may resent outward displays of affection.

The Gang

This is the gang age when children's interests turn from themselves to a group of boys or girls their own age. There is deep loyalty to the gang,

because belonging to a gang is all important. They want to do everything "other kids" do: talk alike, dress alike, stay up as late at night, have the same kind of hair cuts, the same possessions, and to develop similar mannerisms and interests. This tends to be a trying time for a boy or girl whose family fails to understand, and sometimes resents, this turning towards one's peers. A complete break between the boy or the girl, and the family, may result either because the child's friends may not measure up to the social background or to the expectations of the family. Acceptance or disapproval of one's friends is very important.

At this age gangs are usually small, of one sex, of short duration, and constantly changing in leadership. Each gang may be identified by its own special language, signals, ritual, meeting place, and definite code of behavior. As boys grow older, their gangs tend to increase in size and have more permanency and deeper loyalty; leadership tends to center in one or two boys. The strength and character of this leadership is of the upmost importance; it may be a force for good or for evil. No one knows better than those dealing with the problems of juvenile delinquency how powerful this force may be.

In addition to their gang affiliations, they usually have special bosom pals with whom they have a greater intimacy. Despite frequent quarrels, they are protective, confidential, and extremely loyal to one another. The way their friends feel toward them is important.

Hero worship is closely identified with the later part of middle childhood. Great loyalty and idealism may be generated by a "chosen person." The breach within the family may be widened if the chosen hero or heroine is contrary to the ideals of parents. Their attachment to certain persons may be in open defiance to parental dictates and authority, such as a girl worshipping a female roller-derby skater and the boy, the popular wrestler of the day. They "collect" people somewhat in the same manner that they collect autographs, trophies, trinkets, and pictures. These are the important possessions of the moment. As boys and girls pass through this hero-worshipping phase, they need understanding of their points of view and mutual appreciation of their idols. Woe unto the parents or teachers who openly defy, make fun of, or show disinterest in these chosen heroes.

Boys and Girls Are Social Beings

Because of cultural patterns, or because of the structure of American society, there seems to be some drawing apart of the sexes during this period. This is recognizable in different interests, playing, social activities, conversation, and reading selections. Girls have a tendency to choose other girls, and boys other boys, in their "choice time play." One group may even be scornful of the other, and teasing, bickering, envy, and rivalry may result. It seems open to question whether this drawing apart of the sexes is natural or artificial. Is it something parents and society seem to expect? Some adults openly discourage boys of this age playing with girls, or even associating with them. Boys and girls may have to deal with such terms as "sissies" or as "tomboys" if they play with the opposite sex. In many neighborhoods, where boys and girls have grown up together, and in schools where clear understanding of boys and girls is the prerequisite for teaching, there is evidence of cooperation rather than antagonism or separation of the sexes. In such instances boys and girls continue to get along amicably. Have our puritanical backgrounds influenced the development of these sexual antagonisms? What effects have social mores had upon the development of such attitudes and resentments? There is no doubt that the customs and habits which influenced the growth of certain attitudes in parents may continue to have a direct bearing upon the relationship between parents and children. Many of these parental attitudes in relation to sex may possibly have caused the feeling, in some areas, that dance and rhythms are activities more appropriate for girls than for boys. The nature of folk, square, and social dancing provides for fun experiences and a chance to participate in wholesome, vital boy-girl activities. This would support the contention that more should be done in our school programs in the direction of helping boys and girls grow up together more under their own standards, rather than according to complete adult dictates and prejudices. In schools where activities are meaningful, where the interests of boys and girls are challenged, and where cooperation rather than separation of the sexes is stressed, greater respect for the roles they play may follow.

Accomplishments of boys as compared with those of girls may be another determining factor in widening the breach between the two sexes when emphasis is placed on all reaching the same level of achievement. It has been recognized that girls of this age mature before boys. Thus, many differences between boys and girls can be explained in terms of rate of maturation. Boys, at a given age, continue to achieve and behave in a manner consistent with those of somewhat younger girls. If school programs are to be really productive, maturity factors must be taken into consideration. As boys and girls work together in small groups, particularly in such activities as creative rhythmic movement (where the emphasis is upon a sharing of mutual and cooperative effort), they tend to break down some of this competitive animosity between the sexes instead of striving to "beat" the other fellow. This would tend to de-emphasize competition for "the best" and focus more attention upon cooperation and respect for the role of *each* boy and girl. A group of twelve-year-olds was given a problem to work out their ideas about the dances and cultures of the Scandinavian people. They were asked to divide into groups of no less than four, nor more than seven. The problem was approached from the standpoint of a space factor, or an idea. They had many choices to make: social groupings, country to interpret, and by what means they would illustrate their choice. When given a chance for choices within this framework, they made decisions according to their experience and level of maturity. The emphasis was on the problem, not boy-girl relationships.

Feelings

The emotional needs of boys and girls must be met. If deprived of deserved praise and recognition, they are not likely to continue to make adequate progress. As in early childhood, boys and girls of this next age need a variety of opportunities to provide for achievement and a chance to excel. They need to develop confidence in self and establish a feeling of worth. They exhibit greater self-control but desire to be dealt with directly and individually. They accept suggestions from adults and criticism from their own group more readily than formerly. They feel they are old enough to set up some of their own standards. They have developed a concept of "right" and "wrong" and can apply it to themselves as well as to those with whom they come in contact. They are continually constructing their own codes and sets of values. Their codes may be influenced appreciably by family and teacher. If these codes differ from parental ones, emotional conflicts may result in and create serious adjustment problems. Often boys and girls act as they do because parents and teachers fail to recognize the difficulties imposed upon them by conflicting codes. This is the time, too, when boys and girls are ready to ask, "Why doesn't she practice what she preaches?" If boys and girls are treated with respect, sincerity, fairness, kindness and are given encouragement, understanding, and are allowed to grow up as boys and girls in their own boy and girl world, they will probably develop into more secure, stable, and happier men and women.

They need a certain amount of wholesome competition. Realistic competition of their own selection and planning, and on their own level, produces enjoyment and benefit. However, when competition merely points up "bests" and "failures," it may have devastating effects upon those who do not measure up. To be singled out as having failed to do as well as a classmate can cause deep-seated resentment. Frequent and repeated failure may result in the "I don't care" or "What's the use" attitudes. The child always chosen last is likely to withdraw or develop antagonistic forms of social action. Competition which leads to improvement of and within self, rather than to the proof of self against another, is a means of growth; it is realistic; it is the right kind for boys and girls. It is quite different from the superimposed adult competition, which encourages children to prove that they are the best, the first, or the fastest.

Boys and girls are acutely aware of their own strengths and weaknesses. They are conscious of their performance in contrast to that of others. If given opportunity and encouragement, they will likely make a conscientious effort to improve. Honest achievement, not make-believe, rates high with children. They cannot be fooled into thinking something is better than it really is, because they are their own best judges about their accomplishments. Boys and girls will so often say or intimate, "Flattery will get you nowhere." They want honest appraisal but fear public humiliation. Many times they may have inadequate techniques, and in such cases, adult guidance is needed to protect these youngsters from a feeling of frustration and failure.

Encouraging Creative Power

Creative power needs protection and revitalization, for this is the time if opportunity is offered, when children start to express, through line, color, design, and rhythmic movement, more of themselves ·and less of their surroundings. It is often difficult for these expressions to emerge in the desired form. Given adequate encouragement, the extent of their creative possibilities cannot be predicted. If creative activity is suppressed, because parents and teachers do not understand the degree to which boys and girls mature, or if their efforts are compared with previous products, or with those of younger children, the spark may be lost forever. All too often, parents and teachers thoughtlessly exclaim: "What's the trouble with your drawing? You did better when you were little; now you just doodle." Children normally aspire for perfection, but lose interest quickly if discouraged or pressured. If teachers firmly believe in helping boys and girls develop feelings of worth and accomplishment, they must enlist their thoughts, behavior, and attitudes and avoid making harmful comparisons.

A feeling of inadequacy caused by feelings of insecurity with a gang (or with chosen friends), resentment of adult authority, failure, lack of appreciation, or thwarted expressions of creativeness may be evinced in many ways. The result may produce unruliness in school or at home, or it may be evident in their language, because the language of children often reveals much of what they are thinking. Troubled thoughts are often deep-seated and do not readily appear on the surface. Coughing, weeping, throwing and breaking things, withdrawing, sucking thumbs, biting nails, wrinkling noses, and pulling and twisting hair may be outward manifestations of tensions, worries, jealousies, and feelings of insecurity or rejection. Worries may be caused by peculiar notions which children may acquire. These all interfere with the development of the kind of persons they would like to become. These worries are numerous: They concern freckles, straight hair, getting fat or staying small, and wearing glasses. These child problems often cause untold distress. Boys and girls need sympathetic and understanding guidance. Nervous mannerisms may increase in number and intensity during this age, especially where they are continually confined, cramped, and held in. They need space; they need movement and opportunity for stretching out, for letting go. Modern living makes it all the more necessary that boys and girls have room to play, move, and work. Observations of classroom settings indicate that nervous mannerisms increase when boys and girls are required to sit and listen with restricted movement, in comparison to periods when free activity is permitted. Energetic boys and girls need a program which includes alternate periods of rest and exercise. Every now and then they must be permitted to let go, and let go they must, by singing, hammering, finger painting, or by moving through space.

Interests Change

This is an age of varied interests. A careful analysis of interest is most revealing. Interests change with age and may serve as an indicator of the rate of maturity. Unless they encounter disapproval of adults, enthusiastic youngsters will talk at length about their interests. Play is still important. Not only do they like to play in larger groups, but they soon become interested in more highly organized sport activities, such as softball, football, swimming, ping-pong, and a variety of winter activities. Playing "cops and robbers," "G-men," "F. B. I.," "gangsters," "Hop-along-Cassidy," "space cadets," "commandoes," and "guerrillas" is an outlet for fun and adventure. The popular game of *Monopoly* provides for barter, exchange of fake money, and the usual arguments which also mark this period. They are interested in what is happening at the United Nations, at the World Series, and at the Olympic games. They will stay closely to a radio or television set throughout the football season or World Series to help pull their favorite team through or to enable them to emulate their hero of the moment. Their interest in collecting has increased and may include everything from the latest popular jazz recording, to autographs of their heroes. This is the constructive age, and they like to build their own stage sets and make drops, costumes, and scenery for plays and class projects. From the stories they read they enjoy making up games and constructing rules. Frequently this is an urge to make up their own dances, originate their own calls, and then to discuss and evaluate them. As a group they love to assume responsibility for younger children. At times, interesting experiences have resulted from a fifth or sixth grade inviting a first or second grade to dance or participate with them in a musical experience or a dramatic production. Pets are still important. They are now lively, friendly companions rather than the objects upon which early childhood laid the blame for its own failures. They are friends for whose care and affection they have become responsible.

At this age they are beginning to recognize the value of money and are apt to strut around with an oversized billfold in their pockets. This is also the age level when a camp experience provides exciting adventures and an opportunity for a variety of new and important interests.

Middle childhood finds boys and girls interested in themselves as social beings, and in knowing how they fit into the social group around them. They like to take an active part in group relations and experiences. These characteristics of middle childhood initiate and guide a program of creative rhythmic movement. Having

Later childhood

lived nine, ten, or eleven years has given these boys and girls a right to their demand to be regarded as people—people with ideas, longings, curiosities, and desires.

LATER CHILDHOOD—"WE" PERIOD

The wonder, fascination, and reason for the "I" of early childhood and the spirit of the "I and we" of middle childhood have now been transformed, by time, into the miracle, enchantment, and the purpose for the "we" of the peer age. Boys and girls, eleven to fourteen years of age, are usually in the seventh, eighth, and ninth grades. This is the peer age. It is the period when it is most important that they belong to a group, and to be recognized and accepted by peers.

This is the age of expansion of physical growth. It is the period when secondary sex characteristics first make their appearance. Maturation is rapid, with girls usually maturing a year or two earlier than boys. Because of the rapidity of growth many boys and girls appear to lack coordination. They seem to be all hands and feet. They fall over things, knock things down, and find the

gymnasium and the out-of-doors better places in which to move than apartments or restricted living quarters. They find they do not know how big their hands are or how long their legs are and need time to adjust to this lengthening. Because of the nature of folk dancing this activity provides experiences in movement congenial to them; it is space for them to fling out.

Boys and girls want to be "in" on everything that is going on. They make it their business to be "up to date." They readily label items and people as "it's not modern," "old foggies," "has-beens." This is the age when constant talking and free expression of radical opinions and actions makes adults aware that they are becoming individuals; they are people. This is the time of much "chit-chatting," telephone calling, and frantic dashing here and there. "What are you going to do after school?" "There is so much to do . . . how about the movies. . . ?" are frequent expressions. Trying to gain status in the group sometimes makes boys and girls extreme in their actions. To be the noisiest, funniest, most sophisticated; to have the most pals; to collect the greatest number of boy friends; or to attract the most popular boy or girl in the group are all actions which are associated with the peer age. In their efforts to become part of their group, often their actions seem to adults to have no rhyme or reason. Whatever they do, they do intensively, with much argument and determination. Boys and girls of this age believe "what they do" is right—at least at the time.

Frequently they give the impression they cannot be "bothered" with the opposite sex; a sure sign that such vital interest has started. Providing activities so that boys and girls can be together is important when they are ready for them. However, not all boys and girls of the same age group are always ready at the same time. It is the skillful teacher who recognizes the signs of "girls keep out," or "no girls allowed," and plans and presents activities accordingly. Activities can help boys and girls make the adjustment when emphasis is not placed upon boy-girl relationship as such, but, on the fun of participating in the activity. In later childhood many boys and girls have come to accept each other, and to enjoy doing things together and yet, in every group, there may still be those who cling tenaciously to the earlier pattern of separate boy-girl interests. In dancing, for instance, teachers who know that the fun of participating in the activity itself is important will not stress boy-girl partners. "Getting partners" will not be a problem when boys recognize "such things as girls" and when girls become conscious there are "such things as boys." Social dancing can help to provide opportunities for recognition of each other in a way that is right for them. When social dancing is presented, it should be done from the standpoint of the fun all may receive from participation. There should be no evidence of stress in having to get partners of the "right" sex. It is the job of the teacher to make *all* boys and girls comfortable.

Skills and Concepts

This is an age when motor skills are essential; they are important tools by means of which boys and girls gain and maintain a place in the peer group. Boys and girls who have not had experiences in play, games, and dance often feel uncomfortable with their group. This is one of the reasons they frequently withdraw and find substitute activities which may not be desirable. The feeling that they are not like the rest can be so strong that they will play the role of the spectators rather than as the active participants. Sports and folk and social dancing are experiences which can help them take a more active part in the important social activities of their group.

During this period they become more and more proficient in the use of the written and spoken word. Increased power in the use of these skills, and in the prestige which they gain, is a vital concern. They write countless numbers of notes to each other, carry on many lengthy telephone conversations, and enjoy "putting on" shows of all kinds—talent shows, variety shows and broadcasts or television shows. They will describe in detail things which are important to them—batting averages, the story of the lives of baseball players, or the recent movie or television show. They will listen attentively to adults tell stories about their experiences or about far away places and people.

Their spheres of interests and knowledge are greatly expanded, and they develop a greater awareness and understanding of people. They want to know more about themselves and others, because they are interested in why things are as they are and in what can be done to improve affairs.

As a group, their interests have broadened but as individuals they are "very keen" about certain people and things. Interests take on a more permanent form. These include art, music, plays which interpret adult life, sports of all kinds, woodworking, doing things with their hands, hobbies, science, and research. They seem particularly interested in those activities—science, health, dance and sports—which help them better to understand themselves. They sometimes become "pals" with parents and adults who will share their hobbies and interests. Stamp collections, making and using short wave radio sets, and building things are experiences they particularly enjoy with adults.

"Watch me—this is what I can do!"

"We have an idea!"

Feelings

This is the age when feelings of insecurity are dominant. Physical growth, expanding interests in people and things, the great drive to "do," the anxiety to measure up to group expectance, the effort to belong, and the need for independence all engender feelings of uncertainty. The tensions produced by these feelings are expressed in many different ways. Some may revert to infantile ways of showing tension—nail biting, day dreaming, and stuttering. Others, at times, appear shy or bold. The "big shot" and "I don't care" attitudes are ways they express what is happening to them. Adults often say to them, "You don't act the way you used to." They are as unpredictable in their actions as seven-year-olds, but the twelve-year-olds have their own reasons for being this way.

It is during this period they display stormy feelings of anticipation. They are anxious to know what is coming next, and how it is going to affect them. The anticipation and planning for what is going to happen is of paramount importance.

Expanding Social World

Boys and girls of later childhood find security in their peers—in the feeling of "belongingness." The loyalty and support they give each other has the effect of "ganging up." The peer age is the time when they continually think up things to do which will bring them together as a group. Family affairs become quite secondary, and a delayed mealtime often ends in "verbal eruptions" because it interferes with the business at hand.

The feeling of "we can do" is so strong that adult interference is apt to bring forth words and actions which may be interpreted as defiance or as a polite invitation to "let us take care of our affairs." All too frequently they will take suggestions from the "goofiest guy" in their group to those of the wisest adult. Group approval of action and dress hinges upon not so much how they look as long as they look like the rest of their chums. This is the age of the "bobby socks,"

lipstick, loafers and/or high heels, "hair-do's" and hair "goo," blue jeans and "dress-ups," identification bracelets and neckties. They can be the most disheveled looking, or the most "dressed up." Adults find it difficult to prescribe when boys and girls should be dressed up. "Dress up time" is a decision of the group and may make little sense to the adult.

A code of behavior is developed by each group. It is a period when values, standards, and techniques of working together are becoming firmly established. They like to work out these understandings for themselves but often seek help and guidance from interested adults. It is the wise and patient adult who knows how to give help and when to give it. Boys and girls do not want the help which "tells" them or which is imposed or which makes them dependent on the adult. They seek the kind of help which gives them a chance to talk things over and allows them to come to their own conclusions.

They solicit the kind of adult approval which helps them gain an accepted place in their group. When they provide opportunities which allow boys and girls to say "I'm captain," "I'm president," "I'm calling for square dancing," "I'm stage manager," "I'm chairman," adults are directly assisting in the recognition of peer group, or later childhood responsibility. Regardless of their outward signs of indifference, boys and girls need to talk about their accomplishments and want to share these with adults who care. In spite of their "grown-upness," they need patience, sympathy, and understanding.

These boys and girls generally have a purpose for doing the things they do. They do them to gain prestige with their peers, to make friends, to excel in the things important to them, to expand continually their realm of people and things, to be one of the group, and to have a recognized place because of what they can do. Anything worthy of their sincere efforts must have a purpose. They are their own best judges of what is worthwhile; their standards are high!

The peer age is active, expansive, purposive, and intensive. If boys and girls could put into words what their eyes frequently reveal, they might say, "There are reasons I act as I do; please understand and help me grow in my own particular way." It is the time when they are growing from immaturity to maturity, begin to find and make a place for themselves, take responsibility for their actions, build ethical standards, and contribute to group living. Only as they are accepted for the things they do and what they represent in the growing process will they be free to learn and later to be one with the adult world. A program of creative rhythmic movement based on the needs and interests of boys and girls can assist in this growing up process.

Summary

Early, middle, and later childhood are not ages apart, but continuations of growth of the most precious of God's gifts—the CHILD—who makes this request of adults in the form of "His Bill of Rights":

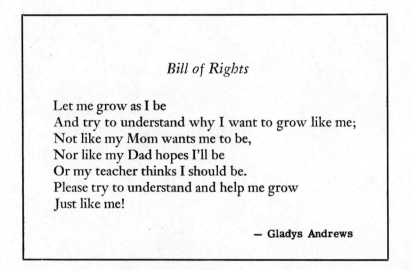

Bill of Rights

Let me grow as I be
And try to understand why I want to grow like me;
Not like my Mom wants me to be,
Nor like my Dad hopes I'll be
Or my teacher thinks I should be.
Please try to understand and help me grow
Just like me!

— Gladys Andrews

Creating "wild horses"

2. Children and Creative Experiences

Creativity is a dynamic element within all children, making it possible for them to do things which they never dreamed they could do. This very vital and latent potentiality resides in every individual, in varying degrees. The extent to which it can be developed is dependent upon the experiences to which children are exposed, the opportunities they are given for expression, and the encouragement they receive in participating in activities.

Children differ in their creative potentiality, just as they differ in their rate of growth, experience, and aptitude for learning. This difference is evident when they are given the opportunity to express themselves through mediums of their own choice: art, music, writing, and rhythmical movement.

CREATIVITY—A WAY OF LEARNING

It is imperative for every child to have adequate opportunity for self-expression. Creative experience is concerned with self-expression. The self is the focal point and remains as such throughout the process of creating. It is what the individual *thinks*, *feels*, *sees*, and *expresses*, in terms of himself and in his own way. The creative process starts, then, with the individual, is directed by the experiences which he has had, and ends in the form of a new expression. The creative process utilizes conscious effort. The child deals with both feelings and concepts which must be "said" by him in a form of expression which is his very own.

It would seem that the creative process expands like a snowball gathering momentum as it rolls down hill. As creative power is set into action by an experience—seeing, hearing, feeling, thinking, or doing—the child responds with his own feelings, ideas, and concepts in some tangible form of expression. The *creative process* involves three phases: (1) the child and his creative power, feelings, and imagination; (2) the action or interaction of his experience; (3) and his outward form of expression. Experience initiates the action; it becomes the raw material of self-expression. Only what a child is aware of through firsthand experiences can be readily expressed in tangible forms.

For firsthand experiences children need opportunities to see, touch, feel, smell, and taste. They need to explore, investigate, and find out things for themselves. Following this they need opportunity, inspiration, and encouragement to express that which they have experienced. Children learn through awareness. They learn to express that which they experience, molding themselves as they grow. Recognition, development, and encouragement of this creative power will lead to the enrichment of their lives.

In the United States creativity has not received the attention or emphasis it deserves, either in research or in actual practice. Creative potentialities in children frequently remain blocked, unnurtured, and untouched. In observing kindergarten or first-grade children, one is impressed with their individuality, their utter abandon, and especially their desire to discover and explore new things. Their wholehearted interest in various forms of expression, such as songs, plays, drawing, conversation, and rhythmic movement, is quite evident. In their need to explore the world around them they vibrate and quiver like young butterflies emerging from cocoons. There is a freedom of thinking which demands expression in terms of their everyday experiences—expression which is spontaneous, meaningful, and direct. It seems appalling that much of this vibrant, natural zest may be lost, or submerged, when children grow older. From the second grade upward, children are apt to appear hesitant, self-conscious, inhibited, bored, and uninspired. When this is true something tragic has happened to their way of learning and to their urge to explore new realms and tell about them. Can it be that natural activities of children are too often upset and disturbed by adult conditioning? Have joyous, natural, creative expressions of children been suppressed by adult-imposed patterns of how children should act as they grow older? Have creative activities been put on the shelf by adults? If so, perhaps this may be attributed to the lack of understanding, direction, guidance, and variety of experiences and opportunities provided by parents and teachers. Perhaps, they have either failed to realize or have been denied the importance to express their own creative potentialities.

EXPERIENCES AND CREATIVE EXPRESSION

The fundamental basis for creative expression is to be found in experiences. These consist of things a child does for the first time, in a way which is *new* to him. They include recognition and interpretation of new relationships in thinking, learning, and doing. For example, a third-grade group became interested in the kinds of boats which might be found on a lake. It was de-

cided to imagine the room was a lake, and each child some sort of a boat. They were asked to form groups of two's, three's, four's or five's to represent the larger boats, or they could work alone and be small boats. Not only did these eight-year-olds have to decide on the kinds of boats they were going to be, but they also had to figure out how they could use movement to navigate on the lake and then "dock up." The sail, sloop, Indian canoe, small canoes, rowboat, kayak, speedboat, and raft were *original interpretations*. These children devised their own method of moving, so that others could recognize what they were. Many of these interpretations were indeed unique, and there were obviously as many ways to interpret a sailboat as there were children in the class.

Creating is exciting because children never "say it" in the same way. The creative aspect is the *uniqueness* of the experience of the individual concerned. This process is affected by something from one's own *experience*, which is modified, reassembled, or given an original twist, and outwardly is manifested as an *on-going* experience. This is the process by which new life comes into being and by which living things continue to grow and to reach maturity. This is progress, growth, and development.

Creative power, the dynamic element within each child, develops with discovery and exploration. The result is creative expression. Children at work, children who are experiencing this process of creativity, reflect in their faces the thrill of vibrant expenditure of energy, the elation of complete satisfaction, and the harmony within themselves. One can actually feel them "think" and can share with them in the enjoyment which comes from expression.

In creative expression the emphasis is on what is happening to children, rather than on what they may produce. Teachers gain an insight into their developing personalities by observing them when they are free to express themselves in an encouraging, understanding environment. It is a common error to suppose that creative activity starts by itself. The act of expressing original thoughts, feelings, and ideas in tangible form has its beginnings in experiences of everyday life and flourishes best in a normal, natural atmosphere.

Experiences surround children! However, they need to be selected, channeled, and arranged according to the specific needs and stages of development. It is not enough merely to expose children to experiences; they need to interpret them in their own way. For example, a school was preparing children for the local appearance of the Boston Pops Orchestra. There was much evidence of the "big affair" in the decorations, in the halls, and in some of the rooms. In the music room, children were being given firsthand experiences with various instruments which made up the orchestra. Sixth-graders were seriously demonstrating their instruments to a group of seven-year-olds. Kim was taking his horn apart,

showing what it was made of, and how sound came out of its various parts. The potential musicians announced the selection they had decided to play for their second-grade audience. A cello, violin, French horn, and flute were never more appreciated by any group of listeners. After the applause had ceased, the music teacher announced that the performers had another surprise. Every youngster was given an opportunity to play the instrument of his choice. The seven-year-olds were asked to think about the instrument which they most wanted to play and then to go to the spot in the room where the sixth-grader would help each one. Not only was this an experience in sharing, but also the tremendous concentration and the joy registered on faces when a sound was produced gave thirty second-

Sharing experiences—moving the way it makes us feel

graders and four sixth-graders a happy learning experience. The genuine appreciation evidenced by Kim when he said "Good" as he looked down at the "little tyke" trying to make sound come forth was something to be remembered. Each of four sixth-graders handled his pupils in his own particular way, determined to give each of the seven-year-olds a successful experience. Thirty children left that room as potential musicians—each an artist in his own realm.

This experience was intensified by the opportunity of moving the way the different instruments made them feel. The children explored the different qualities of movement suggested by the violin, cello, flute, and the French horn. Creativity had started.

If children are to develop creatively, they must be provided with a chance to experiment with a variety of media. When the expressions of creative effort are given form, they need to be received with understanding, encouragement, and appreciation. As sympathetic atmosphere is evidenced for creative efforts, all of those who are privileged to explore, share situations with, and provide media for expression will be gratified and astounded by what is happening. The tremendous air of concentration, release of tension, pulsating output of energy, and the enjoyment which emerges from expression are symptomatic aspects of growth and development through the creative process.

One cannot share a creative experience with children without realizing that something important has happened. This reaction is visible in the eyes and on the faces of the creators; something revealingly important is manifested in the genuine pride in individual or group effort. Children express their satisfaction when they glowingly say, "Look what we did!" "Bet you can't guess what we are?" or "I did it all myself." This is the basis of respect for self and others working in a co-operative endeavor.

Up to the present time changes in children through creative experiences have not been scientifically measured. These changes—acceptance of oneself and others, and the ability to communicate and work with others—are the outcomes of creative education. That important changes do take place cannot be questioned! Everyone who has worked with children over a period of time knows this to be true. One can actually see such changes taking place and can observe that the children have important contributions to make to their world.

Media for Creative Expression

If children are to have opportunities to explore those experiences which are within their realm of understanding they need to experiment with a wide variety of media, which may include such activities as drawing, poetry, playmaking, singing songs, writing stories, painting, puppetry, making maps, and making and playing percussion instruments, as well as exploring movement.

Children should have at their disposal many kinds of materials. They should be encouraged to explore the materials and use them freely. This in itself is a means of learning. As children vary in their creative potentialities, and in their abilities to express themselves, so they vary in their choice of media for expression. The important factor is that children actually have the opportunity to utilize these media—the doing, the exploring, the making. Through the media of expression children convey to others their inner feelings, meanings, and values.

One Medium of Expression—Creative Rhythmic Movement. What is meant by creative rhythmic movement? Much confusion exists in the minds of people about the terms creative movement, rhythms, creative rhythms, and dancing. Tradition, religion, association with physical education and music programs, previous experiences of teachers, and adult forms of dance are some of the reasons for confusion. Additional misunderstandings have been caused by the way in which rhythms or dance experiences for children have been provided.

The terms creative rhythmic movement, rhythms, creative rhythms, and dancing are often used interchangeably. To most teachers they mean the same thing: They are the expressions of children in the use of movement, rhythm, and creativity. It is the *meaning* and purpose of these experiences in education which is important, rather than the terminology used. When movement becomes fully recognized as fundamental in children's learning, and becomes a recognized part of the total educational program, then perhaps, schools and communities will be ready to give this area of experiences a standardized term, such as "dance" or "children's dance." *It is the meaning of the underlying concept which is important.* If the term dancing prevents schools or communities from providing these important learning experiences, then it would seem advisable to use a term which will assure children the opportunity for this form of expression.

Creativity, rhythm, and movement are the three constant and common elements, regardless of the terms used. The way children use movement and rhythm to express themselves creatively varies with individuals and age groups. For instance, the peer age group may think of these experiences in terms of social dancing, middle childhood in terms of folk dancing, and younger boys and girls in terms of "just galloping like a bucking bronco"; all three symbolize movement and expression. It is creative; it is dancing!

Creative rhythmic movement is the individual's interpretation of thoughts and feelings expressed through the use of the body. Discovery and exploration of body parts by a child, and his use of them to express or interpret in *his own way* that which is within *his* experiences, constitute creative rhythmic movement. When a child is given an opportunity to use movement, it is as expressive for him as it was for primitive man. Through this medium the child can react to the world about him, use it as a means of communication, and express the thoughts and feelings which are deep down inside. His life is enriched through experiences in creative rhythmic movement, and they contribute vitally to his development through moments of exploration. Movement is the child's universal language, *i.e.*, his most convincing form of communication and a way of learning.

Experiences, carefully selected according to the varying needs of boys and girls, contribute to growth if emphasis is on *children* and their development, rather than on *activity*. Because children are different, their expressions are different.

Therefore, no one standard or pattern can apply. When given opportunity to express themselves, the results must be considered in terms of continual self-improvement. In this area of expression teachers are concerned with the education of all children. They should see that opportunity is provided for all children to participate in a program of creative rhythmic movement, rather than for producing star performers. It is exciting to watch children discover the wide variety of movement of which their own bodies are capable and the pleasure which comes from using these movements in patterns and relationships to interpret feelings and express thoughts and ideas.

Movement is influenced, enhanced, and intensified by experiences in space and rhythm. As children explore movement, they become aware of the various elements in space which are related to the area their movements cover and the directions which they take. Likewise, as children explore movement, they become cognizant of the various rhythmic elements. As these experiences in rhythm and space become interrelated with movement, additional tools are developed to give added meaning to movement. These tools or techniques the children use to interpret more complex movement patterns or to create studies and compositions.

As children develop the tools for expression they are further influenced by additional experiences growing out of their own surroundings from things they can see, touch, feel, and hear. They may translate these perceptions into movement expressions, or they may use them to modify movement. For instance, children may hear the ticking of a clock and translate this into a swinging movement, using their own bodies as the pendulum. Movement may be further modified by the ever-present feelings which children possess. Children feel happy, so their clock pendulums become a happy swing, and they express their feeling of happiness in the manner in which they swing. As Joan said, "I wanted to be the cuckoo part of the clock 'cause I felt that way today." These are the expressions of feelings which come from within, giving added meaning to movement. Probably the largest group of experiences related to movement are those concerned with ideas and thoughts of children. These may be consciously translated into movement, or may influence movement, or may serve as the stimulus for movement expression. A clanging fire engine transposes children into the biggest, the best, the noisiest, and the busiest engines and firemen at hand. A picture of trees hanging with moss turns children into big, old, slow, droopy trees. The sound of street calls,—scissor sharpener's calls, e.g.—caused a fifth grade to collect street calls and use them as accompaniment for their movement composition.

A variety of experiences adapted from the school and camp program and from the everyday living of children provides stimuli for movement. Percussion, songs, music, pictures, nature, or graphic representation often provide some of these experiences. Classroom activities, language arts, science, and social studies may also give impetus to movement. Other experiences may result from holidays, field trips, or experimenting with the effects of words, sounds, or colors. Seizing the opportunity to relate folk or social dancing with studies of cultural, national, or geographical backgrounds are all too often missed as an opportunity to include rhythmic movement as a part of the school or camp programs.

Movement is the very essence of creative rhythmic expression. This form of creativity differs from all others because the body is the instrument of expression. Awareness of this sensitive instrument is one of the first steps in exploration in a rhythms program. Children discover that they are made up of arms, legs, trunk, head, and so on. As children become familiar with their wonderfully constructed bodies—instruments of expression—they discover they can manipulate them in many ways, as a whole or in parts. They find out that their bodies are instruments of their will and they are at the controls to set it in motion. They soon realize they can use their bodies to express experiences, translate surroundings, and interpret feelings. Often they respond to incidents with their whole bodies, not just isolated parts, by jumping up and down with the "Christmas feeling," pushing or pulling with "I can do it" determination, or dancing a polka with a feeling that "all's right with the world."

As children become accustomed to movement, they enjoy it for its own sake, for the exhilaration they receive from galloping through space, for leaping higher and higher, and the fun of just finding out how different parts can move. Learning is accomplished by "doing." Through the use and development of skills and tools in creative rhythmic movement, children have a chance to explore and to grow. They give vent to their imaginations and interpret meaningful and timely happenings. In this process of creative expression what happens to the boys and girls is of vital importance.

Children Say

Through their own words children evaluate outcomes of creative rhythmic movement.

"Let's Go!" "Can We Skip?" "Let's Do It Again!" These are spontaneous exclamations denoting children's movement expression which they become aware of as they learn to direct their wonderful bodies. By developing expressive body instruments they are fulfilling a need for effective bodies, bodies that are strong and have power and endurance to perform vigorous locomotor and body movements. As they explore movement they develop important physical skills of balance and body coordination. As they gain better control of their bodies they experience the fun of using them as a means of expression and communication. They soon realize the challenge and pleasure which comes when they can work out combinations in movement that feel good and that others like to watch. An execution of a combination of movements, which they hitherto have been unable to achieve, brings forth "I didn't know I could do that." They become aware of their instruments of expression. Because they have increasing opportunities to explore and use movement, they are forming the basis for further learning experiences. One of the primary values of this form of creative expession is to provide movement experiences to care for the child's urgent need for action, which is characteristic of childhood.

"Look Out!" "Here I Come!" "Look at Them!" "Feels Like We're Going to Touch the

"Swing your partner!"

Sky!" Children discover that Space is a world to explore. They realize that they can move through it vigorously or quietly; they can push it aside by moving in different directions and according to a variety of designs and patterns of their own making. Children gain knowledge of spatial relationships—tallness, smallness, highness, lowness, bigness, littleness, nearness, distance, geometrical designs, and so on; when they do this they are expressing various *important concepts*. They love to move through space—to polka, leap, and swing, for the sheer fun and feeling of exhilaration which comes from moving through space.

"*That Felt Good!*" "*That Makes Me Want to Jiggle All Over!*" Children discover rhythmical relationships when they move at different rates of speed, with different combinations of "strongs and weaks" and to the accompaniment of different patterns of sounds. As they are able to respond with a sound, they can adjust their own rhythmical response to the rhythm of another, or to the rhythm of a group. When they can clap out a beat, walk out a pattern of their own making, or dance with others they say, "That felt good." This also leads to a fuller appreciation of music.

"*Gee, That Was Fun!*" "*Look What I Can Do!*" "*It Worked Out!*" "*We Need More Time!*" Fun, satisfaction, and growth take place when children can let go and use movement to express that which is within their own experiences. When they can interpret an idea, feeling, picture, or a sound through the use of movement so that others can understand what they are trying to say or to portray, they realize satisfaction in accomplishment. Children grow as individuals and as members of a group when they are not ashamed to let their feelings come out, or when they are not afraid to express that which is within them. They gain confidence in themselves when they are able to give expression to an interpretation which they have worked out. They take pride in the satisfaction that they receive from a product of accomplishment or when another group member says, "That's good, Carl!"

As children gain in self-respect, they have the conviction that what they discover for themselves or work out for themselves is worth while. They grow in stature when they lose the fear of presenting their creation to a group, or of sharing their creation with a younger or older group. Their eyes light up when their creations are genuinely accepted, due to their sincerity of purpose, ability to organize an experience, or to establish a logical arrangement of ideas expressed in a form others can understand. Their verbal outbursts of "Let's do it again" are recognizable expressions of achievement. The glow mirrored on their faces is another manifestation of the good feeling which children have about their accomplishments. Seeing Tom grow "inches in height and degrees in personality" when directing a group through a square dance, which he had written, is a satisfying experience which teachers and children share. This recognition, resulting from accomplishment, helps children to "let go" and to shake loose from strains of cramped quarters, periods of mental concentration, tensions from heated group discussions, or from "inside" hurts.

"*I Think.*" "*We've Got an Idea!*" "*Guess What We Are!*" "*Let's Find Out!*" Children take responsibilities for their own learning when situations and opportunities are provided for them to solve problems. They grow in their ability to find things out for themselves by working with movement problems or responding to experiences from their classroom, neighborhood, or community. As children discover things for themselves, they are less apt to be afraid to tackle problems and to work them out to completion. They will share their findings with a group and thereby gain in perception, appreciation, respect, and judgment concerning self and others.

"*Can We Be Next?*" "*Our Jig Is Better Today Because Red Is Back to Help Us!*" "*Peter, You Be the Piston and We Will Be the Motor Parts!*" "*Gosh, We Have to Have a Tail. Who Is Going to Be That?*" As children grow in their ability to find out and in the desire for self-realization, they also gain values in human relationships. When they work with groups of varying sizes, and experience the give and take of group action, they grow in their development of the skills needed for working with others. Their attitudes, appreciations, and understandings of self and others are affected as repeated interaction takes place. In creative rhythmic movement teachers and children are constantly working together to determine goals, to make plans, and to evaluate accomplishments. As boys and girls learn to assume effective roles as members and leaders of groups, their appreciation and understanding of others comes through the personal experiences they have shared. The respect of self which comes from the feeling "I can do," or "We can do," gives deeper and more effective meaning to group living. Good feeling about one's self, good feeling about the group, laughing together, concentrating and working on solving problems together, having fun together, sharing, evaluating, and letting go in action are all outcomes provided by creative rhythmic movement experiences.

Summary

Creativity is a way of learning. Children must have experiences to express themselves creatively. These experiences consist of things they do for the first time in a way which is new to them. These include the making of interpretations and the recognition of new relationships in thinking, learning, and doing. Creative rhythmic movement is the individual's interpretation of thoughts and feelings expressed through use of the body. The body is the instrument and movement the medium of expression. Children evaluate and say in their own words the desirable outcomes they receive from participating in creative rhythmic movement.

"We need room to go up and down and stretch out."

3. *Creative Movement Experiences*

Helping children to develop as creative individuals and helping them to live together cooperatively is the main concern of education. School programs which are meaningful to children place emphasis upon their development, rather than on mere skills and subject matter. This calls for curricula based upon the interests and experiences of children. Curricula developed cooperatively by children, teachers, counselors, principals, supervisors, and parents are most likely to achieve this objective. Such cooperative efforts are all too few, but some communities and camps are recognizing their importance and value.

CREATIVE EXPRESSION—A PART OF THE SCHOOL PROGRAM

Creative rhythmic movement as a form of expression should be part of all children's school experiences. Creative rhythmic movement is not a frill, or a minor part of physical education, or music, or an extracurricular activity. Awareness of children's need for action, desire for expression, and urge to create necessitate thinking of creative rhythmic movement as an integral part of the curriculum.

There are many conditions which retard the development of creative rhythmic movement in the educational program, such as failure on the part of administrators to "set the stage," inadequate feeling of classroom teachers toward participation in (and presentation of) forms of creative expression, and illogical attitudes toward the place of play, movement, and expression in children's learning.

However, more and more administrators are recognizing how children learn and how they can help teachers provide broader experiences for groups of children. They are better interpreting school programs to parents and other lay groups and are encouraging teacher workshops, conferences, and other in-service experiences. When this is apparent, administrators are beginning to assume the responsibility for inclusion of creative rhythmic experiences in the school program.

Often, classroom teachers lack the confidence to guide creative rhythmic experiences. Usually they have not had sufficient experiences in moving themselves, or, the experiences have not been satisfying. The so-called "method courses" in physical education, games, rhythms or dance offered them are often completely divorced from the needs and interests of children and are presented from the standpoint of teaching physical education activities, rather than teaching *children* through physical education activities. For this reason teachers have not recognized the potentials of movement as learning experiences for children. Frequently they have been led to believe that the area of movement is the concern of the specialist. However, teachers who work with children every day recognize children's urgent need for activity, and often seek help. This help for teachers can be provided through pre- and in-service courses (under the leadership of one who knows activities for children, current practices in elementary education, and who is appreciative of the needs of classroom teachers); through workshops, demonstrations, sharing experiences with other teachers; and through referring to current literature.

Too few physical education specialists have had the type of training which would give them an understanding of the place and purpose of activity for children. The training of many of them has been geared to secondary or college level; therefore, a majority of them have had little work with children of various ages, and are quite unfamiliar with children in the elementary school setting. For the most part, teacher training institutions have been remiss in interpreting the whole area of play, movement, and expression and have tended to assume that the acquisition and performance of skills are the qualifications for teaching children. If physical education teachers are to be qualified to handle elementary physical education programs in elementary schools or teacher education institutions, then more emphasis must be placed on the specific interpretation of *how to help children grow through activity*.

All too often, men particularly in physical education have had little, if any, preparation in rhythmic activities—the very basis of sports, skills, and techniques upon which so much emphasis has been placed. Men as well as women teachers should be able to guide rhythmic experiences, such as folk and social dancing, if these experiences are to be valuable to children. Rhythmic experiences in their rightful place in the school program should challenge teacher training institutions in their offerings of creative experiences for teachers.

SCHOOL SETTING

Creative rhythmic movement experiences in the school program cannot happen in a vacuum; it requires a receptive environment, time, space,

and teacher guidance. A congenial atmosphere, with freedom and spontaneity, exists in schools which are adapted to children's needs. One of the major tasks of the administrator is to develop a "working together" atmosphere within the school which helps teachers and children feel free to realize they are surrounded by a democratic environment. The attitude and approach of the administrator to teachers and children will, in many ways, motivate and encourage, or thwart, creative expression. Rarely does creative expression have an opportunity to flourish in an environment which is stilted, authoritarian, or repressive. The elements of security, understanding, encouragement, and comradeship will promote creative rhythmic movement.

Congenial Atmosphere

The atmosphere within a school and the attitude of the administrators and teachers are reflected in the relationships of the various groups. Children need to know that they will not be laughed at or derided for their efforts in creative activities. It is discouraging to be laughed at by an older group of children or members of a teaching staff who do not understand or appreciate creative effort. It is a wonderful experience for different age groups to share in creative endeavors.

An understanding of what happens when children are "at work" is essential. They are noisy! Noise associated with creative rhythmic movement is wholesome, purposeful noise—the sort of noise happy children make. Noise comes from thuds on the floor, leaping or jumping, the "calling" and response "calls" in square dancing, the bursting into song, vocalizing to accompaniment, and hand-clapping and foot-stomping. Noise is necessary as group action and interaction take place. This has to be understood by the teacher and administrator. Percussion is noisy business at best, and when a group of children are playing a variety of percussion instruments, their noise increases as they experience a release through their response to rhythm. This noise, however, is not unlike that of a big orchestra tuning up, which is an acceptable type of noise for grownups. The need to vocalize from the sheer exuberance of living is not a unique characteristic of children. How many times have adults been heard to say, particularly at vacation time, "I feel so good I'd just like to scream." Why should teachers and administrators deny this emotional release to children? Thwarting a release because it involves too much noise is as cruel as giving a child an ice cream cone and telling him he can only look at it.

Time to Create

Time should be allowed for creative rhythmic movement to emerge naturally in correlation with various aspects of the school program. Undoubtedly the spontaneity and value of an experience is diminished if one must put it aside and wait for a specialist to come and provide opportunities to give it expression. When planned this way, it eliminates any necessity for programming rhythmic movement for ten- or twenty-minute periods on any given day or month, only to be forgotten the rest of the time. Flexible school programs allow rhythms to function as part of the total school experience. For example, a child's movement responses or expression about the circus are usually most vivid after a visit to a circus, or after reading about or discussing circus animals. Initiating a circus project comes most naturally when instigated by meaningful experiences. A Swedish folk dance fits into a child's program more adequately when there is a reason for doing Swedish dancing. This may be because he is studying about Scandinavia in social studies or because a child who has been living in Sweden has just become a new member of the class.

"Polishing up" the two-step or rhumba is more important as boys and girls make preparations for a coming school party where emphasis is to be placed on social dancing. Such factors have definite relationships when they are within the immediate experience of children.

If, because of scheduling difficulties, there has to be a specific period set aside for creative rhythmic movement, then time should be allowed for utilizing experiences in the classroom which may have been initiated during the rhythm period, or vice versa. Specialists or consultants need to know what goes on in the classroom and, by the same token, classroom teachers need to know and experience what goes on in the rhythm or activity periods in the playroom or gymnasium. The element of time is important. It takes time to explore, to create, to share studies and compositions, and to discuss and evaluate them. Firsthand experiences with materials are essential. In addition to time, materials are needed with which to express ideas. These materials may consist of a piano, percussion instruments, or a Victrola and records. Children must have access to, and personal experience with, these things as well as with art materials, blackboards, paints, papers, chalk, and other items. Children need to touch the piano and dabble in the paints and to bang, rattle, or shake the percussion devices. Thus they will recognize the characteristics of these instruments of expression through sight, touch, and sound.

Space Available for Movement

Room in which to move is essential to the establishment of a program of creative rhythms. A large gymnasium is not necessary. In such a large space the teacher and group may lose the intimate feeling which helps to encourage freedom of communication. The ideal space is a large classroom, kindergarten, music, or playroom. Children need room for stretching their legs and for the large locomotor movements—the leaps, gallops, and jumps—that carry them through space. They must have room to go up and to stretch out. Because their urge for activity is so great, it can be best satisfied only by a space which gives them opportunity to move freely. Space should be available where they can lie on the floor to relax after vigorous activity and continue to explore movement while in a resting position. Adequate space is also essential for various groups to plan and work out their movement interpretations.

Classrooms Are Usable. Many experiences in creative rhythms may be carried on in the ordinary classroom, especially if the desks are movable. If desks are not movable, a limited program in creative rhythmic movement can still be offered. Exploration of body movements, combinations of body movement, and various rhythmic elements can be initiated. Dance songs (samples of which are included in this book) also lend themselves to use in a classroom. Colorful pictures, charts, maps, drawings, and sketches found in the classroom provide further stimuli for movement.

If no other place is available, a limited program can be carried on in the halls. If administrators and teachers are concerned with children rather than facilities, they will utilize the end of a corridor, basement room, or make an exchange with a kindergarten. Often the music room is a good possibility. A basement boiler room, auditorium, a stage, corridors, an attic room, classrooms with nailed-down desks, music and art rooms, gymnasiums, playrooms, kindergarten rooms, out-of-door council ring, tennis court, and recreation hall and playground have been used successfully. If movement is important, then some space can be found for providing these experiences for children.

Using the kindergarten room

TEACHER GUIDANCE

Teachers are directly responsible for the development of meaningful experiences in creative movement. They play the major role in selecting and motivating opportunities for self-expression with children. They either provide or deny children the opportunity for release of this kind of expression which is so necessary for growth. They are responsible for initiating the situation in which cooperation and creativity prevail.

Creative rhythmic movement experiences can be so closely related with all that is going on in the classroom that teachers, if they are willing to explore with children, can provide many opportunities.

All Teachers Possess Creativeness

All teachers possess some degree of creativeness, though many of them may not have learned how to make use of it. Teachers who can raise an eyebrow, swing a foot, clap their hands, or beat a drum can release creative possibilities and share enjoyable experiences with children. As they start to explore movement with children and release some of their own creativeness, they may surprise themselves by rediscovering their abilities in movement. Teachers who believe in children, who are concerned about their growth and needs, and who are not afraid to explore can successfully guide creative rhythmic experiences. The teacher who recognizes the urgent needs of boys and girls for activity and expression will find that participation in creative rhythmic movement will aid and abet him, both as a person and as a teacher of children. The extent to which teachers can develop creative rhythmic movement with children will depend to a large degree on their understanding, knowledge and appreciation of movement, and their ability to express themselves through this medium. The realm of creativity provides a "togetherness" of teachers and children in a world which has no barriers. Teachers who can share in the process of creativity gain insight of children and themselves.

Teachers Set the Situations

All aspects of creative teaching must be original, and associated with experiences. This type of teaching must include a willingness on the part of the teacher to explore. It is not concerned with the superiority with which a child may perform a technique or set dance pattern; it is

Creative Movement Experiences

concerned with the development of each child and his own improvement and desire for participation. It is replete with experiences which come from, and are related to, children. An expressive rather than an impressive experience is sought.

Creative teaching is concerned with helping children to understand themselves better, evaluate their experiences in terms of themselves or the group, and work cooperatively with others. It is a process of expressing ideas and experiences, and there is no right as opposed to wrong way to react or respond. Cooperation and accomplishment for *all*, rather than competition (as to the "best"), is the goal of creative teaching. Teachers can rarely determine how great the creative spark, the extent of development, or the effect on the lives of children which a good program of creative rhythmic movement can make. *Teachers who work in this way with children recognize that something exciting, genuine, and important has happened to each child, to the group, and to themselves.*

When working creatively, teachers are more inclined to view education from the child's point of view, and see the reason for, and the meaning of, expression. This is the very essence of good teaching, because children's work is seen as important. Time and encouragement is given to creative efforts, and joint evaluation is continuous throughout the process of creative teaching. Children will evaluate in terms of their own readiness when they are free to make self-appraisal. Teachers understand children and their ability to achieve as indicated by their willingness to try and their earnestness to do better. Thus teachers witness the purest form of evaluation: letting children look at themselves honestly and unafraid, through their own product, and ask "How can I do it better?" There is no pretense or no barrier, only individual achievement and that goal of self-improvement—*learning*.

Success in creative teaching comes when teachers actively participate in the process. After initiating movement explorations, teachers set the situation by such a leading question as "We all have arms; what can we do with them?" Teachers do not have to be active participants in all the movement explorations. However, they continue to be active participants in the process by helping with accompaniment, encouraging children by the "verbal pat on the back," helping children to think through their problems, and suggesting other ways in which movement can be made. Using the voice as a motivating factor is another means of active participation on the part of the teacher. Taking *clues* from children, rather than always giving children clues, is another way of remaining active in the process. When the teacher asks such questions as "Why is Frank's gallop so good? What makes him go so high?" a group starts thinking about gallops and how they can improve their own. *Teachers set situations which make creativity possible.*

Summary

Some form of rhythmic expression is usually included in school programs but with little relationship to the total program. These forms of rhythmic expression are often included as bits of subject matter rather than being concerned with the needs and interests of boys and girls, or as a means of creative expression.

If one of the major functions of the school is to help children become creative individuals, then schools must provide creative activities adapted to the needs and interests of boys and girls. When creative rhythmic movement is one of the creative forms of expression in school programs, then it is dependent upon a place in the curriculum, time, space, a congenial atmosphere, the administrative understanding, and teacher guidance. The wider and richer the school program, the greater are the possibilities in creative rhythmic movement for the development of children.

All teachers possess some creativeness. They are responsible for setting the situation and initiating the creative process. Those who will attempt a creative approach to rhythmic experiences with children will gain deep satisfaction for themselves and a better understanding of how to work with children. By using this book and making use of some of its suggestions, teachers may find help for providing meaningful experiences for children in creative rhythmic movement.

"Jumping as high as we can!"

4. *Movement*

Children use movement as a medium of expression. Movement is the substance of this form of creative expression, and it is the framework around which, through which, and from which experiences are introduced and interwoven. Movement fundamentals are the same for all children and adults, regardless of age or grade. All should understand these fundamentals before progressing to more organized forms of dance.

By understanding movement fundamentals, and helping children to develop the body as an instrument of expression, we are encouraging boys and girls to be creative, express concepts, and solve problems. We are also bringing about better body coordination by providing opportunities for children to express themselves through movement. If all children were given this opportunity, it would not only be fun itself but also provide the basis for an easy and natural progression to folk and social and more organized dance forms. Children are helped to realize how simple social and folk dancing can be when they are an outgrowth of movement fundamentals.

MOVEMENT IS THE MEDIUM OF EXPRESSION

There is no one classification of movement, or a particular sequence for presenting or developing the fundamental movements. If there were, it would not only kill creative teaching but also stifle creative expression. Nor can movement be developed in isolation without a recognition of elements of space and rhythm. As movement is developed it is also affected by experiences, thoughts, feelings, and ideas which children continually have. The way in which these movement fundamentals, and the elements and experiences which affect them, are initiated depends upon the teacher, the situation, and the particular group of children. The following list and description of activities may serve as a guide:

MOVEMENT FUNDAMENTALS

Locomotor	*Body*	
walk	swing	twist
hop	bend	strike
jump	stretch	dodge
run	push	shake
leap	pull	bounce

Locomotor Combinations   *Body Combinations*
(See suggestion 3, on page 83.)

skip (walk and hop)	bend and stretch
slide (walk and leap)	swing and push
gallop (walk and leap)	push and pull
polka (hop, slide, walk,	strike and dodge,
hop, gallop, walk)	twist and shake
schottische (walk, walk,	bounce and pull
walk, hop)	

Locomotor and Body Combinations
(Examples)

leap and swing	skip and bounce
hop and shake	walk and twist
polka and bend	

Movement   **37**

ELEMENTS AFFECTING MOVEMENT

Space	*Rhythm*	
direction	tempo	
level	accent	rhythmic pattern
range	underlying beat	phrase
focus	duration	measure
floor pattern	intensity	

OTHER FACTORS AFFECTING MOVEMENT

experiences   thoughts
ideas   perceptions
feeling

Movement Fundamentals Described

To help clarify meanings of these various components, the terminology of children and illustrations of their explorations have been used. These illustrations have been taken from the recordings of stenographic notes resulting from working with many different groups of children and teachers in various situations.

Locomotor Movement. Locomotor movements are those which propel the body through space. They are the large free movements to which the legs give impetus. Children think of the movements in terms of "going some place" and how to get from here to there. There are five fundamental locomotor movements: walking, hopping, jumping, running, and leaping. All other locomotor movements which propel the body through space, such as skipping, sliding, galloping, and traditional dance steps, are variations or combinations of these five. (For instance, the skip is composed of the walk and the hop—a combination of two locomotor movements.)

Body Movements. Body movements are the nonlocomotor movements of which the body is capable. These emanate from a fixed base of sitting, standing, and kneeling. Children think of body movements as those they use "while staying right here, or what I do with my body without going any place"—*i.e.*, the way they can move their body while staying in one spot. Body movements are swinging, bending, stretching, pushing, pulling, twisting, striking, dodging, shaking, and bouncing.

Combination of Movements. Combination of movements may be either a series of locomotor

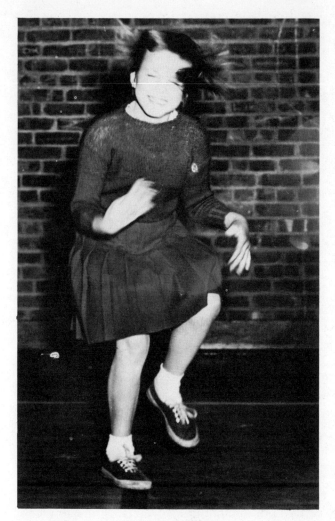

Mapes shaking like jelly

movements, (walking and leaping) or a series of body movements, (bending and stretching), *or* a series of locomotor *and* body movements (jumping and bouncing). Children think of combinations of movement as "putting two or more things together." It is natural for children to put movements together—to skip (walk and hop), to gallop (walk and leap), and to slide (walk and leap). Other illustrations of combinations, which are numerous, include skipping and swinging, sliding and pushing, and galloping, bending, and stretching, as well as such traditional dance steps as schottische, polka, two-step, waltz, and tango.

Acquisition of these fundamental skills and the awareness of them as tools to be used are basic to a program of creative rhythmic movement. Other experiences in this medium of expression result from, augment, or affect movement in some way or another. When children have had opportunities to explore movement fundamentals and to use these in combinations which feel good to them and which they understand, they have acquired tools (movement) for expression. They can concentrate on the spirit and fun of using these movement fundamentals in meaningful, organized patterns of expression.

Qualities of Movement. The way in which children execute movements characterizes the quality of their movements. Children think of these as "jerky," "bumpy," "smooth," "stiff," "loose," "hard," "soft," and "booming." For example, the way children execute a loose walk is quite different from the way they look or feel when they are doing a jerky walk. Qualities apply to all movement which helps children to express themselves more adequately.

ELEMENTS AFFECTING MOVEMENT

Movement is influenced, intensified, and affected by elements in space and rhythm. To start, concentration is on movement, and as we become familiar with locomotor and body movements we realize that there are elements which relate to movement. These elements which affect movement are readily observed when children *walk around* a room. They are moving through space to a rhythmic response; they are walking (means of a locomotor movement) around a room (going through space in a given direction) in accordance with certain rhythmic elements (the speed with which they move and the beat to which they respond).

Elements of Space

As children are given opportunities to explore movement, they become aware of the various elements in space which are related to the area which movement covers and the direction it takes. Children analyze, by saying, "We are going in a backward direction, using big steps, to cover a lot of space." The elements of space which relate to movement include: direction (forward, backward, sideward, and around), levels (high or low), range (small or large), focus (the attention of movements toward a specific spot, or point, in space), and floor pattern (the

picture, path, or design on the floor that is made while moving). Children understand these terms, and they become a part of their vocabulary as they discover them in connection with movement and space experiences.

Elements of Rhythm

As children continue to explore movement, they become cognizant of the various rhythmic elements. These rhythmic elements which relate to movement include, tempo, accent, underlying beat, rhythmic pattern, measure, phrase, duration, and intensity. Children have their own terms for these. The following terms in parenthesis illustrate this point: tempo (fast or slow), accent (loud or different beat or sound), underlying beat (steady beat or pulse which goes all the time), rhythmic pattern (pattern of beats or sound like a song), duration (even or uneven—short or long combination of sound or beats), intensity (loud or uneven—short or long combination of sound or beats), intensity (loud or soft—heavy, weak, or light sound), measure (divisions of beats or sentences of sounds), and phrase (ending and beginning again, like a paragraph of measures).

Yellow makes Bob feel light and happy

"Can you guess what animal I am?"

OTHER FACTORS AFFECTING MOVEMENT

When children are helped to develop movement tools for expression, they are more deeply influenced by additional experiences growing out of their own surroundings from those things they can *see*, *touch*, *feel*, or *hear*. Children may either translate these perceptions into movement, or the perceptions may provide the impetus for movement expression, or they may simply modify movement. For instance, nine- and ten-year-old children may perceive a design in the room, in the form of a picture, and with a body movement follow this design, making it in the air with their arm. They may also translate the design to the floor in the form of a floor pattern.

Children *look* at various colors and discuss the way a certain color makes them feel. Yellow usually makes them feel light and happy. (This has been tried with a number of groups of children and, almost without exception, yellow has made them want to take high, light skips.) They *hear* different sounds which stimulate them to move in response to the way they perceive the sound.

Movement may be further modified by the ever-present *feelings* or emotions which children possess. These are the experiences which come from within and give added meaning to movement or enhance movement expression.

Ideas and Thoughts

Probably the largest group of experiences related to movement are those concerned with the *ideas* and *thoughts* of children. When children have had a chance to explore movement, and have become conscious of and begin to use their bodies, they then need to be provided with innumerable experiences to help them express the many feelings, thoughts, and ideas which they have. These changing thoughts and ideas may be consciously translated into movement, may influence movement, or may serve as the stimulus for movement expression.

Other School Experiences Related to Movement

Percussion, songs, music, pictures, or graphic representations and a variety of other experiences adapted from everyday school happenings provide stimuli for movement. Units, classroom studies of different topics from divergent areas of language arts, arithmetic, and science or social studies also give impetus to movement. A host of other experiences may result from holidays, field trips, and everyday living in the city or the country. Seizing the opportunity to relate folk or social dancing with studies of cultural, national, or geographic backgrounds are all too often missed as an opportunity to integrate dance into the total school program. A detailed description of experiences and their relationship to movement will be found in the succeeding chapters.

The following account illustrates how the elements and experiences which have been discussed in this chapter affect *fundamental movement*. This excerpt is taken from the stenographic record of a period with a fifth-grade group of forty-three boys and girls. The main point of emphasis during the lesson was not on movement as such, but on space—particularly range and levels and how they affected and stimulated movement. Because the group could move freely it took only a few minutes to get them in motion to explore these elements in space. (Writing about an experience takes longer than working it with a group.)

T.: Teacher's questions, remarks, and suggestions
C.: Children's responses, answers

_____: Action

T.: If we said how tall could you be, what would you do?

C.: I'm stretching with my neck. Stretch _____.

T.: If we said how small could you be, what would you do? Let's see?

C.: Roll up; squeeze up; shrink _____.

T.: How wide can you be? _____. Make yourself even wider _____.

T.: Now shall we put ourselves in a box—a nice, tall, skinny box. (Children pulled various parts of them in _____.) And now let's break ourselves out of the box and see how much space we can use; let's change the range of our movements as we break out. (Some started head first, others started stretching feet first _____.)

T.: Let's put ourselves back in a little box and then make it go up like a tall box of flowers, like a gladiola box.

T.: How do we get to go higher? (This was the first question that elicited verbal response from the majority of children; most of the other responses had been motor responses up to this point.)

KAREN: We could jump.

T.: What could we put with a jump?

CLARK: We could hop and jump.

T.: Why don't we try this? Hop-jump, hop-jump. (The children went up and down and sideways, circling.) What does it say? Can you clap it?

GEORGE: "One foot, two feet" is what it says.

T.: Shall we try it? (Music followed the group, and was used for the first time.) Why don't you really let go? See how much space you can cover. Let's clap it again while you catch your breath _____. Shall we do it narrow and then wide? _____ Think of being back in that box and then springing out _____. See if we can go farther out if we use the upper parts of our bodies, too _____.

T.: What would help to remind us to jump and hop?

DAVE: We can say to ourselves as we do it, "Jump and hop," or, "Two feet and then one foot."

T.: That's a good suggestion. Let's try _____. Some of us aren't quite doing it. What do you suppose is wrong?

CLARK: It's because we are jumping too far to the side.

SHERAN: Maybe we are forgetting to hop and just jumping all the time.

GEORGE: Yes, but do we want to move just up and down or out to the side?

T.: Maybe we should try both—jump and hop in place, and then in space out to the side, and then in place again. Now let's move out every time we hop _____. That's it, jump where you are and then move out on your hops _____. Maybe if we say what we are doing, it will help _____.

GEORGE: Golly, I didn't hop because my jump carried me too far. I kept forgetting to hop. Suppose we watch George and all say "Jump, hop," while he does it _____.

T.: Is he covering space?

C.: Oh yes, just look at him go. Whee!

T.: Suppose we think of another way to cover space, using first a little kind of movement and then a big one, changing our range as we move. While you are resting think of ways, and then we shall try them.

T.: Could we work on different levels? What levels are we now?

C.: Low and medium.

T.: How long can you get? Now let's see if we can move our head; our feet; our hands. Now let's go way up tall. Now can you move some way in-betweenish? Now as high as you can go. Is this _____ high or low level?

C.: High, high.

T.: What else can we do?

JOYCE: We could bounce. We could bounce our heads and our fingers, too.

T.: Can you bounce sideward?

C.: Sure.

T.: This time try a little bounce with a small part of you, and then a big bounce with a large part of you _____. Good. Now let's see if you can change your levels while you keep on bouncing _____.

T.: Suppose we all get into three's, or not more than four's. Let's watch this group of three for a minute. Jackie, suppose you be the pivot and establish a level you want to start from _____. Now the other two take another level so that we see three levels. Good _____. We said that there were three levels, and now we can see those three levels. Now, do you think that you could change your levels so that we would continue to see three different levels? Let's make a game out of it.

JOEL: Can we do it? One can be high. One can be low, and I'll be in between.

T.: Shall we all work now at the same time, and see if we can continually change our levels within each group? Use any movements which seem good to you. And be careful to stay close enough together so that you can watch each other and we can tell that you are a group changing your levels. Let's see the pivot person _____. Now the others in relation to your center of pivot _____.

PETER: This is like statues.

T.: For just a second, let us watch Peter's group, working out their pattern of levels _____.

PETER'S GROUP: One jumping and turning (high level)
Another hopping, all bent over (medium level)
Another slithering around on his tummy (low level)

T.: Now let's see if you can change your levels, moving slowly from one to the other.

T.: Let's all try. You have to concentrate and keep your eyes on the rest of your group. Try moving a little slower. When we say "stop," everyone stop right where he is, but move all of the time in between. Stop. Hold your different levels. What is another way we could call "stop"?

BARB: We could freeze.

T.: O.K. Let's move, changing levels until we hear the call "freeze." Freeze.

T.: This time, suppose that we watch Penny's group _____.

PENNY'S GROUP: Jumping and reaching with alternate hands (high level)
Slow and fast shakes (in between level)
Bending and stretching down low and sidewards (low level)

C.: Jack looks like a cat; he looks like a shaggy dog to me moving close to the ground.

T.: What level is Jack?

C.: Low.

Levels—high, low, and in between

T.: George's group was doing something very interesting. They have quite a level's pattern started. Let's watch them _____.

GEORGE'S GROUP: (Moving in and out and up and down progressively, they turned in toward the center as they changed levels.)

T.: Let's all try changing levels once more, using another kind of movement and making it a jerky quality. We shall go on with this another day.

T.: It's choice time. What will the activity be today?

C.: Duck and Dive; more Freeze; Levels again; Hokie Kokie (and so on).

T.: The Hokie Kokies seem to be in the majority. Suppose we turn to the person nearest us for a partner and start singing and clapping to the chorus part (*see Chapter 12*). This time on the chorus part, ". . . and we do the Hokie Kokie and we do it Okie Dokie . . .," partners figure out something to do together. Let's try them out.

BOBBY AND PARTNER: (Jumping in opposition to each other, away from and toward the group circle.)

PETER AND PARTNER: (Swinging up and down in opposition.)

DANNY AND PARTNER: (Nonplussed Terry by saying, "Can you do the Mexican Jump?" and then proceeded showing. Both were soon doing it.)

JOEL AND PARTNER: (Jumping in opposition to partner—up and down.)

These are a few examples of the activities done by partners during the chorus. Although no mention was made of space elements, there was a carryover from the previous experiences—particularly levels.

Summary

Movement is the framework of this form of creative expression. It is fundamental to folk, social, and other dance experiences. How to get movement started and how it can be explored and developed as a medium of expression depends upon the teacher, situations, and the particular group of children.

"It's fun to move!"

5. *Movement Exploration*

Children crave *activity*. They love to move. As boys and girls vary in the length of their arms and the length of their legs so do they vary in their rates of maturity, levels of achievement, and aptitudes for learning. All these affect the way children move. As deep seated as their urge for activity is their desire for *expression*. They need to express themselves, individually, like Tad, Susy, or Teddy. As children vary in interests, experiences, and rhythmic responses so do they vary in their creative potentialities. These, too, affect the way boys and girls express themselves, so given a chance they will move, write, talk, paint, and sing out their thoughts, feelings, and ideas. When boys and girls are given this chance to express themselves through rhythmic experiences, they are fulfilling two fundamental and urgent needs of childhood—to *move* and to *express*.

THE CHILD'S INSTRUMENT OF EXPRESSION: THE BODY

Creative rhythmic movement is the child's interpretation of thoughts and feelings expressed through the use of his body. This medium of expression consists of a child's exploration of movement, and his use of it to express and interpret in his own way, in tangible form, that which is within his experience. Creative rhythmic movement differs from all other media of expression because the *body*, the child's instrument of ex-

pression, is always at hand. It takes desire, confidence, and motivation to set it in motion. When given opportunities, a child soon becomes aware of his wonderful instrument of expression, delighting in discovering the many ways in which he can make his body move. He discovers his body can move as a whole, or in parts. It is made up of arms, legs, fingers, toes, shoulders, a head, and a trunk, all of which have infinite capacity for movement variations. He finds his head can go up and down and around; it can go from side to side; it can swing, shake, and push; it can be made to move slowly, quickly, or jerkily, giving expression to some of the feelings which are within.

When a child discovers for himself the many different parts of his body, and how he can make it move, it becomes a joyous procedure, for he is learning by exploring, thinking, and thrilling at his own findings. He discovers he has large parts and small parts which can be moved simultaneously. Responding to the question, "See if you can move the very smallest part of you," such parts as fingers, toes, eyes, nose, tongues, and sometimes, even ears can be observed. "Now can you move two parts" may result in a variety of combinations. "What do you suppose is the biggest part of you, and can you move it?" brings forth response with trunk, hips, and shoulders.

When the concentration of finding out results in a series of movements that feel good, often one hears enthusiastic outbursts of "See what I can

Movement Exploration

45

do," or, "Whee, look what Mapes can do with her middle."

As children have opportunities to explore movement, they find they can make discoveries while sitting down, lying down, kneeling down, sitting at their desks, or in the way that is most fun of all—moving through a lot of space. They soon become aware of the many ways they can use their bodies, and they learn to enjoy movement for its own sake. For them it is the sheer joy and fun of the exhilaration they receive from going through the air when skipping, the energy they expend from leaping higher and higher, and the delight of just finding out how different parts move. Gradually, they gain control over all their parts and come to realize that they have an instrument of expression which can help them communicate their thoughts and ideas. In time, movement becomes so automatic that they can concentrate on other experiences which affect movement—space, rhythm, and ideas and the ways of organizing these into tangible forms: studies and compositions.

WHAT TEACHERS CAN DO TO GET MOVEMENT STARTED

Teachers must realize at the outset that the way of starting is unimportant. The essential element is *to get started*. How one approaches a group, and what one starts with, depends on what one knows about children: their needs, varying stages of development, interests, and former experiences.

Suggested Questions for Beginning

Having a few key questions pinpointed to the particular group will pose enough problems for starting to use bodies as instruments of expression. The following questions are only a few of the hundreds which have been used with various groups of children and adults to set them in motion. These questions suggest many more. Each of these involves concepts, thinking for one's self, finding out, exploring, and expressing in terms of movement.

Can we walk fast—faster—even faster?

How slowly can we walk?

What happens to our steps as we walk this way? (faster or slower)

What other ways can we walk?

Can you swing your shoulders? How can you swing your shoulders while you are walking?

What is another way we can move around the room besides walking?

Let's see if we can move our very smallest part. Now, can you move two small parts?

Can you move the biggest part of your body? What different ways can you move this big part of you?

Do you suppose that you can move a part from your neck up and at the same time a part from your hips down?

How heavy can you make yourself? Think of something very heavy, the heaviest thing in the world; can you make yourself that heavy?

How do you think you would move if you were in a very tiny box? Now, how could you move if you were in a great big box?

Is skipping forward the only direction you can go?

Why do you suppose Bob goes so high when he skips?

Can you skip and move your arms or head at the same time?

Can you take a jump and then a hop?

What is the difference between a jump and a hop?

How can you move while sitting at your desks?

While playing your percussion instrument, can you move another part of you?

Look at this picture, how is the horse moving? Who can show us?

These are only a few of the many questions which might prove helpful when beginning a movement approach with children or adults. Each teacher finds questions which can be used to good advantage. Because groups of children, situations, and teachers vary greatly, there is *no one question* which can be used. When movement does start, however, it will become an active experience for the teacher as well as the children. "Timmy, that was a terrific gallop. Show us how you did it. Why do you think Timmy gallops so high? How could we gallop higher and higher?" This does not mean the teacher necessarily has to gallop continually around the room with the children. If she desires to do so, all the better. However, she can participate actively by playing a gallop on the drum, clapping a gallop rhythm with her hands, making sounds with two sticks, or carrying the gallop beat in place with the feet.

Here are some other things we can do. If it is a group of first- or second-graders, the approach might be from a locomotor movement—*walking*. In response to such questions as "How did you walk to school this morning? Let's see. Did anyone have to get here in a hurry?" they usually discuss other ways of coming to school. (There often are some children who had to get to school in a hurry, and are ready to show how.) This may involve a discussion of coming on bicycles, in automobiles, in busses, and in other modes of transportation. When this happens the teacher has two choices: She can go back to the original question concerning the walk and explore it further, or she may pursue the cue concerning transportation. If, however, it is the very first approach to movement exploration, sticking with the original question of *walking to school* is usually better.

Defining the problem for the entire group in the beginning limits the situation and sets the framework for further exploration of the locomotor movement of the walk. (Transportation cue can be tucked away and used later.) "Did anyone have loads of time to get here? Did anyone walk with another pal?" are examples of questions which might help children start thinking about walking. Further questions and discussion may elicit the many different ways people can walk: high, low, bumpy, smooth, cross-legged, loose-legged, with a sore toe, with a walking cast, and many others. Exploration of animal walks may result if we are alert to cues from children. Susie says, "Look at me, I'm a turtle." Sure enough, Susie is a turtle. Then, immediately, there may be forty-two turtles, because Susie suggested it, and because it is fun to be a turtle. However, this might be a cue to talk about different animals, with each child suggesting the animal he wants to be. Perhaps the group needs more time before they can suggest a variety of animal ideas and walks. No two groups of children or all children within a group, will react in the same way to these questions or to this approach. In any case, the children are moving, and exploration has started.

The entire first experience in movement need not be confined to one activity, such as the walk. Rarely is one period of rhythms confined to one particular movement. Such a procedure not only causes boredom and loss of attention for some children, but does not constitute good teaching, any more than does spending an entire reading period on the comprehension of one word.

The following is a similar approach to movement exploration. "How can we get from here to there, from this spot to that spot, from this door and around the room and back to the door again?" When movement is started in this manner, children have opportunities to devise new and different ways of moving from one place to another. Exploring movement becomes a game which children call "How to get there."

With a fifth- or sixth-grade group a first approach to rhythmic movement may be quite different from the approaches just discussed. These children are not the same in their responses, reactions, and experiences. We often hear them comment, "No sissy stuff for me." Creative rhythmic movement can be as vigorous as a football game. Boys and girls of middle childhood desire and need strenuous, vigorous activities. Their motor coordination helps them to do many a spatial feat of movement. They particularly like the thrill of getting up in the air to see how high they can go. This calls for the use of jumps, hops, or leaps which get them into the air. Therefore, a first approach might be one to get them in the air. "Let's see if we can hop on one foot and just let the other one go where it will. Now let's see if you can swing the other foot while hopping. How low can you hop . . . and now how high?" As they are exploring, Dave starts hopping low, going sideward. This gives a cue to explore hopping in different directions: forward, backward, sideward, and around. And, so they are *moving!*

In a group of sixth-grade boys, the jumps and leaps seldom miss! The first approach to this group might be, "Let's see how high we can jump. Can you go even higher? What helps us to go higher? Can you turn around in the air as you jump?" Thus, movement exploration begins.

Another approach to any group is with the help of two rhythm sticks. Movement explora-

"Here's an arm—what can we do with it?"

tion responding to the hitting together of two sticks can be fun, for it has a game element which readily attracts a group. Children often ask for the "Stick Game." It goes like this: As two sticks are hit together the children are asked to respond to the sound; as the sound gets louder they go higher and higher, as the sound gets softer they go lower and lower. The same idea can be used in the discovery of range and direction and other variations of movement.

Some exploration of body movement can be started while groups are sitting on the floor, or even if they are on chairs or at desks. "Here's an arm . . . what can we do with it? Can we move it? How? Let's see if we can move it another way?" "Sure," says Ginny, "I can move mine around and around like this." "Can you move any other part of your body besides your arms? Let's see if you can move five different parts, one right after the other." Again, movement exploration has begun! Encouraging children to think further and to make associations we might use such questions as "What does it make you think of when you shake your 'middles'?" A universal response is "Santa Claus' tummy" or a "bowl of jelly."

Moving heads, arms, legs, or eyes while singing peppy songs may be, for these boys and girls, another way of exploring movement. Dance songs (action songs—see Chapter 11) designating specific movements are good motivating devices. Songs originated for this purpose, such as the one below, are found in Chapter 11:

FOLLOW, FOLLOW

Movement Exploration

Follow, Follow (Cont.)
Movement

As the group sings the song, they follow the movements of first one and then another. The teacher or a child starts with such a movement as swinging the arms, and the group does likewise. During the last line another person is designated to continue by pointing to, calling out name, taking turns by seats, and so on. The song is continued until all have had a chance to suggest a different movement. Lack of space is not prohibitive as far as opportunities for discovering movement are concerned.

Additional opportunities may be provided by using children's drawings, sketches, or paintings, all of which can give impetus to movement. A horse in action, an airplane taking off, or a rocket ascending may suggest a discussion of something fast or slow. "Could you make your arm move fast . . . or slow? Could you gallop fast like that horse in the picture suggests? Could you make a slow movement with your body which would be like the plane approaching a landing?"

Use of percussion (see Chapter 9) may afford another way of initiating movement exploration if each child has some piece of percussion to play so that all may participate at once. Percussion devices may be drums, rattles, pencils, sticks, keys—anything that will make a sound. Even though a tumultuous din may result in the beginning, controls which are set up by the teacher and the children can arrange order out of chaos. Just as an orchestra has a leader, we may have ours, helping to keep us together; starting and stopping with a signal which has been agreed upon. The discussion of an orchestra recently seen on television might be an introductory cue. As children become more familiar with their instruments, one of them is bound to move some part of his body, thus giving the cue. "Look, Margie is playing her instrument and moving her head at the same time. Could we move a different part of us while playing our instrument?" One more movement exploration is underway. This method has been used effectively with beginning adult groups who are reticent about moving out on the floor. Sitting together and having the percussion instruments in their hands often gives them the security needed to start relaxing, releasing, and responding. After discovering the many ways their instrument can be played they often forget about the instrument and are moving body parts before they know it.

To get movement started, it helps to have some kind of accompaniment (the kind of accompaniment that *follows* the children and picks up patterns, tempos, and beats from the group, rather than accompaniment that sets the pattern for the group). A piano helps to make the experience a more pleasurable one, but it is not a *prerequisite* for offering movement opportunities. Regardless of whether a piano, drum, or Victrola is used, the instrument supplies accompaniment that responds to the group. (See Chapter 9 for discussion on accompaniment.)

Listed above are but a few of the ways of getting movement started. Many other suggestions should occur to the teacher as she reads the following chapters, remembering that no two children or two groups of children will react in the same way to an approach. They react in terms of their own experience.

How Children May React

Unlike adults, boys and girls need no warming-up period before their bodies can be put into action. They are warmed up all the time; one has only to watch a group of children burst forth from home or school to recognize their readiness for action. Vigorous movement experiences can be a part of the very first rhythm period. In fact each period should include a mixture of strenuous and relaxed activity, because this is important to the way children learn.

Children's first opportunity to explore creative movement may cause untold reactions. The experience in itself may be so *needed* that it is like "uncorking a bottle." For a time it may seem as though there is no controlling the spirits. Such response may only serve to show how much these children need just such an "uncorking." On occasion, the reverse may happen; children may have had the cork put in so tightly that they will need repeated experiences to loosen it. Before long, though, out it should come, and the teacher who helps children give vent to their feelings may witness miracles before her eyes.

Boys and girls may react immediately, but as in anything else, it may take a little time to "unloosen" them. If one approach does not work, another will, especially if teachers are on the alert for the cues of children. Some children may have been conditioned by suppression and, therefore, need time, encouragement, and security in order to venture forth with ideas of their own.

Others who have been held in by close quarters are apt to stick together despite open space. If they have been continually confined to a small circle painted on the floor, they tend to herd together. All we know about child development tells us that children need to spread out, that they need freedom instead of a small, painted circle, and that they need space to move unrestrictedly.

Due to overcrowded conditions and safety hazards in the school setting, children may not have had opportunities to move freely—going and coming through various parts of the school. Therefore, they may not react at all, or they may giggle, or they may become rampant when they make their initial approach to movement expression.

These reactions should tell us much about these children. We should be hesitant to interpret such reactions as meaning that there is something wrong with the rhythm activity, or the approach to creativity. Rather, it should indicate how much the children need some form of movement experience. Further, it may mean that several attempts are needed before movement exploration is productive.

After a movement experience is introduced, the tangent it takes depends on the teacher and children. Cues will emerge to help in the selection of experiences which may be pursued further. As long as everyone is given an opportunity to explore, to let loose, and to give out, there is sure to be discovery, especially if all children are encouraged to feel their discoveries are worth while.

Swinging like a cow's tail, railroad signal, clock pendulum

When children are kept busy discovering, trying things out for themselves, and then sharing some of these findings, there is little time for mischief or wasting time. Instead, there is an atmosphere of working, thinking, moving, and having fun together.

Situations in which children and teachers together are exploring rhythmic movement require a give-and-take in the group. Experiences of this sort are natural for developing a spirit of cooperation and a feeling of being together to define the limits and controls. Since we are responsible for building the environment in which we work and live with children, our attitudes are most important. If we are truly desirous of an environment which will encourage genuine respect and a give-and-take, then we must evince willingness to explore and create with children, rather than only a reluctance "to put up with them." Creativity doesn't just happen. It isn't disorder, bedlam, or just doing as one pleases when the spirit moves; it is a series of well thought out situations which involve planning of experiences that are meaningful to a group. Providing situations takes into account the cues children offer. The boy who decides to be a bucking bronco when the children are being horses; the girl who can't be a flower because her stem broke; or, the child who can't go any lower because the floor is in the way are some typical children's responses which, if respected by the teacher, contribute to the give-and-take feeling—a part of working together. These experiences in creative rhythmic movement offer vital opportunities for teachers to thoroughly appreciate, enjoy, and better understand what children are like.

Planned ideas, where the teacher says such things as "Let's all be automobiles," should be avoided in the beginning before boys and girls are acquainted with movement as a means of expression. Saving the idea approach until later, when children have become familiar with the movement approach and are secure in the ways they can use their bodies freely as instruments to readily express ideas, will avoid embarrassment and humiliation at the outset.

Movement Experiences Initiated with a Second Grade

The following account illustrates how movement experiences were initiated with a second-grade group. These children were working with the author for the first time, therefore exploration of movement was necessary to become familiar with them and their knowledge of movement. The lesson was given as a demonstration for elementary school teachers. It was developed and stenographically recorded as it appears below. The use of questions, cues, and reactions of the boys and girls and the progression within the lesson should be noticed.

Demonstration Lessons

TEACHER: Let's all move out and take a little space. Now let's see if we can go way down as low as we can. How low can we go? Lower yet?

CHILDREN: Uh! Uh!

T.: How high can you go? Peter, how high can you go? And Jean? Still higher? What would make you go even higher?

FRANK: Jump _____.

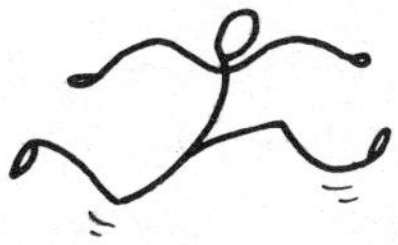

T.: Let's go way up. What would help us to go high?

FRANK: Jump and push.

MARGIE: Use your arms.

T.: Let's try that jump and move our arms. Jump, jump. _____. Let's clap our hands and make them say jump. Do we jump with one foot or two?

C.: Two.

T.: Let's watch and see _____. Could you jump around the room? What else could you do to move around?

MARGIE: Gallop and gallop.

T.: Could you clap what a gallop says? Is it fast or slow?

CHARLEY: Fast, fast, fast.

T.: Let's gallop; faster, faster; and gallop, gallop _____. Whoa. Can you make your hands gallop? Now your heads, shoulders, arms? Let's really let them go—your hips, knees, too. Shall we clap it again? Now your tongues, and fingers. Frank, will you show how you galloped? Let's clap the way he galloped.

CHARLEY: Why doesn't he do it again, and we'll clap what he does?

T.: What was good about that?

MARGIE: His feet.

CAROL: He *really* looked like a horse.

BOBBY: He did it so quietly.

T.: What kind of a horse do you think he was?

MAPES: A pony.

T.: Good! Do you think we could gallop slowly? And slower—and faster—and slower—. Poor old horse; he can hardly make it.

C.: Whew!

T.: Poor old Raggedy Andy; he just let his head go flop, flop, flop, and then his shoulders go flop, flop, flop, and pretty soon his hips flop, and his knees go flop, and his ankles go flop, flop, flop until. . . . Poor old Raggedy Andy and poor old Second Graders, they couldn't stand up any more so they went flop right down on the floor.[1] While you are lying on the floor, how heavy can you be? What's the heaviest thing you can think of? You don't look heavy Peter. I'll give you about one minute to decide what the heaviest thing is that you can be. Joan, can you decide?

JOAN: I'm just heavy in my feet.

T.: Can you be heavy in your hips? your shoulders? your head? Watch Bobby, see how even his fingers are heavy? I can't lift him.

MAPES: Well, I can lift him; well, anyway, I can lift his feet.

T.: See if you can turn yourself into something heavy.

C.: Alligators, a train, a floor, a tree, elephants.

BOBBY: Well, I'm the iron on a train.

T.: Let's turn and lie on our backs and see what the lightest thing is that we can be now. Be oh so light! Can you make your fingers light? and your shoulders? and your hips? (At this point there was much wiggling and waving of fingers and toes.) Peter, that's good. What is the lightest thing you can be?

PETER: A toy truck.

JOHN: A breeze.

BARBARA: A cushion.

CAROL: A pillow.

VICKI: I guess I don't know.

MIKE: Air.

MAPES: Toilet paper.

T.: Shall we sit up and just move our fingers and keep them light? And now move our toes.

FRANK: Let's move our heads.

MAPES: Let's move our tummies.

PAULA: Whee, look what Mapes can do with her middle!

MIKE: I can wiggle my shoulders.

T.: Shall we see if we can move all over? How else can you move around?

CAROL: We could skip.

MIKE: We can shake.

T.: Let's see you shake, shake, shake _____.

PETER: I can bend and str_____etch.

T.: What bends and stretches like we are doing?

MIKE: A rubber band.

PETER: Putty will too.

---

[1] Gladys Andrews and Marion Bozenhard, *Creative Rhythms for Children* (Master's thesis, University of Wisconsin), Mimeographed edition, copyright, 1939, by the authors.

T.: Show us how your body bends and stretches; that's good, Carol.

MAPES: I'm "stretching" like a snake.

T.: What else can we do? How else can we move?

PETER: We can move our legs.

CAROL: I'm shaking.

PETER: Look at my legs.

MIKE: I'm swinging myself.

JOHN: I'm still shaking.

CAROL: I can pu-u-ush _____.

MIKE: And I can pull.

T.: Let's all push, push, push _____ and pull. Now, let's see if we can shake with our toes, our heels, our knees, our hips, our shoulders, our heads—all over. Shall we do it again? What is it that shakes all over?

BOBBY: Well (*in the most serious and gravest tone of voice*), I would say that I was one of those little toy trucks that go up and down.

PETER: I'm a top.

CAROL: Horses. But I'm shaking way inside my shoes and all the way up.

T.: Shall we try a shaky skip? _____ That wasn't very easy, was it?

C.: No-o-o-o-o.

T.: Shall we see if it's easier with a swing—like with your arms? Let's skip in place. Can you clap a skip?

FRANK: I can make my fingers skip.

T.: Can you make your tongues skip? Let's clap a skip on our knees, keep it skipping. Let's make every part of us skip. Let's move with it now. See what you can do that feels good with your skip. Let's stop. That was very good; I saw all kinds of skipping. Would you like to see what Bobby was doing? He crossed his legs over as he skipped. It was hard, wasn't it?

DORA: I walked and stepped.

T.: When I first met you today, what did you tell me you were studying about?

GINGER: We've been studying about turtles, and we've been studying about dinosaurs.

T.: What's the difference between a turtle and a dinosaur? And how would they move?

MAPES: Turtles are funnier and dinosaurs real bigger. Look, I'm a turtle.

T.: What other animals could you be?

STASSIE: Monkeys.

T.: What does a monkey do?

SUZIE: Tricks; he can hang by his tail, but we can't do that.

T.: What are some other animals?

MAPES: Cave men.

JOHN: Deer.

T.: What does a deer do?

FRANK: He runs and leaps.

T.: How would you like to have a zoo? (They were divided into seven groups and given about three minutes to work out what they were going to be.) Stay in your spots and decide on your animals, and then you can come back to the zoo in your little groups. Where shall we start?

Frank's group

T.: What are you?

CAROL: I'm an elephant.

T.: Oh, you're all elephants.

CAROL: No, I'm the elephant, the only elephant.

FRANK: I'm a deer. (He ran lightly and swiftly and softly and was beautiful in motion.)

NINA: I'm a horse, and I can prance.

Peter's group

C.: We're great, big dinosaurs.

GENE: I'm a wild one.

Vicki's group

C.: We're kangaroos.

"How light can you be?"

"How small can you get?"

Movement Exploration

A group of four boys
C.: We're monkeys.

A group of two boys
MIKE: We're frogs, watch us hop.

A group of one boy and two girls
C.: We're birds.
T.: What kind?
C.: Cardinals, we guess.

A group of four girls
T.: What are you—turtles?
MAPES: I'm not—I'm a big gorilla. (Her arms were dragging all over the floor.)
T.: Of course, you know the gorilla got to the zoo before the turtle. Now that all the animals are back in the zoo, that's all we can do today.
C.: Oh gee.

Summary

A teacher might say, "Why explore movements with children when they come so naturally?" That, however, is the crux of the matter; often this medium of expression is overlooked as a means of learning, because it comes naturally.

Helping children to explore movement by using their bodies is the starting point. There is no one order, no right order or sequence. How we initiate these movements—how we include different elements which affect movement—depends on the teacher and the group of children. We select questions, cues, and experiences that will best motivate a particular group. We start a group with a simple suggestion or question concerning a fundamental movement (such as a hop), build on this locomotor movement, and then continue to the other movements (jump, walk, and so on). We may start with a body movement (swing) or with a combination of movements (push and pull). We discover many possibilities concerning the movement selected: how we do it, what we are doing, how we can do it better, what it reminds us of, how it feels, and how it looks. These are but a few of the ways we can start to work and become familiar with fundamental movements.

Children in action

6. Development of Movement

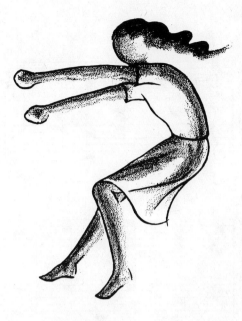

The way each child is constructed and the kind of body he has determines *his* kind of movement. The basic fundamental movements are natural to a child; he can explore them in many ways, talk about them, and analyze and use them to express that which is within his experience. Fundamental movements have been defined in general terms, but this chapter is concerned with specifics. No attempt will be made here to indicate the extent of development of any one locomotor or body movement. Instead, samples will be presented to indicate how children have considered them, how boys and girls have explored and developed them, and how movement has been used to express experiences.

It is difficult, if not impossible, to portray through the written word a true picture of the spontaneity, intense concentration, exhilaration, electric atmosphere, and the give-and-take that is evident when children are exploring, expressing, and *creating*. One large factor contributing to this difficulty is the fact that children move and think very quickly. The samples recorded here may be considered as the kinds of things which can be done with children in the various aspects of creative rhythmic movement. *The examples, suggestions, teaching hints, ideas, and descriptions of experiences are related as they have actually been developed and recorded from accounts of working with teachers and children.*

LOCOMOTOR MOVEMENTS—NATURAL EXPRESSIONS OF CHILDREN

The way in which children are constructed determines to a large degree their performance of locomotor movements. Since we have only two legs we can do only so many kinds of locomotor movements. Of the basic locomotor movements (walking, hopping, jumping, running, and leaping) the most common is walking.

Walking is basic to many other step patterns. It is a transfer of weight from one foot to the other, or stepping from one foot to the other. Children say, ". . . on one foot and then on the other." One foot is on the floor at all times.

WALKING

FLORENCE BURNS

Hopping is on one foot. If we put our weight on *one foot* and elevate ourselves by pushing off the floor and landing on the *same foot* it is hop-ping. Children say, ". . . up in the air and back down again on just one foot, the same foot, like a puppet on a string."

HOPPING

JOYCE ELDRIDGE

Development of Movement

Hopping (Cont.)

Jumping is on two feet. If we have our weight on two feet and elevate ourselves by taking off from the floor and landing on the floor again with both feet simultaneously, it is a jump. Children tell us that they take off and land on the same two feet.

JUMPING

FLORENCE BURNS

Running is a faster movement than the walk and includes more elevation. If we do a faster step, pushing a little harder against the floor, suspending the body in the air for just a moment, so that we transfer weight while getting some elevation, it becomes a run. According to children, this is "being in a hurry in the air just a little."

RUNNING

JOYCE ELDRIDGE

Leaping is the elevation, or suspension, of the run, which is held in the air for a longer period of time, with a transfer of weight from one leg to the other. Actually there is little difference be-tween the run and the leap, except in range of the movement. Children analyze the leap as "going away up in the air, stretching out from one leg to the other—like going over a big puddle."

LEAPING

JOYCE ELDRIDGE

These are the locomotor movements. Other locomotor movements or steps are combinations of two or more of these five movements or steps. Some of these are easier for children to perform than others. For instance, in working with about six- to nine-year-olds, if the run is developed be-fore they know how to manage this kind of free-dom, or before they have had many opportunities to move freely, a group may get out of hand. The very nature of the run, with its accompanying exhilaration, often makes children "let loose" like exploding firecrackers. As in anything else with children, their readiness for an activity is an im-portant consideration. Similar difficulties may be encountered when the leap is introduced. Young-sters of middle and later childhood particularly enjoy the leap because it requires a fair amount of coordination. To present it to first- or second-graders who have not acquired the necessary coordination may cause discouragement. It can be used most satisfactorily when the group has learned to respond to individual and group tempo. There are, of course, some first-graders who can execute beautiful locomotor movements without exception. For the most part, though, children of this age are not ready for the leaps.

Let us explore some of the locomotor movements. What we discover about the walk could be applicable to any of the other locomotor movements. Many of the same questions and cues for motivation could be applied as effectively to any of the other movements. When a child explores one element, such as the walk, it holds his special attention. He is rarely conscious of other elements entering in until they are pointed out to him, or until he suddenly discovers them. Let's look at all kinds of things we can develop from the walk. The walk progression in this chapter is developed with children of early childhood, while the jump progression, which follows, is carried out for middle or later childhood. It cannot be too strongly emphasized, though, that while certain age groups were kept in mind in developing these progressions, they may be used for any age group by making certain adaptations. (These adaptations are largely concerned with readiness in terms of language, coordinations, and experience.)

Walk Progression

The walk, the most basic of all the locomotor movements, is the foundation for folk and social dancing. It is important that each child be encouraged to develop the kind of walk that is best for him. This should be a free, easy walk—his kind of a walk—rather than a stylization of someone else's. Restrictions and stiffness, such as those frequently resulting from marching, should be avoided. The music which accompanies walking should likewise avoid stylization and should have an easy, natural quality.

To begin with, we could say, "Let's just start with an easy walk, going around the room toward the door. The music will pick up our walks as we move." With the walk (hop, jump, run, or leap) we discover that we can go high, low, or somewhere in between. We have short, long, fast, slow, hard, soft, heavy, and light walks. We can walk quickly and then slowly, up high and then down low, or we can walk and then stop, and then walk again. We can walk, turn around, and walk the other way. (With this exploration we need plenty of room to avoid bumping.) This often necessitates a discussion of what is meant by controlling our walks so that we will not bump into one another. This can be presented to the class by comparing the situation to a problem concerning traffic and automobiles.

In answer to the question "What other ways could we walk?" children discover all sorts of variations. They walk on heels, peg-legged, with a goose step, on the outside or inside of the feet, with the toes turned in or out, with the knees in or out, or they may just lumber along or be crooked all over. Exploration such as this often gives us a cue for finding out about animal walks. "Look at Red; he reminds me of a duck, the way he is walking." "Nat looks just like a penguin." And that is just what Nat was. In fact she became so much interested in penguins and how they waddled, that she talked about it, and as she talked she developed a story about penguins. By saying her story over and over it became a part of her. She was encouraged to sing it rather than tell it, and soon a tune emerged and became Nat's Mr. Penguin song. It was recorded, and music was arranged. Since the time it was originated it has been used in many ways with children. Sometimes it has been used when exploring walks; other times when working on qualities of movement, because there is a definite quality about a penguin's movements. Once it was "just right" to enhance a story about penguins which a first grade had been reading.

Pets which children have in their classroom or at home or a visit to the zoo, circus, or museum may occasion a discussion about animal walks. A group of first-graders were concerned with their setting hen. They became interested in the way Henny

Mr. PENGUIN

Words and Music by NAT

Arr. JOYCE ELDRIDGE

O! I'm a pen- guin in a full dress suit, I'm al - ways travel-ing in a crowd. Tho' I'm a mem-ber of a state - ly crew, I some - times de - vi - ate, don't you?

Penny walked. This instigated finding out how Henny Penny walked. A lively discussion resulted, which called for "let's find out."

Other discussions have centered around which animals do walk, how they walk, why they walk, and ascertaining whether they do not walk. Children become walking ducks, penguins, hens, lobsters, tigers, dinosaurs, and turtles. This may lead into a discussion and further exploration about the way a turtle would move in contrast to a dinosaur. We may all be the same kind of an animal, or we may all be different ones. We could all be animals which are small, and then, animals which are big. Sometimes we decide that because Jeannie is a cute, little, lively monkey who toddles along with her walk we all want to walk like monkeys. As we explore how our monkey is moving, we often say or call out things, such as "Look, we're all monkeys in the zoo," or, "I'm a monkey, so are you," or, "Aren't we funny?" Out of this might develop a poem or a song from ideas and words which fit together. From just such an exploration among seven-year-olds, the following ditties resulted:

Development of Movement

We're all monkeys, we're in the zoo
I'm a monkey, so are you
We can do all kinds of things
Watch us close . . .
Now aren't we funny.

I'm a monkey, so are you
Come and see me at the zoo
I am happy, I am gay
You can see me every day
I eat bananas brown and yellow
Come and see me at the zoo.

To the first ditty they sang an original melody which was recorded as they composed it. The second they sang to the tune of "The Alphabet Song", as the group walked and moved around.

Another approach to walking might develop from a discussion about people. "Look at the way Ralph is walking; he makes me think of my mailman," someone says, so such questions as these follow: "As you were walking to school today, whom did you meet on the street? What kind of a walk did he have? Could you walk like someone you know? Will you let me guess whom you might be?" This may bring about a wide variety of such responses as "milkman," "policeman," "barber," "grocery man," "garbage collector," and many more.

Ginny may say, "You know what? This is the way my Granddaddy walks!" This cue starts us exploring the way baby walks, Mom and Dad walk, and sometimes points a discussion about how "we" walk. We try to find out what helps us walk and what we do with our head or arms and other things. Sometimes the way we walk affects the way we feel, and we find we have certain "qualities" in our walking. Our walks can be *smooth* like a skier, *jerky* like a robot, *bumpy* like a cowboy, *stiff* like a stilt man, *loose* like Raggedy Ann, and *booming* like a firecracker.

We learn that we can walk in various directions, in response to a question like, "Can you only walk forward toward the door?" Responses of "backward, sideward, or around" are elicited. Sometimes recognition of various types of walks

"How does Henny Penny walk?"

takes a little prodding, but it is fun to go forward and then back up. (We find as we start to back up that sometimes we have collisions. This means a discussion about the ways we can avoid bumping into one another. We need to remind ourselves often about the problem until we can all go in various directions without danger.) We explore many items in connection to direction of movement. We find that as we walk sideward different things happen to our legs, and that we can walk sideward with our legs crossing over in front or in back, or with our legs going side by side.

After this discovery we might divide into small groups (about two to three in a group for seven-year-olds, but larger groupings for older children) and make a walking study by combining different directions in which each group moves. We may come from the different corners of the room to our opposite corner (the backward walkers, then the sideward, and then the around walkers). All this walking movement makes a design and leads easily to more discoveries of walking in larger and larger space.

Another approach to walking might be: "Could you walk so we can hardly hear you?" "What kind of a walk might we call the one you are doing?" In exploring further this soft light walk we ask the questions, "What does this make you think of? Does walking lightly make you think of anything?" The answers usually come tumbling out. Walter starts, "Yeah, snow or quiet rain." Others follow: "Tick of a clock, baby asleep, airplane 'way in the distance, sail boat, the desert, soft breeze, candlelight in a dark room, church, ghosts." To deepen the problem solving experience we might ask, "How could you walk so that we could hear every step?" The answer is, ". . . heavy with both feet, making loud sounds." "Do you feel any different when you walk lightly or heavily? Let's watch and see if we look any different when we walk heavily or lightly. Can you think of anything that seems like a heavy walk?" Robert says, "Sure, hail stones," when given time to think; others venture such suggestions as squeaky shoes, riveter, steam roller, rubber boots, horses, elevator, redwood tree. When

an elevator was mentioned, a lively discussion followed, which is typical of those which might evolve from any exploration. (It is here that the teacher has to know when to let it be discussed, how far to let it go, when to channel it, and when to change the topic.) Mickey picked up the idea of the elevator immediately: "Huh, an elevator doesn't make a noise like a loud sounding walk." From Toby: "It does, too; I listen to it every day when I go home—I ought to know. It grunts and groans and makes a terrible sound, just like this groany, grunty walk." This particular group of seven-year-olds were "loosened up," and well on their way to discovering movement. They were secure within their group and able to talk freely about their discoveries. This discussion led into a serious conversation about elevators: the different kinds, how they worked, how they were controlled, the noises they made. The children became different kinds of elevators—express, dumb-waiter, freight, old-apartment house, and automatic. (Of course, the teacher doesn't know all the answers, so teacher and children have to find out from those who do.) All this makes for exploring movement.

Playing a walk on a tom-tom often starts endless explorations, incidentally bringing in elements of rhythm. Using percussion frequently helps us discover more ways of responding to a walk. We say to a child who is playing a tom-tom, "Do you suppose you could listen while we walk, and then, try to play our beat?" To encourage children to think more about their movement, and to help them get the rhythm of the walk, we often pose the question, "Can you clap the walk? Let's try to keep our claps steady and not let them get faster and faster."

We also find we can make other parts of our bodies "go like a walk." We say we are walking with our heads, eyes, tongues, fingers, knees, and so on. This way children get the feel of the walk throughout their bodies. They find that they can make certain rhythmic patterns.

movement pattern	walk walk walk walk walk
rhythmic pattern	▬▬ ▬▬ ▬ ▬ ▬▬
movement pattern	long long short short long
rhythmic pattern	slow slow fast fast slow

Children can accent the first walk of a series of walks:

accent >
movement pattern  *walk walk walk*

They can make up walking songs and make their song say what they are doing. They can respond to poetry (see also source material), such as Elinor Wylie's "Velvet Shoes":

> Let us walk in the white snow
> In a soundless space;
> With footsteps quiet and slow . . .[1]

or Vachel Lindsay's "The Mysterious Cat":

> I saw a proud, mysterious cat,
> I saw a proud, mysterious cat,[2]

Through walking discoveries elements in space are easily recognized. Children may discover, or it may be pointed out to them, that as they walk they make certain patterns or designs on the floor. This may be a good time, then, to start working on floor patterns. (Full development of floor patterns will be discussed in Chapter 7.) We may discover rangy walks, walks which have focus to them, and those which are concerned with different levels.

When given opportunity children find various kinds of combinations of movement based on the walk—walk and leap, walk and jump, walk with a twist, walk with push and pull, walk with a bounce. Discovering the combination of the *walk-hop* is fun, because children find out that it sometimes becomes the *skip*. As they go faster in this combination, and pull their knees up, first

SKIP (or SLIDE)

With a lilt   (See suggestion 3, page 83.)   JOYCE ELDRIDGE

[1] Elinor Wylie, "Velvet Shoes," from *Collected Poems of Elinor Wylie*. Copyright, 1921, 1932, by Alfred A. Knopf, Inc.

[2] Vachel Lindsay, "The Mysterious Cat," from *Johnny Appleseed and Other Poems* (New York: The Macmillan Company, 1925). Used by permission of The Macmillan Company.

one knee and then the other, and *change their rhythm from even to uneven*, the *walk-hop* combination becomes the *skip*. This is something they can figure out for themselves, especially if we make it a game or a problem to solve. It is not too difficult for them to find that the rhythm is uneven; the hop is shorter than the walk. Joel says, "It doesn't sound like a walk anymore; it sounds like two different sounds and they say dummmmmmmm da, dummmmmmmm da."

movement pattern	walk hop walk hop
rhythmic pattern	—— — —— —
underlying beat	———— ————

Skipping is probably the most loved of all the locomotor movements. It isn't often that the skip needs to be taught. When there is a "one-footed" skipper in the class, however, this device of pulling up first one knee and then the other, together with decreasing the tempo, may help a child to analyze his own movement difficulty. Sometimes we find that children have difficulty skipping because of their balance. Working with body movements and combinations of movement, in order to help children use body and locomotor movements together, may aid children with their balance. In addition, it is fun to sharpen wits by analyzing movement, gaining in ability to clap sounds that feet make (and sounds that we hear others do), and recognizing the difference between a skip which is uneven in sound, or an even walk-hop. "Close your eyes and listen. Can you tell whether Joan is skipping or walking? Listen to the tom-tom; is it skipping or walking? What is the piano saying—even sounds of walking or hopping or is it saying uneven sounds of skipping? Look at Butch's skip. Is it fast or slow? Why does he go up in the air so high with his skip?"

Studies and compositions often result from the walk. Children come to know the walk as their most fundamental movement. It is basic to folk and social dancing which they should experience when they are ready for this form of dance. *This discussion on the development and progression of the walk is directly applicable to any of the other locomotor movements.*

Jump Progression

Six- and seven-year-olds have as much fun discovering and exploring the jump (or any of the movements) as do ten-, eleven-, or twelve-year-

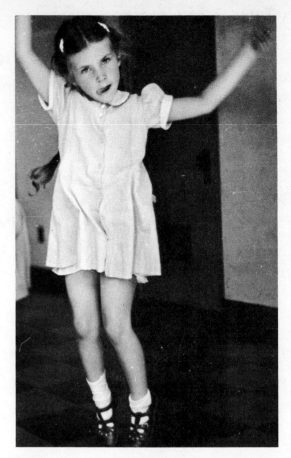

"And—jump!"

olds. (In any approach to the jump we need space. Children should spread out so they will have space to go up and down and out.) First of all, they should spread out so they have plenty of room to themselves in order to really move, because that is exactly what they are going to do. An initial question might be: "How could you get yourself off the floor? Let's all start to jump. How could you go higher? Could you go faster, then slower and slower until you are not jumping anymore, but just sort of bouncing? What makes you go up in the air? What will help you to get a good jump?" Children discover that if they use their arms, keep their heads up, bend their knees to get started, and land on the balls of their feet that they can spring right back. We discuss; we watch demonstrations; and we all try.

One child could be instructed thus: "Bernadette, suppose you clap a jump for us." This could be followed with: "Now, let's all clap and really make it say 'jump.' What would we clap if we wanted a sound to help us get ready to jump?" As they jump they discover how different it feels to do it with something that says ". . . *and* jump."

Children discover they can jump sideward, backward, and around and that they can jump in straight lines and in curves. All these take skill and coordination. It also requires control of the arms and upper body to help them turn in the air. Trying these things often leads to a good discussion of the body as a whole or in parts and of what particular parts help us to jump. Boys, particularly, have a wonderful time trying to spin in the air on "around" jumps. When it was said to the children, "Let us watch Pat jump while turning around. What does it make you think of while you watch him?" some of the answers have been an electric fan, a pin wheel, and a half gainer. Flash might say, "Watch me, I can make a propeller of the DC-6," and the group would watch Flash do a series of jumps with cartwheels, coming out of the cartwheel with jumps.

Things happen to children's legs when they jump; they find that they can jump with their legs crossed, apart (one foot forward and the other back), or astride, weight on one side and then on the other side. With their jumps they can touch their hands with their feet, bend their knees up in front, or in back—to mention only a few. Time needs to be given to explore the different ways. Not all children within a group can explore jumps with the same speed; at a slower

tempo sometimes more complicated explorations result, and with other children many need a faster tempo. They find that they can discover all kinds of combinations of the jump with the other movements. Jumping with different movements helps boys and girls to see that jumping and bouncing is quite different from jumping and pushing. These combinations are usually used to help them express different kinds of experiences. Some patterns with the jump which have been worked out with children are:

> Jump, hop, leap, leap
> Jump, hop, jump, hop, jump
> Walk, walk, walk, jump
> Run, run, run, run, jump
> Gallop, gallop, jump, jump

It was St. Patrick's Day, so starting with the jump and adding combinations of the hop, we developed an Irish jig. This was the start of a St. Patrick's folk dance which a group of twelve-year-olds composed:

Groups have fun with parts of songs, whole songs, or jingles which they make up on the spot. For example, one day when a group of eleven-year-olds were working on jump patterns, they were asked if they knew the tune "Bell Bottom Trousers." Most of them did, so we all hummed

"All jump up and never come down."

it. It was suggested that they take the first line of the melody and try to work out a jump pattern. The following sample was given:

Jump, jump, jump like a funny jumping bean.

Six boys and girls working together in a group completed an entire song; the following accompanied their jumping pattern:

I'm a little jumping bean
I'm happy as can be
I jump and bounce and jump and bounce
And jump and bounce around
I jump, and jump, and jump, and jump,
Like a funny jumping bean.

Another group started their jump pattern this way:

Jumping up and bending down
And skipping in a circle
Jumping up and bending down
And . . . .

For accompaniment they used a tune of a popular song which was fresh in their mind because they had been singing it in assembly. These jump patterns and songs to accompany movement were not completed the first day. They finished the Jump Songs, however, with the help of their classroom teacher.

To such questions as "How does a jump make you feel?" or "When you jump what does it make you think of?" the following responses have been recorded from a group of ten-year-olds: roller coaster, ferris wheel stop, going over gutters, football passer, high jumper, space cadet, frogs, fireflies, jumping horses, cheerleaders, the occasionally wavy lines of television channels, neon signs, Times Square, balloons bursting, firecrackers, soda fizz, square dancing, and "jump 'n' jive."

Children find that they enjoy jumping with accent. They identify accents from the piano, Victrola, drum or wood-block beat. They also identify accents in songs they can sing. They may move accordingly with one group jumping with the first accent, the second group with the second accent, and so forth. They listen to square dance calls, such as "All jump up and never come down

. . . ," and their jumps seem to take on added meanings.

A group of thirty-eight peer age boys and girls were asked to form groups according to colors—everyone with brown on to be in that corner; all with red on in the other corner; all with green over there, and all those with none of these three colors to stay here in the middle of the room. They were asked to work out some kind of group pattern using the locomotor movement of the jump. They could add any other movement, space, or rhythmic element to their study, just as long as the pattern was predominately jumps. (This was setting the situation or posing the framework of the problem.) The group of "nones" composed of four girls and five boys started working on a square dance. When time was called, they had only begun. Being disappointed, they groaned, "Oh, we need more time!" They were excited about the beginning of their group effort and asked if they could wait and give theirs next time. The next time the same group asked if they could work the entire time " 'cause they had a keen idea." When their effort was proudly presented to the class it fully warranted the time spent; it became a favorite square dance call of that sixth grade. With one calling and the others dancing this was their presentation:

All join hands
And circle the track
Keep on going
'Til you get back
When you get home
All jump the track
And swing your girl like thunder

There goes first couple
Jumping the track
Others circle left
Going around the track
Keep on going
'Til they jump back
Keep on going
Around the track

Whoops there goes seconds
Jumping the track
While others turn
And circle back
Keep on going

'Til they jump back
Keep on going
Around the track

(Repeat with third and fourth
couples jumping the track)

(Repeat first call)

Sometimes we start with one movement, such as the jump, and add others to it. At times, we just work on combining movements. A group of seventh-graders were busily working on combinations of locomotor movements. They were in groups to work out a pattern of movement or a combination of movements in space. The "movement study" came as a result of putting their group patterns into a class study. The groups showed their movement patterns to the class. It was discussed how they could put them together to make a larger study, and they also talked about which patterns might go together easily, tried them out, beat them out, and listened to the sound of the pattern. Up to this time no sound accompaniment had been used, but after the class had decided on the way they wanted their movement patterns to fit together, Nina worked out the music with them. This took the better part of four class times to complete the study.

1. They divided into two groups that started from two sides of the playroom and galloped diagonally across the floor.
2. Ran into a circle.
3. Forward walk toward center of circle.
   Backward walk away from center.
   (Repeat)
4. In place, facing center of circle.
   Jumps, accenting with a clap on first of every three jumps.
5. Half of group, alternating, going toward center. Other half going away from center with two walks and a jump turn, alternating going toward circle and away from circle.
6. All sliding around circle and back to original starting spots at side of playroom.

This study was used many times during the year with that group. Since that time, it has been used in different ways with various groups of children and teachers' classes for exploring movement, reviewing movement, listening and picking out underlying beats, and rhythmic patterns. It has also been used when working on direction (changing direction when the music changes).

Considerable group work can be accomplished by ten-year-olds and eleven-year-olds as they work in their chosen groups or gangs. With some groups it may be necessary to discuss ways of forming groups but with others it may not if they have had previous experiences with group or committee work. Sometimes children may select the group they want to work with, and at other times they are just divided up informally as they happen to stand. As a group starts to work out a pattern with the jump, such as:

Jump, jump, hop, hop, hop, jump, jump
or
Jump, hop, leap, leap, leap, jump

and as they are progressing easily, we talk about other things we could add to this pattern to make it more interesting. Their suggestions have been to combine movements with space elements (range, level, floor patterns). (See also Chapter 7.) We might decide, then, on a particular combination, such as their original pattern on the jump (or leap), together with a body movement and a direction which seems to go with it. For instance, the first pattern as indicated above (jump, jump, hop, hop, hop, jump, jump) was worked out by five boys. Two of them took low jumps, and three boys took high jumps, with all boys on the same level when they hopped. They used a swing with their arms, repeated their pattern four times, ending with one large jump turn. Thus they added three elements: levels, swing, and turn. When the teacher is setting the situation, this is the type of framework she might use. The suggestion might be given to select three elements to combine with their jump pattern— one from space, one from rhythm, and one from the body movements. Of course, there will be disagreement with some groups, and at times few groups spend most of their time arguing because each individual wants to hold to his particular pattern. When this happens they will find they do not have a pattern or study ready to present to the rest of the group. (Sometimes we have to talk these things over, for sharing is terribly important. Children have to learn how to share not

MOVEMENT STUDY

NINA COFFING

Gallop

Run
Vivace

Development of Movement

Movement Study (Cont.)

Walk

Clap
Jump Jump Jump

Walk Walk Jump

Slide

only their ideas but also their accomplishments and their evaluations.)

When studies have been worked out, usually it is important that they be shared. If time should run out, it is the teacher's job to see that those groups which have not presented their particular studies have a chance at the next opportunity to share other accomplishments. When studies are presented for a group, the presentations usually are followed by a discussion and evaluation. These are the points discussed: Did we stick to the problem? How could we improve it? What did you particularly like about the study? What did the group combine with (in this case) the jump pattern? Did you notice a definite beginning and end? Many of the ideas used for motivating and developing the jump could be used effectively with any of the other fundamental locomotor movements.

BODY MOVEMENTS

Body movements are different from the loco-

motor movements; as children say, "They are the movements which do not take us any place," or ". . . the way I can move while staying right here." Body movements may apply to the body as a whole or to specific parts. *One* body movement can never be entirely divorced from the other body movements. For instance, it is difficult to think of a bend without thinking of a stretch; therefore, the body movements which children have explored together and which logically go together will be considered.

Swinging consists of a pendular, arc-like movement executed by the arm or the leg, or the body as a whole. Children think of this in terms of back and forth or side to side, like a pendulum on a clock, and say "swinging like" a camel, boat, monkey, railroad signal, lantern, trees, leaves, rainbow, tennis forearm, windshield wiper, elephant's trunk, cow's tail, yo-yo, lasso, and the way some people walk. Sometimes they say, "We can swing over like this ⌒ , or under like this ‿ ."

SWINGING

FLORENCE BURNS

Bending and *stretching* are flexing, or contracting. When we extend, we stretch. Children consider this as "how small" or "how tall," or when we squeeze all up, we bend, or when we reach up all the way, we stretch. They say bending and stretching like an accordion, rubber band, alligator, bedsprings, snake, crepe paper, gum, smoke, midget, stilt man, and somersaults. The impetus to bend and stretch comes from within us.

BENDING AND STRETCHING (Study 1)

JOYCE ELDRIDGE

BENDING AND STRETCHING (Study 2)

Pushing and *pulling* occur when we impel or shove away from our fixed base. If we draw toward our fixed base, we are pushing. According to children, pushing has to do with a car, doll carriage, being in a subway, animals who push with their heads (buffalo, elephant, goat, bull), wheelbarrows, lawn mowers, doors, crowds of people, and Christmas time. Pulling is connected with a wagon, taffy candy, oars, gum, dogs on leash, swimming, little brother, rocks, anchor, sled, and curtains. Pushing and pulling includes the movement of bending and stretching, but the force

PUSHING AND PULLING

JOYCE ELDRIDGE

Development of Movement

exerted against or toward an object makes the pushing and pulling movement different in quality from the bending and stretching. (For instance, in pushing a lawn mower, our arms bend and stretch, but we are applying force to the object, and we call this "pushing.")

Twisting results when the upper part of body is rotated around and the lower part of the body remains stationary. *Turning* results when the body completely revolves. Children say, ". . . twisting as far as you can go without moving your feet or your seat." Twisting is like corkscrews, pretzels, eggs, ice cream cones, trees, hurricanes, tornadoes, currents, and fishing lines. Turning is like a top, nickel, fans, swinging doors, and egg beaters.

TWISTING AND TURNING

FLORENCE BURNS

Twist and twist and turn a-round, Twist and turn down near the ground

Twist and twist and turn up high, Let's twist up to the sky.

Striking is an explosive kind of movement toward something. *Dodging* is an instinctive recoiling or drawing away from something. Children say "to hit or pound," or "to get out of the way" instead of "striking" or "dodging." They think of striking and dodging as hitting at a ball, slapping mosquitoes and flies, and hammering, or dodging bats, a ball, or automobiles. Striking and dodging include the movement of bending and stretching and swinging of body parts, but a differentiation is made by the quality of the movements and the external stimulus which causes a reaction: the striking toward someone or something and dodging away, to avoid someone or something.

STRIKING AND DODGING

JOYCE ELDRIDGE

Shaking is caused by quick, successive tensions of muscles. Children think of this as being like shivering, the chattering of teeth, the vibrations of a refrigerator and the quiver of jelly, the jiggling of riveters, the steps of the Hula dance, and the agitation of mechanical toys, windows, dust mops, and milk shakes.

SHAKING

FLORENCE BURNS

Bouncing occurs when people make themselves go up and down or back and forth, in quick rhythmical sequence. Children know this as bouncing a ball, bobbing for apples, bouncing on the bed and on chairs, the occasionally wavy lines on a television screen, part of babies' actions, divers on a spring board, and the bouncing of clowns, trapeze artists, and tight-rope walkers.

As children discover the body movements, they come to realize that they can swing just their arm forward or back or sideward, or they can swing their whole body. They find out that they can start shaking their toes, then their heels, knees, middles, shoulders, head, and then every

Development of Movement

part of them. They explore the many ways they can push, with their shoulders, their heads, feet, knees, and their whole selves. They realize that they can pull toward their middles, and that they then can pull down or pull up. They can discover the smallest part of their bodies that they can twist, and then the largest part that can be twisted or the different parts they can twist. They come to realize that some body movements can go together easily and that others cannot. Often they sing about what they are doing. To illustrate, a group of teachers taking a creative experience workshop, originated this song "Swing and Sway." It has become a favorite with children.

BOUNCING

JOYCE ELDRIDGE

Children realize that some body and locomotor movements feel good together, such as the bounce and the jump, and that the leap and the shake are hard to do. They soon associate body movements with other things. All locomotor movements are greatly enhanced when children have enough control of body movements to coordinate the two. As nine- and ten-year-olds often say, "I feel like I am polka-ing all over," or "My leap makes me feel like I'm flying." Usually, twelve-year-olds discover the rhumba through combining body movements with the walk.

Let us look at some of the ways a body movement may be approached and developed. The bend and stretch will be used for this purpose, because it serves as an illustration of the manner in which any one of the body movements may be developed.

SWING AND SWAY

We'll swing and sway and turn a-way And come back to-geth-er a-gain,

We'll swing and sway and turn a-way And do it all o-ver a-gain.

Bending and Stretching

Bending and stretching can be developed in the same manner as any of the other movements. Here are a few suggestions from a recording of

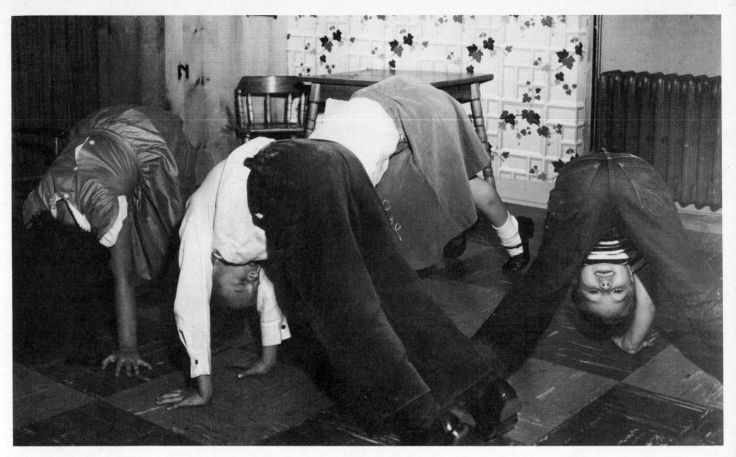

"Look! We are bending like haystacks."

a group working on stretching and bending. Not all these items were developed at the same time, but are presented simply to show examples of explorations which can be started.

The initial approach by the teacher might be something like this: "How tall can we make ourselves . . . taller . . . still taller? And how wide . . . still wider? Can we reach with our hands and arms, too? Esther is even reaching out with her legs and feet. What do we call what we are doing?" "Reaching," replied Esther. "Stretching," says Frankie. "Sure, now let's see if we can stretch every part of us, starting from our feet up . . . way, way up to our very finger tips. Bobby is even trying to make parts of his face stretch! Do you suppose we could discover all the different parts of our faces that we could stretch? Now, see how different it feels to bend those same parts of your face." Children discover things they can do with noses, forehead, ears, and eyes. They have fun, too, sharing these discoveries with others. "Look at Johnnie." "See Peggy. Wonder if I could do that?" Thus exploration begins in another way of moving.

"Shall we forget all about stretching ourselves for a minute, and see how small we can make ourselves . . . still smaller . . . every part of you make smaller? What would you call what we are doing as we make ourselves smaller and smaller?" From the children, "We are making a little ball, curling up, stooping down, bending every bit of us." (Here is the teacher's cue.) "Suppose we call what we have been doing 'bending.' Let's try to bend our fingers and hands . . . now our arms and shoulders. How does it make you feel when you bend each part of yourself?" Children say, "I feel shriveled up, old, awful, or tiny," or "Hey, look I'm a haystack!" (So we all decide that we will be haystacks.)

"Now, let's see if we can bend, bend, bend, and then stretch, stretch, stretch." This was repeated several times. "Do you know what we call the tall man in the circus?" Phyllis spoke up, "The man on stilts?" Others said: "The stilt man, the skinny man." Discussion followed about stilts, walking on stilts, and so on. Then the teacher asks, "What do we call the tiny man at the circus?" "Midgets," said one child. "I saw a circus with Tom Thumb," said another. "Now, let's see if we can stretch up like the stilt man; then bend way down

Development of Movement

THE STILT MAN

FLORENCE BURNS

There was a great big stilt man who was tall, tall, tall There

was a lit-tle midg-et who was small, small, small And the

midg-et who was small would try and try and try To

reach up to the stilt man who was tall, tall, tall.

like the tiny midget. See if I can really tell which you are. I know a song about the stilt man. Would you like to hear it?" (This is just one example of the ways words, music, or songs can be written to assist in the exploration of movement. Sometimes, the songs come from the children as they are working; at other times, teachers compose songs as a result of working with chil-

dren. Sometimes, teachers and children work them out together; at other times, the music is original, or the songs are adapted to appropriate music. When piano accompaniment is not available, a repertoire of simple movement songs which the teacher can sing, or speak out, or which the children can sing, will help exploration.) "The Stilt Man" is a good illustration. The

Exploring body movements—swinging and swaying

teacher sang the song, then the group discussed it together. The teacher started singing it with the children, even though it was written for the original purpose as stated above. With one group, it fit in when they were discussing a circus. The song has also been used in connection with high and low levels when children have been exploring space.

Occasionally the teacher needs to give hints like, "What else can you think of that bends and stretches besides the stilt man and midget?" "I know," says Warren, "crepe paper." "Suppose we all make ourselves into crepe paper like Warren. Now, make your paper bend and stretch." Often the teacher can inject humor and warmth into any lesson by commenting, "I see Joan as red crepe paper and Sammy as brown and white stripe" (suggestive of the color of the clothes that they are wearing). "Suppose you try to think of something which bends or stretches, then we'll see if we can all guess what some are." Again all kinds of purposeful ideas and movement execution follow. If some children can't get started, a casual hint or some "drawing out" from the teacher helps. It is easy to say, "Henry, what's that attached to the top of your pants that helps to hold them up?" or "Does your father ever wear anything to help hold his trousers up?"

The following means of exploring lend themselves very well to two or more children working together to figure out bending and stretching ideas or other movement explorations. One could start with: "Do you suppose you could bend or stretch any *one* part of your body while you are sitting on the floor? Let's try. What part shall we start with?" In another position they try bending their trunk, legs, and so on. They may

get on their knees, backs, or sides to try other bend and stretch explorations. Sometimes, they draw their bends and stretches on the blackboard; at other times, they explore movement with finger painting. (The finger painting included in this book was done following a rhythms period. The illustration is a graphic representation of bends. The same idea has been captured with all the locomotor and body movements.)

Poetry and stories help us to become more aware of such movements as bending and stretching. Hilda Conkling's poem "The Old Bridge" is an example.

One of the most delightful studies to come from a group started with the idea of bending and stretching. The children were bending in such a fashion that they looked like turtles. The teacher asked, "Do you know what you make me think of while I watched you?" (Vachel Lindsay's poem "The Little Turtle" was most appropriate and enhanced the experience).

> There was a little turtle.
> He lived in a box.
> He swam in a puddle.
> He climbed on the rocks.[3]

[3] Vachel Lindsay, "The Little Turtle," from *Johnny Appleseed and Other Poems* (New York: The Macmillan Company, 1925). Used by permission of The Macmillan Company.

Blue finger-painting

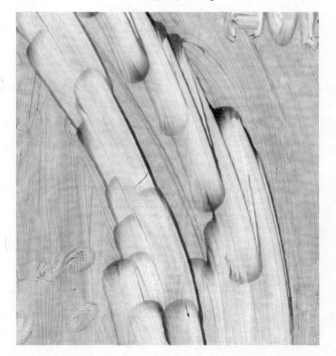

Development of Movement

More discussion about turtles resulted in a class study, with the music consultant helping the children to write their own music to fit the poem.

Another way in which interest has been stimulated in bending and stretching has been through a conversation, such as the following: "Can you imagine you are in a very long box, such as a long, flower box? You have to stretch and stretch tall . . . to fit into it. Yes, make yourself very, very skinny. Now, can you be in a tiny, tiny box so that you have to be very little? Can you put yourself in the long box first, and then very quickly put yourself in the small one?" Reva said that it made her want to be a Jack-in-the-Box. (Again, this is a cue for the teacher.) "Let's see if we can make ourselves into some kind of a Jack-in-the-Box. When you hear the tom-tom, stretch out any way you think your Jack would go." (This particular experience of the Jack-in-the-Box ended with Reva playing the wood-block. She went around to two and three of the Jack-in-the-Boxes and had them pop up when she gave them the signal.)

"Sammy, can you think of a new way of bending and stretching your body?" A leading question like this caused somersaults to become the exploration of the day. In this one instance it was possible to follow up the idea. (In many places it would be impossible for even a demonstration of forward rolls, because of the safety factor.)

The picture which Geital (seventh-grader) painted of cartwheels was the result of working

Cartwheels

with stretching and bending in a rhythms activity. She put her feelings about this body movement into action on paper.

Sometimes brown paper is rolled out on the floor, and a crayon or chalk is selected by everyone. Then bends and stretches (or other movement factors) are drawn the way it is thought they should look. Other times it is done on the blackboard. The children usually say "bend and stretch" as they draw a movement. One day, as Rita was "feeling" and saying "bend and stretch" she started to say other words which were recorded:

> To roll and stretch, to roll and stretch
> Makes me think of the sea;
> The ocean with its great big waves
> Goes on so merrily.
>
> How I would like to be a wave
> That comes to meet the shore
> I'd roll and stretch,
> And roll and stretch,
> And roll and stretch some more.

This was put to music which seemed readily to come from the class as they picked up her words.

There are infinite combinations of movement emanating from the bend and stretch. In answer to the question "Could you combine a bend and stretch with some locomotor movements?" the following was recorded: bend and jump; bend and stretch; walk, stretch, and walk; bend and run; skip and stretch, skip and bend; and bend and gallop. Another group found it was fun to hop and stretch. They ended by being puppets on strings. They worked this into a script which they wrote and a composition which they produced in their classroom.

A group of forty-six fifth-graders was exploring bending and stretching combinations. They divided into groups taking twelve to fifteen minutes (which they had agreed upon) to work out combinations of bending and stretching with jumps. The following compositions resulted, and were entitled: Piano Keyboard (to which they sang an accompaniment of "Three Blind Mice"), Rabbits, Tennis match (two boys as players and one boy the ball), Kangaroos Go Dancing, the Story of the Kangaroo (one boy narrated a story

"I can bend my knees—that's what I can do!"

Development of Movement

which they wrote on the spot to accompany their movement), A Fire. Another group interpreted the Fight Between the Grasshopper and the Worm. The last group composition was a variation of the square dance.

Summary

The locomotor and body movements presented in this chapter serve as illustrations of the way in which any of the other movements may be developed. When children use movement as a medium of expression they become aware of the other elements which affect movement—elements of space and rhythm.

Suggestions for Development of Movement

1. Start a run of moderate tempo. Increase tempo and run in place. Go around the room and decrease tempo. Suggest the children go higher and higher and cover more distance on each stride until the run becomes a leap. It helps to make such suggestions as going over puddles of water or over hurdles.

2. Start with an ordinary gallop (combination of walk and leap, two sounds of uneven rhythm). By changing the tempo, vary the gallop—fast and slow, smooth, low and high. Gallop changing directions as forward, backward, and around. Gallop in place, gallop with tongue making a clacking sound, gallop with shoulders. Have the group think of different animals that gallop, and let each child be the animal he suggests.

3. The skip, gallop, and slide are alike in that all three have two sounds of an uneven rhythm, include the walk, or are a combination of locomotor movements and have elevation. They are different, in that the gallop and slide are made up of a *walk* and *leap* but the skip is a *walk* and *hop*. In the gallop and in the slide the same foot is always in the lead and the walk always comes on the lead foot. In the skip the leading foot changes from one foot to the other. Have individuals, small groups, or large groups develop five ways to vary the skip, the slide, or the gallop. The variations may be slow and fast, low and high, smooth and bumpy.

4. Sitting at desks or on a floor in the classroom, have children discover various ways they can move different parts of their bodies by asking questions or by using such a dance song as follows:

I've got a head
You've got a head
I can shake my head
That's what we can do

I've got two feet
You've got two feet
I can tap my feet
That's what we can do

I've got hips
You've got hips
I can twist my hips
That's what we can do

Suggested Tunes: "Farmer in the Dell"
"I've Got Rhythm"

5. Have the group sitting down, pushing and pulling forward and back with their feet and legs. Have the group discover other ways they can push with their feet besides out and back. Have them push with some other part of the body while still sitting down, or push with one part while pulling with another. Ask: "What pulls?" "What does it make you think of while pushing?" Have each individual or small group work out the action of something which pushes and pulls.

6. Start the group with the hop suggesting that they let the other leg go where it will. Same with the other foot. Add turning. Add hopping high and low. Add other locomotor and body movements. Have individuals, small groups, or large groups work on combinations using the hop. (Exploration may result in a schottische, an Indian step, and many others. This may be the time to develop any of these steps or patterns with the entire group.)

7. Have children either individuals or small groups go across the room with a leap, a gallop, or any of the locomotor movements. Then have each group decide how they can get across the room with any locomotor movement except the one used at the beginning. Have each group combine their locomotor movement with any of the body movements.

8. Explore such possibilities of the swing with the group as swinging one arm, two arms, one leg, entire body, and so on. Vary swings by changing tempo, changing levels and range, and so forth. Individually or in small groups, work out combinations of the swing with a locomotor movement. Individually or in small groups, work out combinations of the swing with another body movement.

9. Divide the class into groups, and have each group select either body movements from the hips down or body movements from the hips up, and use these movements to build a study.

"It's fun to discover space."

7. *Effect of Space on Movement*

When children can move freely, and know and understand the ways in which they move, then it is fun for them to discover elements in space and to explore the many ways in which their movements can be affected by these elements. Space is the area through which we move. Because we can reach out no farther than our human frames will allow, the actual amount of space we cover is not great. It may be that some of us can cover a bit more space than others, but this, too, is because of the way we are constructed. The illusion of more or less space can be created as we move and are conscious of the fact that we cover space by change of direction, level, range, and focus.

ELEMENTS OF SPACE

Elements of space affect movement. To illustrate, let us first walk across the room, turn around, and walk back to where we began. This is a common procedure and one we ordinarily do not think very much about. But, now, let us walk across the floor in a forward direction, *consciously* turn around, and with *emphasis* walk back to the point from which we started. Our movement has assumed a definite emphasis due to the

direction we have added. We walk down the street every day unaware of the space about us, but our walk changes when we purposely walk toward a specific object, or concentrate upon arriving at a designated spot. The entire quality of our walk has changed.

Direction of movement is the line of motion that the body follows: forward, backward, sideward, or up and down. Children label these as they explore. In the beginning they often call "around" a form of direction, because they cannot seem to understand that it may be a combination of the other three. Youngsters often think of backward as "backing up." This takes more skill for them than going forward. Therefore, we set up controls within the group to prevent collisions as the children change their directions. To follow the leader, follow the orchestra leader, follow the policeman, and follow singing directions are ways of having young groups work with direction, and with which they can have fun.

When we move we can do so at certain *levels*. Children think of levels as "high, low, and in between," and they say, "way up, high to the sky, down low to the ground, and just in between." "Look how I'm walking high" is an example of how they express their concept.

Range pertains to the amount of space we fill

Following the leader

when we move. Children discover this in terms of "how big" they can make themselves and "how small" and "how wide" they can become. They often say "a big movement" or "a little movement" or "Look how wide I can go; look how long my leap is; if I get much wider I'll split."

Focus may be difficult to use as an element in space. However, certain movements cannot be captured without it. Focus is a tool used continually by the dancer. It is a spot upon which he concentrates, or toward which his attention is drawn. This spot may be direct or deviating. Focus has little meaning for younger children because of their short attention span. Older children have enjoyed working with focus, and find it valuable when they want to emphasize particular movements.

In a composition about ghosts, focus gave emphasis and projection to the older boys' movements. The idea has been clarified for children by using an imaginary magnet which draws them toward or away from it, never losing the attention, gaze, or line of direction of the group.

Floor patterns are the designs children make on the floor with their feet or body. As people move through space, their feet make an imaginary design on the floor. Children call this a floor pattern, and they say that the pictures they make on the floor are the square, the circle, the zigzag, or the figure eight. Children of middle and later childhood like to play guessing games, using their own ideas of floor patterns. They realize that they can translate to the floor any design which comes to mind. Floor patterns may be graphically translated to the blackboard, chalked on the floor or on newspaper or on drawing paper rolled out on the floor, developed in the art room, or translated on the floor through the use of movement. Frequently they serve as a basis for a study or composition.

Development of Floor Patterns

In the previous chapter, the walk, jump, bend, and stretch were developed as illustrations of what might be done with any of the locomotor or body movements. It was found that even though one movement was given attention, others entered in, and that elements in space were constantly present. The walk or jump could not be developed without direction, range, and level. (It is true as attention is given to one of the elements of space, the others enter in, and movement now unconsciously becomes the skill or tool used. In other words, the attention now is on *space*.)

As a sample of what might be done with any of the other space elements, let us give our attention to the development of floor patterns.

Regardless of age, the approach for discovering floor patterns might be something like this. "While you were skipping, something very interesting happened. Suppose we watch Stanley and see if we can guess what seemed interesting." Watching Stanley skip brought forth these remarks, "He's pulling his knees up high because he uses his arms." "He's going around in a nice kind of way." The teacher says, "Stanley is going around in a nice kind of way, and as he is skipping he is making a picture on the floor." (This is the teacher's clue—"going around in a nice kind of way"—which she uses as a lead into a new series of explorations about pictures we make on the floor as we move.) In developing floor patterns, associations have been made with snow, chalk on feet, or sand. To illustrate, this question could be asked, "If Stanley had been playing in the tar out there in the middle of the street and then had come in here and skipped around, just as he is doing now, what would happen?" "He'd get the floor dirty and make marks on the floor" immediately comes forth. "What kind of marks?" draws forth such replies as "tar marks that his feet make; whole foot marks." An explanation might be thus: "That's what we call making a picture on the floor—a *floor pattern*. For instance, if Stanley had tar on his feet, he would make a floor pattern of tar foot marks, and the shape or design or pattern he would make would depend on how he moved in the room. Let's watch Stanley again to see what kind of a design or pattern he would make on the floor as he is skipping. Could anyone draw on the board the picture he is making?" (An oval was drawn.) The oval, or egg-shaped, picture that Stanley was making on the floor as he moved started a discussion on different kinds of pictures or floor patterns which could be made. Children often trace with their fingers, toes, or arms patterns which they could make or which have just been demonstrated for them.

"Suppose we move out on the floor and stake out our space claims." (This suggestion was made while this particular group had been studying about the Gold Rush in social studies.) "Let's be certain that we have enough room so that the

"I'm in between."

"I'm tall."

"I'm small."

designs made on the floor, or the floor patterns, will not interfere with anyone else's pattern. Are we all ready? It seems as though some of us could take more room. Can we walk out just a single circle on the floor? Just one circle—and be careful to end up just where you started. Try again and this time skip out your circle floor pattern. Could you skip it backward?" Exploration has begun with various sizes of circles and with different kinds of locomotor and body movements.

Whenever this initial approach has been used with children or adults the problem arises about someone interfering with another pattern and about such remarks as "Gee, Shirley spoiled my picture." This calls for a discussion about more ways of controlling the movements, so that the floor patterns won't infringe on others. The children talk about this and realize that sometimes they are concentrating or thinking so hard that they hadn't realized they were in each other's way. This is an indirect way to develop feelings, understanding, and respect for others, without embarrassing an individual child. Sometimes, space is limited and they cannot avoid interference. When this happens we discuss ways in which we can make our pictures overlap, without actually bumping into another person. At times, it means that they have to take turns in working out patterns on the floor, while others work them out on paper or at the board.

To the question "Can you tell what design or pattern I am drawing on the board?" these three different answers were received from one class: "It's a snake." "It's a zigzag." "Looks like a fly swatter to me." These suggestions could follow: "Try to walk out the pattern you see on the board. Make it very zigzaggy. Maybe we could make it even more zigzaggy if we did it slower and took more space. What other designs might you make? Warren, do you want to put yours on the board for all to see?" Warren drew circles within a circle. To the class it was a curlicue, a spiral, a snail, a sweet roll. They all explored Warren's floor pattern.

Then, the teacher might suggest: "Let's see if we can figure out a floor pattern that is different from Warren's. Donald is doing a pattern of a

Effect of Space on Movement

box or square, so let's try his pattern. How about doing it again? This time when you come to a corner of the square, put in a jump so that we can readily see your square. Think about how you are going to do it before you start to make it on the floor. What could you do to make your floor pattern of the square more interesting?" Some of the recorded answers are: "Do something different at the corners." "Change direction." "Change movement." "Change levels." "Put an accent at the corner."

To continue, the teacher might say, "Let's try some spirals and see if you can get across the floor doing one. Can you finish yours up with a dot? How do you think you can do that?" (If these explorations are with seven-year-olds the symbols should be simple in design and movement. With older children, the symbols become more complicated and may be anything from simple spirals, numbers, or notes to elaborate designs of Indian lore, camp life, animals, birds, fish, leaves, and holiday ideas. These explorations give the teacher an opportunity to point out the products of children who need the feeling of accomplishment or worth. For children who may not have developed as much motor coordination as others floor patterns frequently present an opportunity for them to gain recognition.

Often boys and girls are asked to spread' out over the room so that each has his own spot like an artist with a huge piece of canvas in front of him on the floor. Instead of having a brush and paint or a piece of chalk they are going to make their pictures with the path their movements take. Time is allowed to refine their floor patterns. If the group is not too large, they sit down where they are, and one at a time show their designs for all to guess. The one who guesses is next to show, or sometimes the one who shows may select the next floor pattern for all to see. If it is a very large group and they do not have time to see everyone's pattern, they call for volunteers. If they use a classroom, designs can be figured out at seats or on the board and then space cleared on the floor for demonstrations.

In addition to figuring out floor patterns, they sometimes change the problem to figure out five different ways they can move while doing their

pattern. They might also think of different ways they can vary their design. For instance, they might make a figure eight skipping or "polka-ing" and leaning as they make the curve.

Other times we do floor patterns by following a leader. When this happens we find out that we have to do large simple patterns so that all can follow (this takes room). Sometimes we decide that there are too many of us to do too many designs so we break up into smaller groups, with a leader. Here we set up controls: Leaders can go any place in the room as long as they are careful not to bump into another group and spoil their design. This puts responsibility on the leader and calls for judgment and reasoning. Naturally this calls for "reminders" on the part of the teacher because sometimes leaders become so involved with their own patterns that they forget about other groups. After this kind of an experience, sometimes we recall our designs by drawing them out on the floor, or on the board, with chalk.

The letters of the alphabet make interesting floor patterns. Making floor patterns out of the first letter in names, or one's initials, is fun. In discovering some of the floor patterns to be done with letters, often a remark such as Norton's is elicited: "What sort of a design is Nancy doing? "It's all mixed up, like." The teacher would then suggest: "Well, suppose we all watch Nancy, and see if we can tell what kind of a design she is making on the floor." The puzzled faces of the class having been noticed, Nancy was asked to do it again, more slowly. The children were unable to guess, so she told them it was her whole name. This was difficult for the group to visualize until Nancy repeated, spelling out each letter as she progressed. The third-graders watched with intense concentration as Nancy worked, leaping in between each walked-out letter. When she finished, Joey said, "Sure, good for you Nancy," and Warren grunted, "Yup." (What more can a teacher ask—enthusiasm, concentration, sharing achievement, and children recognizing each other?) As one would imagine, this entire period was devoted to floor patterns of names—first, last, middle, and nicknames. (It may be pointed out that all lessons do not progress as smoothly as

Effect of Space on Movement

this one. Problems are bound to come in, but they are handled as well as possible when they appear.)

Time or space would not allow a discussion of the variety of floor patterns from using just letters and numbers. Children find a variety of ways they can make the picture of the number 1— they can stand still, lie on the floor, walk it out on the floor. When making 3's, they can use direction—forward for the first loop and backward to complete the figure. While working on 3's, Ted exclaimed, "Oh, look at me. I made thirty-three." This was a clue to start on two-digit numbers. They make these working by themselves, or by getting into groups of two or more. Some groups have transferred simple arithmetic problems to the floor, working them out with their floor patterns. These experiences include putting in addition or subtraction symbols, equal signs, decimals. They discover that the number 111 may be worked out by three children lying on the floor horizontally, or they can move forward and back, or stand side by side.

The above ties in well with other classroom studies, such as social studies and arithmetic. Pursuing the topic of transportation one day a class was divided into groups of from eight to eleven to see if they could work out floor patterns of a specific mode of transportation. These patterns included designs of airplanes, train engines, and boxcars (which had an oblong effect, composed of eleven boys). As they started to move slowly around the room keeping this oblong-shaped floor pattern, the other children could not figure out why the smallest boy was making

"You forgot to put a tail on your pointer."

a zigzag line in the middle of the boxcar. It turned out to be a boxcar with a lone cow. Floor patterns denoting transportation ideas have included the entire class forming a picture of a pleasure boat, as well as individuals and small groups forming the pictures of small crafts.

Stars, clouds, leaves, and other studies from nature and science help to reinforce learning when children are given opportunities to use movement and space. One group of fifth-graders had become fascinated with a study of stars. They worked in groups to identify constellations and the frieze that they made, and that decorated the wall of their classroom, became the stimuli for floor patterns, which made the experience more vivid.

Animal suggestions are another source for floor patterns. We have had a complete dog kennel translated to the floor. Drawing pictures on the floor, board, or paper to insure that ears and tails and the vital parts are put in can be done if the children's original attempts are not clear. Children's ingenuity in working out these patterns is at times overwhelming. It is not just any old design when the class says, "If you make those ears more pointed, it would look more like a Doberman pinscher," or, "You guys forgot to put a tail on your pointer."

Floor patterns have also originated from drawings, pictures around the room, magazine advertisements, figures in linoleum, maps, and charts. When older children have been working strenu-

Making floor patterns of something in the room

ously on vigorous locomotor combinations, such as the polka, floor patterns can serve as a device for quieting them down and resting them. The teacher says, "While you are resting and getting your breath, suppose you look around the room and find a design or picture which might serve as a floor pattern." At first, the obvious is noted: If they happen to be in a classroom, then the clock, window, or door are often the first patterns drawn; if they happen to be in the playroom or the gymnasium, the basketball hoop, basketball court, lines on the floor, or light fixtures are the first things children interpret in floor patterns. However, children have worked out such complicated designs as curtains with folds, patterns in the ceiling, a pencil sharpener, piano, ventilator, bleachers, and stall bars.

Many group studies and compositions have resulted from working out floor patterns to mechanical devices: piano, washing machine, Coca Cola machine, bottle-capping belt, pistons, and the machines of amusement centers. Such a composition was developed by a seventh grade working on floor patterns of mechanical devices. As they showed their patterns to the class it was decided that many of them would fit together into a department store theme which resulted in the story "Isabel Goes Shopping."

First, Isabel went through the *revolving* door, passing one *low counter* and one *high counter* on her way to the *elevator*. At the *elevator* (which was composed of four children standing shoulder to shoulder) she pushed the button (the nose of the child on the right). The doors opened with two children moving to the right and two moving to the left as Isabel entered the elevator. Going from one floor to the other was indicated by a change of levels. As they rose from floor to floor, the children stretched up taller and taller, from toes to finger tips. In similar fashion, the doors of the elevator opened, and Isabel stopped at the toy department. She inspected a *typewriter, piano, electric train,* and *mechanical dolls.* Isabel was last seen approaching the floor pattern of the *escalator.* Here was group work, concentrating on group effort and solving problems together. How to represent an escalator so that others would understand it was an intriging

Effect of Space on Movement

problem. Added to this was frank discussion and evaluation of their patterns: what could be done to improve them, how to show the elevator moving by employing other space elements of level, direction, focus, and so on. Then there was the problem of working out the details for the department store idea, the organization of the studies into a larger class composition, and the addition of Isabel as a person shopping. This gave their composition continuity—a beginning and an ending.

It was St. Patrick's Day which gave them a good lead into making floor patterns using symbols connected with this day. Working in groups, they made snakes, harps, hats, Irish potatoes, pipes, and shamrocks. Holidays and field trips furnish additional ideas to be used to motivate problems in space.

As explorations of these floor patterns become a part of children's activities, designs and patterns in folk and square dancing are more easily followed. A group had no trouble whatsoever with the grapevine twist the first time it was called when it was associated with a floor pattern of a figure eight. Children understand concepts in space. They realize that space is the area through which they move. Experiences in moving in different directions, at various levels and changing range, toward and away from a point of focus, and translating floor patterns all help children to express themselves better through movement.

Suggestions for Exploring Space

1. Have the group spread out on the floor. Start moving with a locomotor movement or combination. When they come near anyone they change directions to avoid touching the other person.

2. (Change direction with an accented beat.) Divide class into three groups, and send each group to a different corner of the room. One group goes across the room with a forward direction, another sideward, and another backward. Forward direction group takes a gallop to opposite corner. Sideward group follows with a slide, the backward group with a skip. The groups can eventually follow one after the other with no stop in the accompaniment.

3. Each child decides to move either in straight lines or curves. Have individuals change directions frequently, still moving in a line or curve. (Children will discover in going "around" that a line formation is impossible.) Have several children put their patterns together into a study.

4. Have the entire group follow a leader, changing levels from high to low. Music or percussion instruments follow the leader. Divide the group in two, having two leaders with each group following its leader. Add another leader and another group. Call "freeze" or "stop," and establish levels of the groups to point out idea of levels. Have each group start at different levels, and leaders should watch each other to see that no two groups are ever at the same level. Each group follows its leader. Stop accompaniment occasionally to establish levels.

5. Divide class into groups of three or five of their own choosing. If the group is not divisible by three, a few of the groups could be of two or five. Individuals in the groups should be close to each other. Starting at the three levels, change levels, and occasionally *hold* to establish three levels, passing but never holding the same level. This can be done by using a variety of movements, or by changing quality of movements, tempo, and accent.

6. Take a body movement, such as the swing, using any part of the body—arms, legs, hips. Start with arms moving only in front of body. Gradually increase the movement, making the swing cover more space (range) until a walk or leap is used to cover a greater distance. Gradually decrease until assuming original position. Try the same with the skip, gradually covering more range until turning is employed. (This can be done with any of the movements.)

7. This may be done individually or by groups. Each is to select one of the space factors: direction, levels, range, or focus. Using any locomotor or body movement or combination and the space factor agreed upon, develop a study or composition based on the element.

Getting the feel of rhythm

8. *Effect of Rhythm on Movement*

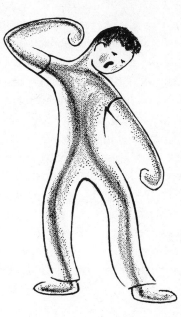

Like space and movement, rhythm and movement are inseparable. Whether we skip, schottische, polka, tango, or duck and dive, we are not only taking up certain amounts of space, but we are also moving according to certain rhythm elements. When we move, when we look at our movements, and when we see and feel ourselves moving we are also perceiving rhythm. We are rhythmical beings completely surrounded by rhythm. It is a part of our very makeup. When we listen to rain on a roof, hear the beat of a drum, squeaky shoes going down the hall, the ticking of a clock, or a dripping faucet, we become conscious that we hear a recurring pattern. *This pattern is a definite grouping of sounds, a regular recurrence of sounds—rhythm.* We tend to group, into orderly wholes, sounds of which we are aware. Our perception (expression) of this is rhythm. The extent to which this sense of rhythm, which we all possess, is developed depends on experiences we have. We often say that we feel, or we get the feel of, the rhythm.

ELEMENTS OF RHYTHM

Rhythmic elements enhance movement, and movement responses give meaning to rhythmic elements: tempo, accent, phrasing. This is especially true when the ten-, eleven- or twelve-year-old is ready and wants to "call" for American folk dancing.

Through movement, music reaches children; it is easier for them to experience and learn about its various elements through movement. Movement responses go hand in hand with music and art. Fascinating experiences can be worked out with the music teacher or consultant in this area. These elements of rhythm and movement become more meaningful for children when teachers work together. Many songs which are popular with children have resulted from such cooperation. The music, classroom, and/or the physical education teacher or consultant need to "talk" the same language when it comes to presentation of these rhythmic elements.

Any program that goes very far with movement exploration cannot overlook the importance and interrelation of this phase of the program. Just as exploration in space may be fun and a learning experience, so may exploration of experiences in rhythm. (Many teachers have had unfortunate experiences with music or music terminology. For many, regardless of area of teaching—physical education, classroom, art—interpretation of rhythmic elements become a chore rather than a pleasure.) The enjoyment and personal satisfaction in music is often overlooked in the teaching of symbols and terminology instead of what is needed for experiences and experiencing. When these elements are presented to children as a part of the everyday experiences which children are having, they can more readily understand and talk about them. They talk about them in their own language.

Tempo is the rate of speed of a movement. When children are conscious of how fast or how slow they are moving, they are conscious of tempo. Children recognize and understand tempo by thinking of it in terms of how fast or how slow they are walking, swinging, or doing the rhumba. The Walking Song is an example of tempo; walking moderately, then faster, then moderately, and then slower and slower.

When working with children in rhythmic movement, teachers need to be especially conscious of tempo. For the most part, the children should set their own tempo, or the tempo which is right for them, rather than having the teacher or accompanist doing it for them. As a group starts to move, they establish a tempo to which most of the children can respond. It is the teacher's job to be sensitive to their tempo and pick up the beat or sound as they move. If the teacher sets the tempo, often it is too fast or too slow for the group and the children's responses are not with the beat.

If teachers, for example, set the tempo for the skip for children, usually it is set according to the way we, as adults, skip. Because our legs are longer and because most of us have developed a greater awareness of the beat, we are apt to set a tempo that is too slow for very young children. When a tempo has been established, then it is the teacher's job to keep it steady and prevent it

THE WALKING SONG

JOYCE ELDRIDGE

Effect of Rhythm on Movement

from getting gradually faster and faster, unless working toward that aim as in "The Walking Song." Some children need many opportunities and much encouragement to listen, to feel, and to respond before they are able to keep up to the tempo of the group. Because children feel comfortable moving and have continual opportunities to express themselves rhythmically, they gain in their ability to hold to a tempo and to adjust their tempo to the rest of the group. Recognition of tempo is particularly important as far as folk dancing is concerned. There is nothing as dead as tempo set too slow, since tempo contributes immeasurably to the spirit of the dance. Tempo, of course, has to be adapted to the group dancing and to the variations within the group. This is just one more reason for children to have a back-

ground in fundamental movement before they attempt folk dancing.

Accent is emphasis. When we emphasize a pulse, a beat (beats), or a sound (sounds), we are giving the accent. If we listen to a visitor from Hawaii, we are conscious that most of his Hawaiian words are spoken with the emphasis on the next to the last syllable, or "wai." In *speaking*, we give *accent* to our *words*. In *moving*, we give *accent* to our *movements*. In the schottische, for example, the accent is noticeable on the fourth part of the step pattern. The schottische is made up of three walks or three runs and a hop (walk, walk, walk, hop). As we move, doing the schottische, we seem to accent the hop. This is the movement accent. This movement accent often differs from the metrical (music) accent. The metrical accent is emphasis given to the first underlying beat in each measure. The movement and metrical accent may or may not coincide. To illustrate (using the schottische), we notice that in the step or movement pattern the accent is given to the last of the four beats or sounds; in the music or metrical accent, the emphasis is given to the first of four underlying beats:

```
movement accent   walk  walk  walk  hop
metrical accent    >___  ____  ____  ____
```

The children know the accent which they hear as a louder beat or sound, or as they say—"extra loud or hard." They recognize metrical accent by indicating the first beat in every measure and say "It helps to keep the music straight." The more they listen to music, and the more they play percussion instruments, the more conscious they are of accent. As they experience percussion and movement, they recognize that there are certain other kinds of accents which are called rhythmical accent. This accent is the natural stress given one or more beats or sounds in a rhythmical pattern. Mary Ann Humphrey's name, as beaten out by Mary Ann, shows the accents she gave the pattern of her name:

MARY ANN HUMPHREYS

As Mary Ann said, "It has a big accent, and then a little accent—or I say 'Mary' louder than 'Ann'." As children become more familiar with movement and as they become more conscious of the rhythmical elements and how they affect movement, their power of perception increases, as did Mary Ann's.

When calling and writing folk dances, boys and girls must be conscious of the metrical accent, so that their "calls" will fit naturally with the music or with the underlying beat of the first measure. Older children realize that accent isn't necessarily a loud or hard sound, but that it can be achieved by emphasis, such as *omission* or *differentiation*. For instance, a group of children accented the first beat of a series of running steps by leaping; another group accented by omitting the first so-called running step. Differentiation of accent or a displaced accent is recognized in syncopation, to which children enjoy working.

Underlying beat is the pulse, or steady beat, that continues throughout. We all recognize units of time. We know that sixty minutes make an hour, or that twenty-four-hour units make a day. We can think of beats in this same relationship; that we measure the length of time of a movement by a unit called beat. This beat (*unit*) is the constant pulsation which exists in all motion. As we attain an awareness of this pulse, we can move with more rhythmical accuracy. *It has equal time and force and serves as the underlying fundamental unit of measure*. Children are conscious of the underlying beat, though in the beginning they are not apt to use the words "underlying beat." Instead they say "the steady beat that goes all the time, or the steady beat (pulse) we are clapping—the bum, bum, bum of the walk or the bum, bum, bum of the music."

```
Movement pattern   walk  walk  walk
Underlying beat     bum   bum   bum
```

Through exploring, the children find that the walk resembles the underlying beat in music. They find as they walk that their feet make the sound of the underlying beat. Children also become aware that the underlying beat or steady pulse is the foundation ("the cellar" as one child put it) for rhythmic patterns. Consciousness of this (being able to hear and feel the underlying beat) on the part of the peer age is necessary in learning social dancing.

Rhythmic pattern is a definite series of sounds or beats related to the underlying beat. When people clap a series of sounds or beats which are even and/or uneven, they are clapping a rhythmic pattern. Children say rhythmic pattern is "the melody or word pattern of a song." "Jingle Bells" is an example.

```
Word pattern       Jin gle bells      jin gle bells
Rhythmic pattern   __ __ ___          __ __ ___
Underlying beat    ____  ___          ____  ___

                   Jin gle all the    way
                   __ __ ___ __       ____
                   _____          ____

                   Oh what fun it     is to ride in a
                   __ __ ___ __       __ __ ___ __ __
                   _____          _____
```

One horse o pen sleigh

— — — — ————————

———— ———— ————

Rhythmic pattern may be an entire song which is made up of many different word patterns. It may also be a shorter pattern taken from the song, such as the last line of "Jingle Bells."

Duration is concerned with continuity of time, which includes even and uneven sound intervals. When we hear rain on a roof we hear short intervals of sound or prolonged intervals of sound. (We hear short intervals of sound and short intervals of silence, or we hear long intervals of sound and long intervals of silence, or we hear a combination of these long and short sounds, plus corresponding intervals of silence.) Children have not defined duration, as such, but they know it in terms of different sounds of *long* and *shorts* and are conscious of it as "even and uneven." This is apparent when they analyze locomotor movement. Children say that the walk, run, leap, hop and jump have even sounds which have a long or a short sound. That is, the walk has a single sound, or each walk has a sound, which we hear as a short interval or a long interval, and it says *walk* (short) or *w a l k* (long).

Even Duration:

Movement pattern	w a l k	w a l k	w a l k
Long even sound	————	————	————
Underlying beat	————	————	————

or

Movement pattern	walk walk	walk walk	walk walk
Short even sounds	—— ——	—— ——	—— ——
Underlying beat	————	————	————

Uneven Duration:

Some combinations of locomotor movements, such as the skip, gallop, and slide, are made up of two sounds which are uneven sounds of long and short "intervals." Often children will say it sounds like "dummmmmmmmmm de," or long short, or "de dummmmmmmmmm," short long. This uneven time interval for a skip is made up of a series of long and short sounds.

Movement pattern   walk leap   walk leap   walk leap

Long and short un-
  even sounds   —— - —— - —— -
Underlying beat   —— —— ——

Intensity is the amount of force exerted or the energy expended within a given length of time. The force of a movement is the intensity of the movement. According to children, they believe, "It is to the amount of hardness, heaviness, lightness, softness, strongness, or weakness that we give a movement." In sounds made by percussion, it is the loudness, softness, heaviness, lightness, or sharpness.

Measure is a grouping of beats determined by an accent. If we listen to a series of underlying beats we find there is an accent; if we start counting the beats from one accent to the next, we can determine the meter or the number of beats in the measure. This grouping of underlying beats constitutes a regular recurrence of a primary (first) or heavy accent which divides the beats into measures. Children say, "Measure is a sentence of beats (or sounds) instead of a sentence of words." Working with movement and percussion and starting their own songs, children become conscious of measures of varying number of beats. Two beats to a measure would include the number (2), a bar line (|) to divide, a symbol for accent (>), and a symbol denoting sounds (——).

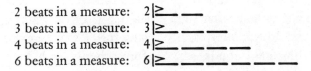

2 beats in a measure:	2|≥ — —
3 beats in a measure:	3|≥ — — —
4 beats in a measure:	4|≥ — — — —
6 beats in a measure:	6|≥ — — — — — —

Phrase is a natural grouping of measures giving a temporary feeling of completion. As we speak, we stop for breath every once in a while. As we write we use periods and exclamation marks. In music or movement, we naturally group to give that same feeling of completion to one thought or one movement before starting over again or starting on another. Phrasing usually means to children "a grouping of two or more measures—a paragraph of beats or sounds instead of a paragraph of words." If we listen carefully to children, we find that they naturally phrase as they talk. When speaking of phrasing, children have remarked, "You can tell when to stop or start by the way it sounds or feels." A four-measure phrase is "tied together" and indicated by the following illustration:

$$2\ |\geq\ \_\ |\geq\ \_\ |\geq\ \_\ |\geq\ \_\ |$$

Development of Intensity, Tempo, and Duration

As children are able to move freely in space, and movement expressions become automatic, it is interesting to watch the way they can respond to elements of rhythm. Usually in working with children, concentration is on one element (rather than on a number of elements), because that is what is being emphasized at the moment. However, rather than to develop any specific one of these rhythmical elements, as has been done with the locomotor movements of walk and jump, and space elements of levels, these three rhythmic elements will be discussed: intensity, tempo, and duration. A treatment of *intensity* follows.

The teacher stimulates thinking by asking such questions as these: "How would I play on these glasses if you walked very quietly?" "Could you start to walk quietly, and I'll try to play your walk on the glasses? Do you suppose you could walk so quietly that if I closed my eyes I would still be able to hear you just a little? What does it make you think of to walk so quietly?" Children responded with such thoughts as birds walking on cotton, baby asleep, going into a scary movie, hospital, clouds, and "before school when I get there early."

The teacher asks, "When I play the drum like this (heavy sound) how does it sound?" From the children comes, "It hurts my ears, boom-boom, loud, like an airplane rumble, like fog horns." Next, the teacher may say, "How does this tom-tom beat make you want to move? Will you try to move so we can really hear you? Now, let's try moving first loud, and then soft. Suppose this group moves softly, in any way you want to, just so you keep it quiet and soft. We will watch and listen. Now let's have this other half of the group move so loudly that we hear every sound. Make it very heavy. This time let's

have the group over there move just their arms lightly and quietly. When you hear a loud sound, then let's have these boys and girls move legs as loudly and heavily as you can. When you hear two sounds together, stop! Did that look any different? Did it make you feel any different when you watched it? Did it sound any different?"

A discussion like the above provokes various reactions. The children give a variety of cues which can be followed. It is a good way to include sounds of words, bird calls, whistles, clocks, and other things. Doing this helps children to get a feeling of *intensity*. The teacher might say, "What does this wood-block sound remind you of? What does this tongue clack make you think of?" The answer might well be "horses." If so, start exploring intensity using gallops.

The children, being curious, would ask: "What does a horse usually do?" "Why don't you show us?" "What other ways could we gallop?" (This means *tempo* which may be brought in, if it is desired to pick up the cues from the children. How fast or how slow is the gallop determines the tempo.) The teacher might say, "Suppose we give our horse a fast gallop? As you were just galloping faster, did you notice anything in particular about the gallops?" Children discover for themselves that their gallops seem to become lighter as they gallop faster. We can then explore making them lighter as we gallop faster, and trying to keep them heavy as we gallop more slowly. The group may be divided into four smaller groups: one group taking a fast quiet gallop; the second group, a loud, slow gallop; the third, a fast, loud gallop; and the fourth group, just a regular gallop. (Here we are combining *intensity* and *tempo*.) We may discuss why we cannot have an accompaniment, if we are trying to do this all together. *Children usually figure out that the piano cannot play for all of them at once, because some of them will go slowly and some go fast and some will be loud and some soft.*

From this, a discussion about gallops, involving intensity and tempo, gets started. For instance, we ask, "Do little, quiet, quick gallops remind you of anything?" This has resulted in a thorough

JOYCE ELDRIDGE

discussion of ponies and horses of all kinds, types, breeds and has instigated reading horse stories. Arguments have arisen about certain strains of horses which have started the children on the search to "find out" because these things are important to them. Visitations to farm and stables and country fairs have helped to provide some of the answers. Often, the teacher learns from the children, or all learn together.

We might want to take the cue of the sound of the gallop and start to explore *duration*, or, as the children say, "evens or unevens." The teacher could say, "While you were galloping, how many sounds did you hear your feet making? Do it again, and listen carefully; did you sound like this (clapping) dum dum or like this (clapping) dummmmm da dummmmm da? Were your sounds even like the first dum dum or uneven like dummmmm da? Close your eyes and listen while Frank gallops. Let's clap with him. Again listen to your own feet and pick up the gallop beat." They realize that the gallop is made up of two sounds or parts, a walk and a leap, and that the sounds are uneven, or as one child so ably

phrased it: "The leap never does seem to catch up with the walk." They discover further that the gallop is different in quality so that they usually go forward and backward with the same foot in the lead and that the higher they go, the slower the tempo and the longer the steps. As they clap it, or move in a similar way with their whole bodies, they get the uneven feel of the gallop. They can take the uneven pattern of the gallop and add intensity to it. They can increase or decrease the tempo, keeping their uneven pattern going. They recognize that the skip and the slide are also termed uneven and made up of two parts of long and short sounds. Often, the group is divided into the gallopers, skippers, and sliders who work on combining movement and rhythmic elements and then compare results.

Boys and girls can respond to duration, intensity, and tempo by playing percussion instruments, by clapping their hands, beating on their thighs, beating on the floor with their hands, and clacking their tongues. Based on these elements, compositions have been made about Indians, primitive life, the rodeo, and city and camp life.

Effect of Rhythm on Movement   **101**

Letting a horse out of the corral

Development of Phrasing

Phrasing can be as much fun for younger children as it can for older children. Children phrase naturally when they speak, and many of their rhymes and song patterns show phrasing. Children identify phrasing as "the end, and ready to start over." Phrasing has been used in different situations: follow the leader with leaders changing after every so many phrases; helping the children identify phrases by the beat of the tom-tom; or by stopping the music, using orchestra leaders and working in small groups with the leaders changing after two or four phrases. Children often listen to phrases in folk songs and change their movements to, or with, the phrase. Singing rounds as well as moving to rounds is also a help in learning to respond to phrasing. Older boys and girls are particularly conscious of it when they folk dance, "call" for folk danc-

ing, and compose their own songs and "calls".

When children have discovered accent and measure, phrasing can easily be approached by using a recording and by following it with the question "How can you tell where the accent comes in this music?" Joyce says, "Because I hear it." The teacher then says, "Now let's put up our hands or nod our heads or move some part of us when we hear the accent. What do we call where the accent comes?" (The answer is "measures" because they have already experienced it.) "Can you take turns going around the circle, each playing a measure?" (This takes time, and not all children can respond as quickly as others. With some groups we may never desire to get into these particular rhythm elements.) "Now, let's see if we can go around the circle without missing a single measure. This time let's try something new that is much harder. There will not be any accent particularly to help you,

Effect of Rhythm on Movement

but let's all clap the beat of this record 'The Syncopated Clock,' while it is playing. Suppose we listen carefully to the song part and see if we can clap to the pattern of the song (what do we call this)? Are there any sounds in the song that are like paragraphs similar to those you have been writing in your stories? Listen to see if you can hear several sentences (or measures). Listen carefully to the record. When you think you can hear where a paragraph comes, move your arm or hand. Do you think this half of the group could clap to the first division or part in the music where it seems to stop for just a second? Then, let's have the other half of the group clap to the second phrase or division of measures. Let's start with Marjorie this time, and each one of you in turn clap until the music makes you feel as though it is time to stop. Then, the next boy or girl starts. We have to listen very carefully so we won't lose the beat. Let's try it again to see if we can make it even smoother—just as though one person were doing all the clapping. Now that we are getting better clapping phrases one after the other, let's see if we can do the same thing moving some part of you. Do you know what those divisions of music are called?" The answer

was, "Yes, they are phrases."

Many games can be discovered from such devices as the above. Circle Phrase and Silly Phrase are always popular. The Circle Phrase was composed as boys and girls were working out this game of phrasing. (Many adaptations have been made, depending on the group and their experience.) Boys and girls are in a circle. One is "it" and moves around the circle or across it tagging off another on the end of a phrase. The game is continuous, starting and stopping with the phrase, using any kind of movement, or each doing a different movement. Circle Phrase has also been played in the classroom while sitting at seats. One person starts a body movement on the first phrase and the person sitting in the next seat starts another body movement on the second phrase, and so on around the room, trying not to miss the beginning of the phrase. At times, this is used like follow the leader.

The game of Snatch the Club or Snatch the Bacon has been adapted and played, using such phrasing as the "go" and "snatch" signal. From the Feet Up is another game version which a group of older boys and girls originated. One starts moving the feet on the first phrase, the

Moving with phrasing

CIRCLE PHRASE

NINA COFFING

SILLY PHRASE

JOYCE ELDRIDGE

Brightly

Effect of Rhythm on Movement

next person moves another part above the feet on the next phrase, and so it goes on up the body until the head is reached, and then they start from "the head down." Magic Carpet, Poison, and Passing Objects have been other games adapted to phrasing.

Silly Phrase, which a group of ten-year-olds originated, came about as a result of one of those days when teacher and children admitted it had been "quite a day." The teacher, hoping that maybe something in rhythms would relax the group, found only that it brought forth more cavorting. After a few futile attempts the teacher asked, "What's the matter with us today, anyway?" This brought forth giggling, until Jake spoke up and said that he guessed they were just silly. Children are bound to be silly now and then, and sometimes it's their way of telling us about them. It's good when they can evaluate themselves in terms of their own actions. The group's behavior was turned into a learning situation which was as satisfying to the teacher as to the children. In ten or fifteen minutes these children learned to identify phrasing by use of their silly actions, faces, giggles, and positions. Silly

Phrase consisted of getting into silly poses on each phrase, either individually or in groups, and holding the position for one phrase and then getting into another silly position for the next phrase. This was an opportunity for the day's feelings to come out. And Bobby, the serious, shy, quiet type, let loose and became a part of the silliness. This game has also been adapted for interpretations of statues and animals. Such an activity as this is an aid in relaxation and in a change of activity when a group has become tired, overstimulated, irritable, or tense.

Writing songs and writing American dance calls, and making up dance or action songs, have also been motivated by using phrasing in various ways with different groups. To illustrate, a group started an action song from the words, "Look at Me, Look at Me," developing an interpretation using two four-measure phrases. They were in a circle formation, and each in the group made up *words* and *actions* to two phrases and the entire group picked up the interpretation and repeated the words and actions of the originator on the successive two phrases. This was continuous, with each child on his phrase, saying something such as:

NANCY: Look at me, Look at me, I'm an elephant.
       I swing my trunk, I swing my trunk, just like an elephant.
GROUP: (*Repeat above.*)
JOEL: Look at me, look at me, I'm an airplane.
       I zoom and zoom, and zoom and zoom, just like an airplane.
GROUP: (*Repeat above.*)
SARAH: Look at me, look at me, I'm a basketball.
       I bounce and bounce, and bounce and bounce, just like a basketball.
GROUP: (*Repeat above.*)
MORT: Look at me, look at me, I am the end.
       I sit and sit, and sit right down, just like the end.

LOOK AT ME

"Look at me!" "Look at me!"

Effect of Rhythm on Movement

This group made up their music, which has been used with many other groups; other tunes have been composed, or the verses can be sung or used with other 2/4 tunes.

When we gain in experience and comprehension with phrasing, we often work to music with *uneven phrases* or an *odd number of phrases*. Elements in rhythm are interrelated, as they are interrelated with movement. Even though one element may be emphasized at a particular time, children are nevertheless responding to other elements of rhythm. An understanding of the use of the elements in rhythm gives quality and meaning to their movements.

Suggestions for Exploring Rhythm

1. Using loud and soft sounds with increasing and decreasing intensity, stay in place, going high with the loud sound and low with the soft sound. Do the same thing with the skip and gallop, going high with the loud sounds and low with the soft.

2. Approach tempo and intensity by using the idea of the gallop. Gallop in place, pawing the ground and with the forward foot increasing speed (tempo) with each successive gallop until the signal "Whoa" is called. Gallop like the tired work horse which starts out quite rapidly for home and slows down gradually until he almost stops, then sees the barn and gallops fast to it. Gallop like the bucking bronco, alternating fast and slow gallop, interspersed with kicks. Gallop like the Lone Ranger coming from a distance. Gallop like Trigger.

3. Play a series of sounds, accenting every other one. Moving in a limited space (or sitting in seats in classroom), have the group move to discover the various things they can do on the accent. The pattern is now established in groupings of two sounds. Have children take turns doing different movement with the accent, the whole group following. Examples: *heel*, toe, *clap*, snap.

4. Analyze and play the rhythmic pattern of any of the locomotor or body movements. Children can clap pattern, play them on instruments, or vocalize them.

5. Have the group listen to and clap the underlying beat of a record. Group can respond with mouth or body percussion to the underlying beat and rhythmic pattern. This can be carried further by having one group playing the underlying beat, another doing the rhythmic pattern, and the third doing the moving.

6. Use music, listen to identify underlying beat and rhythmic patterns, accent, and so on.

7. Have the group as a whole establish the underlying beat. Divide into three groups, and have one-third of the class decide on a rhythmic pattern which would fit the underlying beat; another third could play just the accent. All three groups could then play together (underlying beat, rhythmic pattern, and accent). Each group could also put movement to whatever pattern they are playing.

8. Have the group read the "Congo" by Vachel Lindsay, or, any other poem associated with classroom activities. All should speak it out together to establish underlying beat and rhythmic pattern. On percussion instruments pick up the underlying beat and then the rhythmic pattern. Divide into three or more groups. Each group work on movement abstraction, interpretation of idea, or mood. Groups can be subdivided into three groups, with one part choral speaking, one part carrying the percussion, and the third part the movement. This can be developed into a total class composition by dividing the poem into three parts. The first group does the choral part, while the second group does the percussion, and the third does the movement. This is followed by the first group doing the percussion as the second group carries the choral part and the third does the movement. Finally the first group does the movement, the second group the percussion, and the third the choral part. (It is difficult for the groups to change from one to the other without losing the rhythm.)

9. Divide into groups of three. One child establishes the beat, another plays it twice as fast, and the third does it twice as slowly. This can be done on percussion instruments and then translated into movement.

10. Select a Christmas song or carol, and after having the group establish the underlying beat, rhythmic pattern, phrasing, and measure, divide into groups, and interpret any or all of these. Through movement, develop into studies or composition.

11. Select such folk tunes as one of Joseph Marais' "The African Veld Songs," "Yankee Doodle," or some folk music which has two parts (A, B) or three parts (A, B, A). Divide class into three or four groups. Using a recent locomotive combination, such as the schottische, develop a folk dance which has an A and B, or ABA parts. Have one group start in a circle, one in a square, and another in a line.

Getting acquainted with percussion instruments

9. Percussion and Movement

Using percussion is fun, exciting, and adventurous. Not only does it intensify and accompany movement, but it also helps children get the "feel of the rhythm." Percussion provides opportunity for creative expression by allowing children to discover the variety of things which make sound. Percussion is the act of making noise or sound by *tapping*, *hitting*, or *shaking* something. In this book, sounds made by blowing on or into something are included because children like to explore a great variety of sounds.

Children love to make noise, and at times doing so is valuable. Percussion provides an outlet for release of tension, and can be controlled and directed toward their best interests and development. Percussion may be used as an activity in itself or as an accompaniment for movement.

TYPES OF PERCUSSION

Teachers would not so often feel handicapped when a piano is not available for creative rhythmic movement if they would not overlook the extensive area of percussion. Instead of buying expensive or elaborate percussion instruments the same effect may be had by such simple devices as striking together two sticks, pencils, or rulers; or hitting a stick against a blackboard, desk, wall, or floor. Children can make a game of producing sound by jingling keys or bracelets, shaking bobby pins in a tin can, or stones in a Band-aid box, rattling bottle caps strung on wire or string, bouncing balls, and twisting paper. They can construct their own percussion instruments which serve as an important part of their creative rhythm experience.

For primitive peoples, percussion served as a means of communication. They did not understand natural phenomena. They believed that acts of the gods were responsible for rain, thunder, sun, fire, birth, death, good, and evil. To please their gods, primitive peoples offered prayers accompanied by dancing, singing, and such sounds as hand clapping, foot stamping, and body shaking. As the use of language grew, they repeated the same sound over and over to accompany their movement. They discovered new sounds as they began to make utensils for cooking and knives for hunting. Some of the simplest were made by merely striking together two sticks of wood, or clapping stones against each other. Drums were later made of animal skins stretched over hollowed-out stones or tree trunks. Gourds filled with pebbles created an interesting sound.

Body Percussion

Children use parts of their bodies to help them produce sounds. Soon after they begin working with locomotive movements, they discover that their feet make a certain sound, such as shuffle, skip, or tap, and that they can re-create this sound by using their hands. After children understand movement, body percussion is important in helping them to express better a train starting up, an airplane taking off, and the noises of animals, mechanical devices, and so on. They discover a variety of ways they can accompany their movement patterns, give their movement more meaning, and get the feel of the rhythm. We have one boy and girl moving while the class concentrates on the movement, following and furnishing the accompaniment. This becomes a game of concentration—going fast when the movement is fast, slowing down, picking up uneven sounds, changing and responding to even sounds and dynamics, and even catching the mood of the dancer. This provides an opportunity for improvisation of movement for the one performing and a splendid way to review and enhance the use of rhythmic

elements. For those furnishing accompaniment it provides for concentration, perception, and discovering a variety of ways of using one's body and the floor for sound. There are times when this is done with percussion instruments, but it has been used as effectively with body percussion. Some fascinating rhythms of the accompaniment have been taken down on a tape recorder, and include: stamping of feet, clicking heels, beating heels on floor; beating hands on floor, on knees, on thighs, and on middles; tongue clicking, clacking, clucking; and other mouth sounds— whistles, swish, beep, "tch," "ssss," "shuuuu," "ooooh."

MAKING PERCUSSION INSTRUMENTS

Percussion instruments may take on added

Accompanying Julie's movement

Percussion and Movement

Percussion instruments

meaning when children learn to make their own. Young children can use such available materials as milk and cream containers, cereal boxes, paper plates, shoe boxes, paper bags, shells, and bells. For older children, percussion can supplement social studies and language arts. Study of other cultures might include research on their percussion instruments. While engaged in a social studies unit on China, one group of fifth-graders reproduced several crude Chinese instruments which they used to accompany a dance composition of rice planting. Science classes can teach about sound, and interesting experiments can be pursued. Camps also provide a splendid place for making and trying out percussion instruments. An Indian Pow Wow, a Campfire Evening, or Carnival become adventurous when they have been motivated by a venture with percussion. The ingenuity which children display when given an opportunity to discover materials, construct instruments, and work out stories and designs is satisfying and vital to creative growth. Some of their creations become beautiful ob-

jects with the addition of color and design.

Drums

Drums may be constructed in any size or shape to produce a variety of tones. A drum consists of a *frame* over which is firmly stretched a thin material called the *head*. Some materials that have been used for the frame are barrels, kegs, buckets, tree trunks, wastepaper baskets, flower pots, coconuts, and boxes and cans of different types. The head material may be rubber tubing, shellacked muslin, rawhide (wet before stretching over frame), heavy paper (such as parchment or cardboard), linen, canvas, oilcloth, parachute nylon, or thin plastics. Edges of the frame need to be smooth in order not to cut through the drum head. The head should be pulled *tightly* and laced, nailed, or cemented to hold securely.

Indian water drum—coffee cans filled about one-quarter full of water. Circular rubber head from discarded inner tube should be bound tightly over drum frame with heavy shel-

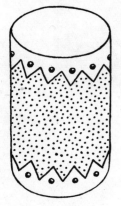

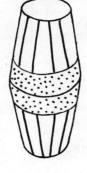

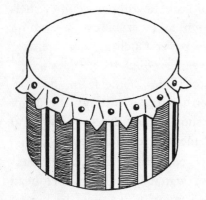

lacked string. Drum then decorated with colorful yarn.

Earthenware drum—sheet of heavy wet paper stretched tightly across top of flowerpot and bound with elastic and gummed tape. Paper shrinks as it dries, leaving tight surface.

Cereal box drums—finger painting cut to size of frame. Stapled on box on top and bottom. Bound with mystic tape. Shellacked to preserve painting.

Tin can drums—rubber tubing stretched over ends of tin can strung with heavy wool yarn.

Round candy box—ends covered with heavy decorated canvas, strung with ribbon.

Painted coffee can—original design. Small bells held in place around edge with Scotch tape.

Wastepaper basket drum—painted rubber sheet tied over painted basket with colored string.

Salad bowl drum—large wooden bowl painted with bright colors. Covered with oilcloth held in place with thumb tacks.

Oatmeal box—shellacked and finger painted, ends covered with rubber sheet held in place with thumb tacks enameled with nail lacquer.

Drumsticks (beaters)—handles made of wood, dowelling, whittled sticks, cocktail muddlers, broom handles, and pencils. Knobs, or drumstick heads, have been made of cotton, twine, elastic, and so on. Spoons and shoehorns make convenient beaters.

Rattles—Shakers—Maracas

Home made instruments (see Suggested Resources) fascinate children, and there is an infinite number that are easy for children to construct. Most of these consist of containers filled with a material that will produce sound when manipulated. A few of the containers that children have used are dried gourds, cardboard cylinder tubes, tin cans, ketchup bottles, salad dressing bottles, cream and milk containers, balloons, bags, tennis balls, and kitchen utensils. Sound is obtained with pebbles, marbles, dried beans, peas, cloves, nails, buttons, small rivets, or other available small materials.

Paper cups and bell—two cups held together with colored Scotch tape. Bell inside. Crayon designs on cup.

Coconut shell—rice for sound. Wooden handle. Painted.

Two cookie cutters—joined with colored Scotch tape. Split peas for sound.

Beer can—painted. Copper disc soldered over open end. Hole made for dowelling handle. Handle nailed at end of can. Decorated. Small rivets for sound.

Two wooden nut bowls—taped together. Handle inserted. Nails, buttons, and bells for sound.

Coffee can—painted. Lid taped on. Hole made with can opener for dowel handle. Nails for sound.

Mayonnaise jar face—jar filled with buttons, covered with twisted crepe paper. Shellacked. Face painted in black. Two bells for earrings. Dowel for handle.

Tennis ball cans—filled with stones and painted. Handle inserted into bottom of each can.

Tennis ball—small hole cut. Pebbles, stones, or buckshot inserted inside. Painted stick put in hole for handle.

Balloons—filled with sand, rice, beans, or a combination of the ingredients. A little air blown in. Knot tied in end.

Gourd—seeds removed from mature dried rind. When rind hardens, lightweight shell is of almost wooden quality, and is filled with gravel.

Boys and girls have their own names for many shaking instruments:

Taper Shaker—milk container filled with rice and Grape-Nuts.

Strain Me—two tea strainers put together with Scotch tape, having pebbles within and bells hanging.

Cup a Tune—two plastic cups taped and glued together. Filled with peas and barley. Bells around outside of cup.

Bel o' Box—top of cream cheese box. Ribbon

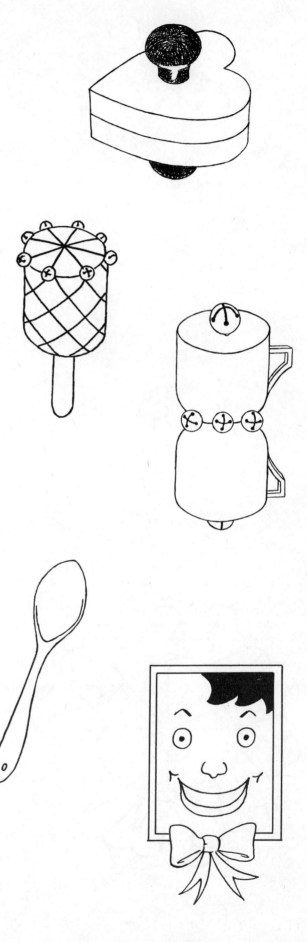

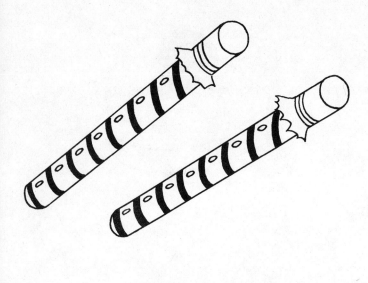

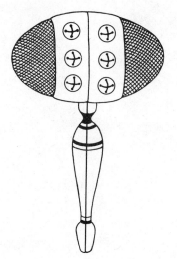

woven on and attached with tacks. Bells sewn on ribbon.

Mr. and Mrs. Rhythm—two hand-toweling tubes, filled with stones, ends covered, painted in stripes.

Rabbit Shaker—papier-mâché in design of rabbit head (tongue and ears go in and out). Buttons inside.

Gun Shaker—two paper cups with handles. Tops sewn together with wool. Peas in one. Lima beans in the other. Painted.

The Shakas—two beer cans covered with plaid material. Dried split peas in them. Open ends covered with sheepskin. Handles from shopping bag put on with Scotch tape.

Rhythm Plate—two paper plates, fastened at edges with strips of gum paper. Filled with rice, tea, or dried beans. Tongue depresser, in between plates, for handle.

Fun o' Bell—bells strung in cluster on shoelace put through two plastic funnels. Cluster of bells in center. Funnels joined with Scotch tape. Ends of shoelace pulled tightly, and more bells attached.

Tin "Can-Can" Shaker—Two strainers put together with adhesive tape. Marbles inside. At times boys and girls talk and sing about their instruments; for example, as a girl was developing a Tin "Can-Can" Shaker she said:

I am Alfy,
The tin "can-can" shaker,
Grasp me with two hands and shake me up and
    down.
Through my strainer-head
You can see my insides get all upset and jump around.

Sounds Made by Hitting or Blowing

There are sounds children make by blowing on or into something, such as shells, reeds, or whistles. They also like to explore noises by hitting together two things, such as cymbals or pie tins.

Reeds—opened at both ends produce tone by letting lips flutter together inside one end of the reed. Tone of trumpet depends on length of reed.

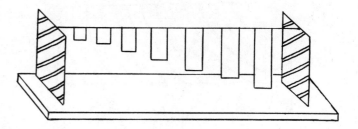

Large sea shells—used as trumpets when blown in.

Oboe sounds—produced by flattening end of straws and blowing through them. The two sides vibrate together to produce tone. Holes burned in straw with hot wire or needle will produce several different tones similar to the oboe effect.

Whistles—if willow wood is available, it may be hollowed out and notched to make excellent whistles. Other whistles can be made of *cardboard cylinder*. Four or five holes punched in a row through the tube about 1½ inches from one end. End covered with square of waxed paper held in place by string or rubber band. Tune hummed into opening. Different notes are produced by covering holes with fingers.

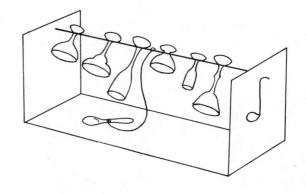

Squeaker—balloon blown up. Opening pinched to let air out. Sound is produced.

Glasses and bottles—used to produce tone. Scale played on glasses filled with water at different levels. The *more* water in the glass, the *higher* the tone. The *less* water in it, the *lower* the tone. Spoon or stick used to strike the glasses. Blowing across water-filled bottles is another method. As with glasses, amount of water determines tone.

Bells and gongs—bell sound made by suspending from a wooden rod three silver spoons of different sizes. Spoons struck with hand beater. Bells have been attached to handle and are played by striking.

Xylophone—eight goblets of various size chosen to produce scale, then hung on wooden rack and played with spoon.

Silver sounder—silver cut into ten pieces of varying lengths. Three-quarters inch wide and from 1 to 4 inches long. Pieces suspended from top of wooden frame at 1-inch intervals. Holes bored in ends of silver pieces and wire used to suspend them from top crosspiece of frame.

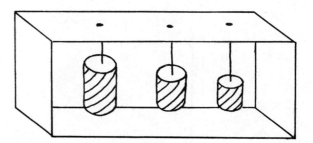

Tin can sounder—three cans hung by wire on board. Marbles inside cans. Wooden stick beater.

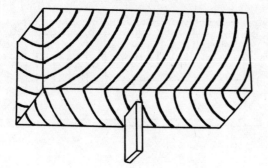

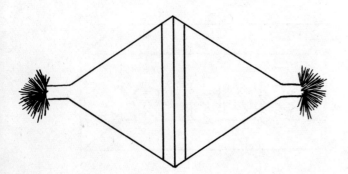

Guillotine—a 12-inch piece plywood for base. Two shorter pieces for sides. One top cross-piece. Three pieces of alloyed tin cut into three different sizes for different tone effects. Table used to hold tin pieces suspended by copper wire in place.

Tinkle—three very large nails of different sizes, separated with string on metal discs arranged along the string. As string is moved, nails tinkle.

Cymbals—made from kitchen saucepan covers or from tops of coffee cans or other tins. Two wooden knobs can be cut from old broom, or spoons may be used as ready-made knobs.

Coffee can cymbals—sharp edges of two tin lids beaten down with mallet. Edges wrapped with adhesive or colored Scotch tape. Handles nailed on center of each lid.

Pie tin cymbals—nail wooden blocks, for handles, to two pie tins. Decorate tins.

Triangles—made from slender rods of brass or steel. Horseshoes or spikes sometimes used. Brass tubing gives best effects.

Castanets—made from shells and walnuts. Manipulation of shells to produce desired sound requires practice.

Tambourines—can be made from the top of round cardboard covers, particularly those coming from cereal boxes, pie plates, tin can covers with edges tapped or hammered down, and paper plates. Shells, buttons, bells can be attached.

Pie plate tambourine—punch holes around edge of rims of two paper pie plates. Insert metal open-hole rivets. Bind with yarn. Small bells attached close to rim. Bottle tops or sea shells may be used instead of bells. Paper plates painted with design in center. Or, fill pie plates with nuts, paper clips, and sew together with ribbon or yarn.

Tin can tambourine—bells attached on a string and taped around edge of cover.

Tamba shaker—two sets of embroidery hoops painted with red nail polish. Plastic table cloth inserted in each set. Hoops decorated with thumb tacks and ribbon streamers, with bells tied on. Rice "alphabets" put in one hoop and sand in the other, the two cemented together.

Cappo—holes punched into bottle caps and strung on wire coat hanger which had been taken apart. Wire twisted together again and bottle caps allowed to move easily back and forth.

Wood Instruments

Children discover that some of the most satisfying sounds are produced by using "woods."

Wood blocks—painted with Indian designs.

Wooden box—size of chalk box, painted. Leather handle. Large wooden bead on end of pencil for beater.

Block of wood—with filed notches. Scrape notches with pencil. Braided yarn handle.

Wooden spools—of various sizes.

Walnuts—hole drilled through. Nailed loosely to wooden broom handle.

Sand blocks—two wooden blocks on which sandpaper is glued.

Rhythm sticks—two slender pieces of wood, such as broom handles, and so forth.

Musical washboards—washboard can be used effectively with other instruments. Different boards make different tones, depending on the material from which they are made (such as glass or metal boards). Board played with thimbles, tin spoons, or metal.

"Washerine"—washboard painted. Bells attached across top and bottom.

"Picket fence"—flat board with eight clothespins nailed on upside down. Piece of wooden dowel or pencil used to play up and down the "fence."

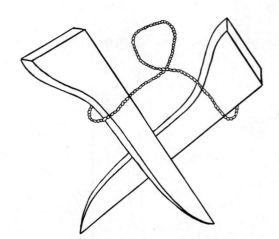

Roller nail—large rolling pin, or any size club-shaped piece of wood. Large nails driven in and spaced along the board at different heights. Hard round stick skimmed along nails for sound; also used to beat the roller.

"Needle Me"—flat board with needles or pins "picked" to give sound.

Percussion and Movement

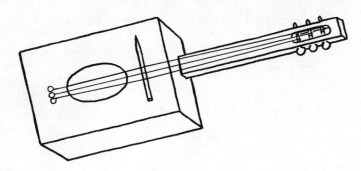

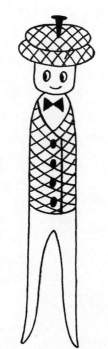

String Instruments

A few instruments have been made by children to resemble banjoes and guitars, but so far they have not proved very satisfactory in producing sound. Rubber bands, catgut, and shellacked string are some of the materials used. If children do make instruments of this kind, there is difficulty in keeping them tuned.

Banjo—made from cigar box. Oval hole cut in lid. Wooden board inserted at one end for handle. Handle and lid held in place with adhesive tape or very small nails. Strings are catgut, raised by pencil or small dowelling, and held in place with adhesive tape. Strings tightened by screw eyes.

"Graslicap"—egg slicer, bottle cap, potato grater. Egg slicer pried apart at the hinges. Only part with the string used. Bottle cap attached to rim of egg slicer with a rubber band. Small potato grater inserted into top of egg slicer where slab of metal overlaps. Hammer down slab. Attach ribbon to top of grater and at each end of egg slicer. Nutpick used to play the instrument.

Salando—salad bowl and egg slicer. End of egg slicer used for bridge for strings. Pick.

Cigar-Anjo—made with a cigar box and ukulele strings. Wooden handle. Paint and shellac applied.

Miscellaneous Percussion Instruments

A variety of "you name them" percussion instruments have been made:

Clothespin kids—clothespins for body. The tops of frozen orange juice cans or beer can tops may be filed and sandpapered, and a hole put in middle of each top. Shellack so paint sticks. Then give coat of tempera or water colors. Two tops with washer between attached to clothespin with firm nail.

Angel Belles—metal sponge or chore boy cemented to Christmas-tree ball ornaments. Piece of wire covered with gold ribbon, shaped into small halo, and hooked on over metal curls. Balls filled with fine rice. Cocktail muddlers or mixers cemented into ball for handles. Faces painted with nail polish.

Hanger-Drummee—drum part made from coffee can. Inner tubing for drumhead. Small metal clothespins and bobby pins in drum. Brown paper painted and cemented to the drum heads for decorations. Bells tied with bows to coat hanger which was attached to drum with two ribbons and another bow tied at bottom of drum. Drumstick of Kleenex covered with paper napkin and woolen yarn and topped off with a bow.

Bellarace Hatzie—cardboard made into hat with top, crown, and brim. Crown filled with small buttons. Small cocktail mixer put through crown, using reinforcement rings on both sides of cardboard. Extra piece of cardboard put inside crown to hold buttons. Large brim taped to crown. Bunches of colored bells put on each side of brim.

Snake—top of old fly swatter cut to resemble snake's head. Strips of brown paper painted and glued over head and wrapped around handle. Hit against hand to make swishing or swatting sound.

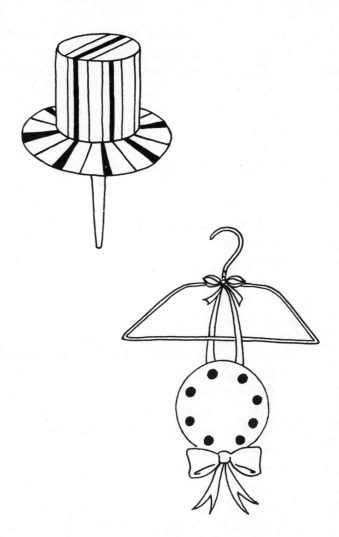

HOW TO USE PERCUSSION

Working together in groups is a valuable and necessary experience for children. Percussion instruments provide an opportunity for cooperation in working and playing with others.

When first bringing together children and instruments (or adults and instruments), bedlam is often apparent. This is a new activity, and children are fascinated with the many sounds their instruments can produce. Their experimentation will be noisy. However, if this is their introduction to percussion, the girls and boys need to become familiar with the instruments, and should be encouraged to beat, hit, and shake and blow them. They need to explore the many kinds of sounds the different instruments make. It is important that each child have something in his hand to play so that all feel that they are participating and contributing—even if the "something"

is nothing more than two pencils, sticks, or rulers.

After they have tried out the various devices, group organization begins. A piano or Victrola may furnish background music to help to keep the group together. If neither is available, the group may choose to sing and play a well-known song. The teacher suggests that everyone start and stop at one time, although she knows this is difficult to achieve at the beginning because children become so absorbed with their new instruments. Selecting an "orchestra leader" to signal when to start and stop can be helpful. While playing, children need to relax, use arms and wrists freely, and play the instruments with various parts of their hands and arms. A tightly clenched fist around a beater will greatly hamper a child in his use of movement and will affect the sound he produces. He also needs room in which to swing his beater up and down, out and around.

Here are some ways to start exploring percussion to such favorite songs as "Syncopated Clock," "La Cucaracha," "Winter Wonderland," "Dixie," "The Erie Canal," and "Jingle Bells." At first, we may have a collection of disorderly sounds. We might have just the drums play (or first the drums, then shakers, bell sounds, and so on), or the drum might play throughout and the other instruments come in at designated times. We can use the drums for accent and play the other instruments throughout. By changing the meter, using a 2, 3, 4, 5 beat, we get a variety of ways of utilizing the drums for accent. We try playing instruments on the first beat and hitting the floor or different parts of our instrument on the next beat.

If we have a leader, he motions to different percussion instruments to come in and to stop. If we have a piano, it can start, and the leader can add shakers (stopping the shakers as the tambourines pick up), then drums, then washboard, and finally motion all to play. Children say, "The piano helps to keep us straight." The piano might be alternated with the percussion, but in so doing care needs to be taken not to lose a beat on the change. If we have a piano, we might have the piano take the first phrase, the tambourines and bells take the second, the shakers the third, and the drums the fourth phrase. (This depends on the former experience of the group; it ties in well when concentration on rhythmic elements are taught.) If we do not have a piano, we can do the same with songs, a harmonica, or accordian.

Children enjoy discovering different ways they can play the drums. They find that drums are not simply "banged" but that a technique may be developed in playing them. The sound will be *drawn out* rather than *beaten* into the instrument. Tones may be altered by playing on different surface areas: top, bottom, sides, rim; by varying the section of the beater used; or by hitting the drum with the knuckles, fingers, fingertips, or fist. Skill in use of the beater is increased when it is grasped lightly between the fingers, with wrists kept flexible and arms used freely. The older children can become proficient in the use of percussion instruments of their own making in the shop, at camp, or as a result of experimentation in science.

Body and Locomotor Movement While Playing Percussion

To keep a steady pulse, we may want to move some part of us with the beat. We may keep our heads going while we play. Sometimes in order to gain a better awareness of the beat, part of the group walks out the rhythm while others play the accompaniment. We may explore with our instruments the many kinds of locomotor movements and try to play a slow walk, a fast one, a run. We realize that the fundamental locomotor movements have only one sound, which is even and steady. The combinations—skip, gallop, slide, and polka—have more sounds, and these particular ones are *uneven* sounds. We can play all of them and thereby furnish accompaniment for movement.

We can achieve interesting effects by moving some part of our bodies while sitting on the floor and playing our instruments. Part of the group may *clap* a movement while the other part plays its instruments. Here are some patterns that have come from a class of eleven- and twelve-year-olds:

They are working in groups with a leader for each group. One group moves on the floor doing gallops and swings. Another group accompanies with some kind of mouth percussion. A third group makes an orchestra with several percussion instruments.

One group moves with a walk for underlying beat. Another moves to a rhythmic pattern they have chosen, which will fit the underlying beat. A third group carries the already established underlying beat on the drums. The last group carries a rhythmic pattern with other instruments.

One group moves with a leader, slowly, and increases or decreases the tempo. Another group follows with percussion accompaniment.

One boy or girl does a variety of hard and soft, heavy and light, fast and slow movement improvisations. The entire group concentrates on the movement and accompanies with percussion instruments or body percussion.

Soon we find that we are no longer producing just any old sound by merely banging drums, shaking rattles and tambourines, and beating gongs. We find ways of getting variations of sound. We learn to improve on the playing of

"Jingle Bells" by hitting the gongs a new way, to realize that there is an appropriate time to use the washboard, and to know that drums are most effective if played for a desired sound. Some experiences require *heavy* drums, while others need the drums only to keep a steady, underlying beat throughout.

Camp situations can use percussion experiences to good advantage, and even adults enjoy this medium of expression.

PERCUSSION ACCOMPANIMENT FOR MOVEMENT

We find that one of the best ways to become aware of patterns is to *move* to them first, and then to accompany them with some kind of percussion.

A rhythmic pattern of gallop, gallop, run run run, leap is accompanied by shakers on the gallops and by drums on the runs and leaps. For example, see the following:

Percussion	shaker	shaker	drums	drum
Movement	gallop	gallop	run run run	leap
Rhythmic pattern				
Underlying beat 3				

To become more aware of the rhythmic elements of accent, underlying beat, and rhythmic pattern we worked on each part separately. The group took four measures of underlying beats (sixteen sounds), then we walked to these sixteen steady beats. We decided that it might be interesting to add accents and put one at the beginning of each measure. This divided up the beats into four measures of four beats each and gave us four accents. We then jumped on the accent. As the group became familiar with the separate elements, they decided to divide into smaller groups, with each taking a part: one group moving with the accent, and others moving with the underlying beat. (We could have stopped there and worked out percussion accompaniment, but this particular group was capable of adding more parts.) Another group was formed and added a

rhythmic pattern of hop, hop, jump, hop, hop, jump, run, run, run, run, hop, hop, jump. This needs to be done slowly at first, because we find it difficult to hold one's weight from runs to hops.

Accent	JUMP	JUMP
Movement	hop hop jump	hop hop jump
Rhythmic pattern		
Underlying beat 4		
Accent	JUMP	JUMP
Movement	run run run run	hop hop jump
Rhythmic pattern		
Underlying beat 4		

One twelve-year-old suggested that it might be easy to practice in one spot, so we faced each other and tried the movements in place. This particular exploration ended with a circle formation with four groups working on the four parts: (1) underlying beat, (2) accent, (3) rhythmic pattern, and (4) percussion. The underlying beat moved about the circle. The accent faced center and on the first jump landed with feet apart. On the second accent they landed with feet together, which faced out from the center and repeated the pattern. The rhythmic pattern faced center except on the runs, which were done in individual circles. When this movement exploration was completely worked out, percussion was added and this fourth group was in the center of the circle and accompanied the movement exploration with appropriate instruments. This group decided their efforts would make a good Indian dance, and it was the next exploration. They added levels and range of movement to their patterns, making them as elaborate as they could, and used percussion to accompany their movement study. (Ventures of this type call for guidance from the teacher in helping to keep the activity within the capacities of the group.)

MOVEMENT ACCOMPANIMENT TO PERCUSSION

Up to this point we have been concerned with movement and have dealt with percussion as accompaniment for movement. Now, let us consider percussion as an experience in itself, and then how movement and elements in space and rhythm affect percussion.

We find that we can play the beat of any song. We can listen to Bing Crosby sing "White Christmas" and then play our instruments along with him. We also play the underlying beat while singing folk and work songs.

We can use rhythmic patterns which children recognize as the *song* or word patter. We recognize the rhythmic patterns of songs and distinguish these patterns from the underlying beat. Part of the group may play the fundamental beat, while the others play the rhythmic pattern. We clap the rhythmic pattern, while some of the instruments keep the underlying beat.

Songs, like "Old MacDonald Had a Farm," provide opportunities to play underlying beats and rhythmic patterns, and to invent many interesting effects of animal sounds. For instance, the children may decide that the drums make the "moo" sound of the cow, shakers the peep of the chick, wood blocks the quack of the duck, and tambourine the "oink" of the pig; the boys and girls play these parts as they sing.

Some groups have called playing the underlying beat the *whole* and those playing the rhythmic pattern, the *parts*. More than one third-grader has asked, "Why don't you play the *whole* and we'll play the *parts?*"

We have found that names have rhythmic patterns. We start with one name, such as Susy Brown, repeat this name together so that all may understand. We clap "Susy Brown," and we play it on our instruments. We find that when we say it one way it has one group of sounds, and when we say it another way, it has a different group of sounds. But whether we say it fast or slowly, evenly or unevenly, there is a pattern to "Susy Brown."

"Guess whose name I'm playing."

rhythmic pattern. We try a few (as a group clapping together), taking turns playing on the tomtom so that all may hear. Sometimes we say names differently, which changes the rhythmic pattern. The teacher may ask, "Which one of these patterns do you like? Could you move some part of you to the rhythmical pattern of your name?" We sometimes go around the room or the circle, playing the rhythmic patterns to our names, or we make a game out of it, with one child playing a name and the others guessing. If we have had some experience with rhythmic patterns, we divide into two's and three's to see how we can play our names together. Sometimes we try to form a finished pattern by joining names. Bobby and Ann found that their best pattern came from repeating their names.

> Bobby Simonson
> Bobby Simonson
> Ann Stoufer
> Ann Stoufer
> Bobby Simonson
> Bobby Simonson
> Ann Stoufer
> Ann-n-n-n-n-n-n-n

Facing each other they moved to this rhythmic pattern, doing walk, walk, run, run, walk. They went sideward on the walk and turned on the run, run, walk, with a complete turn on the last walk.

Movement   W W RR W   W W RR W

Su sy Brown   Su sy Brown

2 __ _ ____ __ _ ____

Each child says his name over and over, the way he ordinarily says it, and then claps the

Rhythmic pattern	Bobby Simonson	Bobby Simonson
Underlying beat	— — —— —	— — —— —
	— — — —	— — — —
	W W W	W W W
	Ann___Stoufer	Ann___Stoufer
	— — — —	— — — —
	Ann_____	
	— — — —	

Sometimes we work with many pieces of percussion, or we may use only single pieces, such as a drum. We have called our drum a talking drum which asks questions to which we have answers. We have answered by playing rhythmic patterns on other kinds of percussion. On occasions the *talking drum* has said something, and, as Joel said, "The shakers just giggled back."

Radio commercials are a source of many rhythmic patterns. Older children from the fourth grade up add movement to the patterns and ask their classmates to guess the commercial. Even though many of the same commercials have been used over and over again, no two have ever been presented in exactly the same manner. Some favorite advertisements used successfully have included:

2 Smoke Kools Smoke Kools Smoke Kools*

—|———— — —|———— — —|———————|

4 Use A-jax the foaming Clean - ser

—|—-————-—|—————————|

Gets the dirt right down the drain†

|——————————|———————|

Many different ways of dividing the class into smaller groups have been used, such as alphabetically by first or last names, dates (months) of birthdays, or by the colors of eyes. Some of the radio commercials or advertising slogans which children called out (when asked to think of a few) were listed on the floor or board. They talked about them, said them over and over, and clapped the rhythmic patterns. When they seemed to understand the process, the groups were given the problem to agree on a commercial or slogan

* Reproduced by permission of the Brown & Williamson Tobacco Corporation.

† Copyright, 1951, by Colgate-Palmolive Company.

which they could play on their instruments, and then to put movement to the pattern. Sometimes this takes the form of abstraction and at other times, an interpretation of the idea, but the rhythmic pattern continues throughout. One group developed an idea to a razor-blade commercial; two boys kept the rhythmic pattern of the commercial going while two children were the bathroom door, two were the medicine kit and mirror, one the tube of shaving cream, two were the faucets, and the last one was the "shaver." Anyone who had watched a man enter a bathroom to shave could not have missed guessing the "take off" on the commercial.

Often a pattern is liked by the entire group, and they will choose it to try out. "Dad's Old Fashioned Root Beer" turned into a conga rhythm. The seventh grade joined in with the group which had set the rhythmic pattern and used voice and drum accompaniment. The entire group developed a conga line.

Other interpretations for percussion patterns have been furnished by rounds and nursery rhymes, rope-jumping verses, peddlers' calls, slogans, quotations, and work songs.

Children have enjoyed inventing codes, radio dispatches, Indian signals, and FBI signals. This may be done by having one group start to play a series of beats and the answer coming from a second group. *Codes* and their *Answers* are another source. One group may be asked to send the dispatch and another group to answer; or the class may be divided into groups, and each group in turn answer the message:

Code

Rhythmic pattern	3 —-—— —	—-—— —
Underlying beat	— — —	— — —
	3 —-—— —	————
	— — —	— — —

Answer

	3 ————	—-— —
	— — —	— — —
	3 —-—— —	————
	— — —	— — —

Another way percussion has been used successfully is by having a child go to the window and "tell" with his instrument what he sees. Christine saw a taxi starting. The effect she gave of slamming the door was fun for the class to guess. She used a beater on a pie tin symbol to produce her effect. Quite different was Clayton's percussion "take off" of the garbage collector he saw. His sounds came from two tin can shakers. Still other percussion interpretations have been used for bird calls, sirens, traffic, street drills.

Percussion is an exciting and stimulating activity, and some groups cannot "take" as much as others. It is a good way to begin a period, especially because it gives older children a better understanding of the elements of tempo, intensity, rhythmic pattern, underlying beat, measure, phrase, and accent.

Percussion has led to composing songs, stories, and dance interpretations. Classroom units have grown from such incidences as the second-grader's discovery that the playing of the wood block sounded like a clock. Sixth-, seventh-, and eighth-graders have formed themselves into orchestra bands to accompany their folk and social dancing. A camp group gave an Indian powwow as a result of working out of doors with a tom-tom (of their own making).

A HELPFUL PIANO ACCOMPANIST

The accompanist is our friend and an important member of the group. She understands and enjoys children and respects and helps them with their creations. She is enthusiastic and encouraging and regards creative efforts as important. She is keenly alert to the ways in which children move and appreciative of the way they use their imaginations to respond to sound. Piano music is a vital and valuable part of the creative rhythm experience when the accompanist adjusts her playing to the mood and tempo of the group. *She* accompanies *children*. When children explore movement, *they* set the pattern, and the accompanist picks up the pattern from them. The children say, "She helps to hold us steady." By

watching children, and getting the feel of their gallops, skips and polkas, the accompanist makes the piano "say the same thing."

Skill in playing is less important than understanding people. We receive little help for creative work from a person whose only interest is in the music before her. If she usually follows definite pieces of music, giving her attention to the page before her, rather than having her attention on the children, she cannot be fully aware of what is happening to them. Her accompaniment should be distinct, purposeful, and well accented and hold the tempo established. A confident accompanist can be of great help to the children.

The accompanist, with a fairly extensive repertoire, cannot always summon the appropriate music to fit the children's movements. Frequently, she needs to improvise to maintain the spirit and catch the idea of the group. The "right music" at the "right time" can add meaning and depth to the children's creations. A background in the classics and folk music supplies a rich source.

Some accompaniment can be furnished by a teacher. Anyone who has just a little skill on the piano can do acceptable jobs for rhythms, if she will watch the children and take her cues from them. A few simple chords may be just what is needed; playing high on the piano for light movements of high levels, low on the piano for low levels, loud for heavy and soft for light movements. As one gains in confidence, delightful experiences often result. Children who have the feel of the movements can provide limited accompaniment on the piano by watching a group. When this happens the piano assumes the same importance as a percussion instrument. In this respect it can be played in the following ways: by increasing or decreasing the tempo and intensity, raising and lowering the pitch to indicate levels, or by taking the underlying beat or rhythmic pattern. *Music* as we know it may not come out of the piano, but *sound* does. It is a fine experience for a teacher or a child to feel movement, watch others move, and then reproduce it in sound which serves as accompaniment.

LEVELS

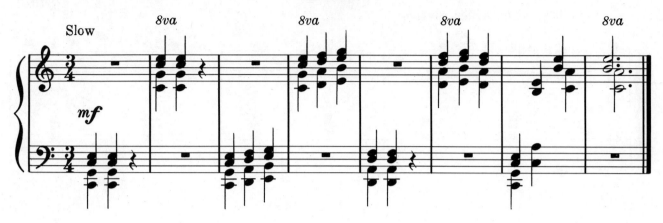

LOUD - SOFT

How the Accompanist Works with Children

One third-grade class always entered the rhythms room skipping. One day they were stopped after skipping around the room three or four times. They were asked to clap the rhythm of the skip while catching their breath, and then to skip again. Nina Coffing (the accompanist), taking her cue from the children, accompanied the skip with a lilting rhythm. As she changed the tune, Bobby asked if Nina would play that same skip again because it made him "skip all over." She recalled it as best she could and so it would not be forgotten roughly jotted it down in a book we kept at the piano for just that purpose. To the delight of the third-graders, Nina surprised them when next they came to Rhythms

and played "their skip." No professional entertainer could have had a more appreciative audience. This particular skip is included to show how simple music can be enjoyed and appreciated by children when it is created for them with their movement patterns in mind.

If the accompanist enjoys improvising, she may become a close friend of a group of children and be permitted to enter their innermost world of imagination. If she helps them in this serious business of working out ideas and interpretations, she in turn gains deep satisfaction. Not only is she repaid by the light which appears in the eyes of children, but such verbal responses as "Gee, that was fun; let's do it again" make her more fully aware of her share in their experiences. She understands that sometimes children's voices are

SKIP

NINA COFFING

Lightly, with marked rhythm

8va

full of exciting tones, while at other times the seriousness of their hushed whispers indicates their fear lest someone else will hear of their creation before it is ready to share. The mysteriousness of the creation may be heightened by the children making such comments as these: "Can you play cornfield music for us?" "We need printing press music." "Do you suppose you can make the press sound?" "Can you play some fast gallop music with bumps in it?" "We need some help with our airplane hangar and in getting the different kinds of Cub's, DC-6's, DC-4's, and Constellations off the ground." "Do you know what kind of music they had in India?" A fifth-grader showed a need for help from the accompanist when he came to her and said, "I made up a square dance 'call' which would be nifty if I could just have some music for it."

The music which has been included in this book is the result of simple piano improvisations, spontaneously played and recorded to fit particular movement explorations and interpretations. With repetition, these improvisations took on definite form, and were recorded and used with many different groups of children.

The Clock and Fire music are samples of group compositions worked out first by the children, and then with the assistance of the accompanists, to help them better express their ideas. These turned into class compositions which were re-lived many times. The music to the Fire began as an idea about going to a fire. The group of children who originated it lived in a section of a city where fire engines were a novelty. One day

BALLOONS FOR SALE

FLORENCE BURNS

Bal - loons for sale! Bal - loons for sale! Come buy a red one, a blue one, a yel-low one, Bal - loons for sale, Bal - loons for sale! Five cents and ten cents to - day.

as a fire engine rushed by the school, everyone hurried to the window. At the time, the fire engine was more important than the rhythmic patterns we were working on, so we talked about the engines. Our discussion led to a rhythmical movement interpretation of a fire department being called to a fire, getting there, and putting out the fire. It took several periods of work before the group was satisfied with this composition. (See section on Fire music in Chapter 10.)

The Clock music (see Chapter 11) followed a study about clocks. This music came from different rhythmic patterns which the seond-graders had worked out for their own clocks. The rhythmic patterns of certain clocks were completed and recorded. Words and movements to the patterns were developed by the children who worked with Nina to find the tunes that their patterns "said." She was able to put their tunes together in a musical composition which accompanied their songs, percussion, and movement patterns.

BALLOON MAN

FLORENCE BURNS

The songs, "Balloons for Sale" and "Balloon Man," came about in the following way. There had been a fair in town, and the children were excited about it. The third-graders said, "Let's have our own fair." After much discussion, they divided into groups to work out their program. The balloon man must have fascinated this group of third-graders, because two groups decided to work out their interpretation of him. As they worked on movements, they made a "patter" of their words. Mrs. Burns (the accompanist) was listening intently and as they worked, she recorded what they were saying. She drew their attention to the fact that they had written a song.

She asked, "How would you like a melody to go with your song so you can sing it while you are selling balloons?" Since they agreed that it was a "keen idea," she accompanied their singing. Another group decided it too must have a "selling song." They wrote some words, and Mrs. Burns created another melody for them.

We make up songs about what we do, to original music, or we may use well-known melodies.

The "Skipping Song" was first originated to encourage children to skip together and to explore a variety of movement. It was adapted to "Sing a Song of Sixpence," but has been sung to a number of other tunes of 4/4 time.

Skipping Song

We'll skip and skip and skip and skip and skip around the room
First I skip alone but I need a partner soon.
  I skip here and choose one; and you skip over there
Come along and have some fun and skip 'most anywhere.

  Sing a song of skipping
A pocket full of things
  Four and twenty children skipping in a ring
When the music stops, then Jonny says "Watch me"
  "Can you do the things I do, they're simple as can be."

This song not only provides an opportunity for children to skip together and to introduce them to folk dancing, but it also, on the line of the song, "When the music stops," then Jonny or (another child) says, "Watch me," allows for individual action to take place. One child then sets the pattern for the others to follow. In this way, a variety of movements may be quickly reviewed. The "Skipping Song" has also served as a mixer type activity for children and parents together, or for different age groups of youngsters dancing together.

Music Listening

There are times when we need to listen to the piano or phonograph to help us become more aware of rhythmic elements or to see if we can get the "feel" of the music. When this happens we talk about the kind of movement that may be done to that which we hear. There are times when we listen to music and then use it for improvisation of movement, because sometimes it is fun to do just whatever we want to music we like. There is *no* one correct movement because children hear the music in their own way. There are times when we move to *specific* music which the accompanist plays for us or which we hear on the

Our ragtime polka

phonograph. The peer age group and adults like to do a Rag Time Polka to Tex Williams' "A and E" recording. (See Source Material.) For this, we need to listen first to get the rhythm and then to adjust a folk dance to the recording. This type of dancing comes *after* we can more freely distinguish rhythm and adjust our own rhythm to whatever we hear. To improve our square-dance calling, we study the work of professional callers on records, noting their style. However, much of our square dancing is done to music with *our own calls*. (See Chapter 11.)

The advantages in the use of percussion are numerous: It requires little space, can be used in a classroom or an auditorium if necessary, and can stimulate a group. Its unlimited possibilities and simplicity give teachers and children an opportunity to use it. Percussion instruments provide a variety of exploration, such as learning about sound and the kinds of things that produce sound in science, constructing instruments in the shop and crafts, using it for expression and accompaniment in schools and camp situations, and furnishing moods and ideas for compositions. Ideas and situations which lend themselves readily to percussion accompaniment are Halloween, Traffic, Industry, the Farm, and Indian Pow-wows.

Children who have had experiences with percussion can recognize rhythms and respond to their basic patterns. It serves as an easy transition to social dancing and the execution of the fox trot, syncopated two-step, waltz, rhumba, tango, and other dance steps.

Changing levels to the sound of the wood block

Piano accompaniment is not an absolute necessity for creative rhythmic movement. It would, of course, be better if an accompanist is available, but she need not be a skilled technician. Chords are often adequate and satisfying accompaniment for children's movement. An understanding of children, how they move, and the ability to "pick up" their rhythm are the essentials for the piano accompanist when working with children's movement.

Suggestions for Exploring Percussion

1. Use a percussion instrument. Explore four, six, or eight ways it can be played. Divide into small groups of two or three. As one plays these various ways, the others move.

2. Start with some piece of percussion with which three sounds can be made. To one sound the group moves at a low level; to the second sound, at an in-between level; and to a third sound, at a high level. Any kind of movement may be used. Using the same idea, change direction of movement instead of levels of movement.

3. Play a rhythmic pattern on a percussion instrument, such as long short long. Ask each child in the group to think of one rhythmic pattern and then clap, tap, or walk it out. When they have their pattern well in mind, have them select a percussion instrument which best suits this pattern. This can be tapping a pencil on the floor, beating on a wood block, tapping two sticks together, and so on. Each one plays his pattern three times. Select one pattern or several patterns for the group to develop in movement. (This can be used in a classroom.)

4. Use a football cheer, a fishmonger's call, or peanut vendor's call. Work out the cheer, call, or saying on percussion instruments. Interpret pattern through movement, having some of the group move while others play and call.

5. Play the polka on the drum or wood blocks, and change direction with the polka rhythm, according to loudness or softness. Dance the polka with partners, and change partners on the loud or soft.

6. Play a polka, schottische, or waltz rhythm on any percussion instrument or piano. When a pronounced accent is heard, change partners.

7. Select and develop one of the following: A narrative, chant, song, famous saying, or proverb (particularly appropriate to birthdays of famous men and women, such as George Washington). The whole group, whether large or small, can all play the underlying beat and then the rhythmic pattern, or part of the group can play the underlying beat while the other is playing the rhythmic pattern. After beat and rhythmic pattern are established, this can be carried into movement.

Fire engines in grandpa's day

10. *Ideas and Movement*

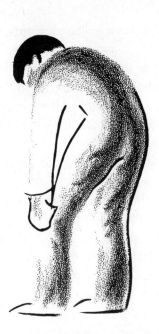

The medium of movement is satisfying to children when they can give a reality to their ideas, activities, and experiences. When children have explored movement and are aware of the effects of elements in space and rhythm, they have acquired *tools* and *techniques* for expression. They have a means by which they can interpret, communicate, and express themselves so others can understand.

Children are concerned with what they *see, hear, feel,* and *touch.* The experiences stemming from these perceptions are motivations for children's expression through movement. The artist has instruments (brushes and canvas) and means of expression (color and paint), but there is no expression (in painting) without experiences (subjects) to paint. The child, too, has the instrument (his body) and the means of expression (movement), but there must be experiences for expression.

As children become conscious of (and begin to use) their bodies, they must be provided a variety of experiences to give them the opportunity to express their many feelings, thoughts, and ideas. Probably the most fruitful field is that of ideas. These may *influence* movement, may be *translated into* movement, or may serve as the *stimuli* for movement. Imagination acts as a force in eliciting responses from what children hear, feel, see, touch, or think about. A fire engine clanging by outside transformed one class into the biggest,

best, and noisiest engines and firemen around. They did not merely pretend that they were these things, but through the force of imagination they actually were firemen and engines.

As children develop their tools for expression, they are influenced by experiences growing out of their own surroundings. The ideas which stimulate movement expression may be found within the total school program, in the everyday activities of children, and through such experiences as percussion, songs, music, pictures, graphic presentation, classroom studies, units, field trips, holidays, words, and sounds.

STUDIES AND COMPOSITIONS

When ideas are used to stimulate movement, a variety of studies and compositions can result. For instance, a child might *hear* the ticking of a clock and translate this into a swinging movement of his body. Or, he might *see* the clock and decide that he wants to be a clock. He might begin with a floor pattern of the outline of a clock, adding movement by designating two children as the hands and the others as the numbers. He thinks about a clock and says something like this:

> This is a funny, funny clock.
> Listen, it goes ah-tick tick-tock.

He starts to move with a quick polka, the way

the sound of saying "ah-tick tick-tock" makes him *feel*.

In all three of these instances the *idea* of the clock stimulated the different movement expressions; experiences modified these expressions. This is how a study starts and how it can be developed into a composition.

The artist who does a charcoal sketch of a tree begins with the *idea* of the tree. He works first with the parts of the tree—the trunk, branches, leaves. Each part might be a *study in itself*, but the picture in its entirety is a *composition*. He pays less attention to the tools or instruments he uses (the charcoal and paper) because his concern is in transposing his idea of the tree onto the paper.

Like the artist's painting, the child's study in movement expresses the idea. Movement should be an automatic tool, leaving the child free to concentrate on the idea. *A study is of short duration, emphasizing an element or idea. A combination of studies, or a variety of experiences (elements or ideas) in sequence, with definite form, unity, and organization, is a composition. A composition has a beginning and an end and a feeling of wholeness.* It may be created in one period or may be extended over several. Studies may be very simple, and even the youngest children may complete studies in the first experience with creative rhythmic movement. One group of children read a story about a horse. Capitalizing on this interest in horses, the teacher suggested that perhaps they would like to be horses. The discussion which followed dealt with about ten different ideas of kinds of horses, with each child interpreting his own kind of horse. To turn this study into a composition, we would group the horses (putting together jumpers, trotters, and walking and racing horses), provide a definite beginning and ending, and make one organized entity of several of the studies.

The purpose of this chapter is to illustrate a few different types of experiences which have been used with groups of children to stimulate movement expression. *The experiences have at times been the impetus for further exploration in the classroom, or classroom interests have supplied the impetus for further exploration through movement.* The kind of experiences, and the manner in which they are interpreted, depends upon the nature of the group. For example, inland children probably would not derive as much mean-

MACHINES

JOYCE ELDRIDGE

ing from a story about the seashore as they would from one dealing with mountains, cornfields, and the activity that occurs in their surroundings.

IDEAS

Mechanical ideas have motivated movement expression, resulting in studies and compositions, and have inspired children and teachers to learn more about these devices. Some of the mechanical ideas which use movement include:

Typewriter	Train switch
Elevator	Air raid alarm
Escalator	Printing press
Pencil sharpener	Garbage wagon
Sewing machine	Television set
Ferris wheel	Jukebox
Concert piano	Pinball machine
Silex	Toaster
Egg beater	Steam shovel
Traffic light	Steam-roller
Tractor	"Coke" machine
Weaving loom	Clock
Shooting gallery	Merry-go-round

Transportation ideas, often stemming from classroom studies (particularly in the third and fourth grade), offer a wealth of possibilities for expression through movement. Different modes of transportation, such as those of the Indian and pioneer, as well as other ideas from the mule pack, water buffalo, and camel to the freight train, the modern, double-decker passenger trains, and atomic plane, have provided sources of inspiration. Boats have been a wonderful motivation for studies and compositions. The music included here of sail boats, canoes, and so on resulted from the exploration of different groups of children expressing their ideas about boats. After exploring a variety of boats, the third grade produced a Lake Scene which they called "Right of Way." Mrs. Burns recorded the music as it was improvised for this composition. The same music was used to accompany some second-grade interpretations of boats which also resulted in studies. Another group of children added the torpedo boat and tugboat, and additional music was recorded. Other boat ideas included:

Passenger boat	Steamboat
Fishing boat	Submarine
Speedboat	Cattle boat
Drifting boats	Lifeboat

SAILBOAT

FLORENCE BURNS

Smooth

CANOE

Light and smooth

FLORENCE BURNS

CREW

Strong and heavy

FLORENCE BURNS

Ideas and Movement

SPEEDBOAT

FLORENCE BURNS

Very fast and bumpy

TORPEDO

Very fast
staccatto

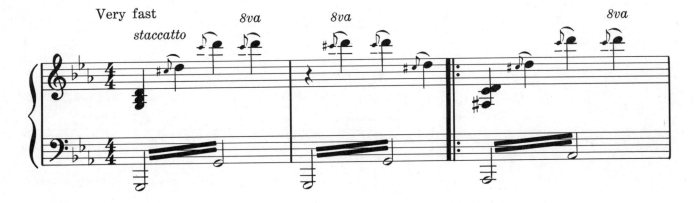

ROWBOAT

Smooth

FLORENCE BURNS

TUGBOAT

JOYCE ELDRIDGE

Ideas and Movement

The settings, surroundings, and people which these boats involved motivated one such experience. The film, "The Boat Trip," used in connection with a third-grade unit on transportation, stimulated movement. The song, "Old Man River," motivated another composition.

AIRPLANE

JOYCE ELDRIDGE

RICKSHAW

JOYCE ELDRIDGE

Airplane ideas of different types have been explored and have led to the creation of sound effects, placement in a hangar, taxiing on the strip, landings, take-offs, and other activities which occur at an airport. Simple chords to accompany movement may be helpful.

Trains furnish infinite possibilities. Not only are the children interested in the engine, caboose, and types of cars but also in what the trains carry, how they are operated, how they stop, start, and change engines, and so forth. The activities are worked out in movement. The children may decide to be one train and depict what goes on in that train, or they may become a string of freight cars with a caboose and engine and each car carrying a different product. Such songs as the "Little Red Caboose," stories as "The Little Engine That Could," or the film, "The Passenger Train" have been used to initiate ideas about trains. Children and teachers have composed their own songs and have used a variety of percussion to accompany their studies or compositions. Additional transportation ideas include:

Rickshaw	Bicycle
Stretcher	Truck
Mail truck	Air mail transports
Elephant	Covered wagon
Eskimo sled	Bus

The picture of the air mail letter, included in this section, served as an excellent motivating force for a movement composition on transportation. It originated with the art teacher asking a first grade, "What can you think of that is *light*? Shall we see how it feels to be very, very light? Let's make a picture about something very, very light." Charles thought that an air mail letter was very, very light and started his picture with that idea. The other ideas expressed in his picture *followed*, for the letter had to be delivered to *some place*, and the *some place needed surroundings* (the farm, flowers, animals).

Airplane letter

JOYCE ELDRIDGE

Animals have given ideas for studies and compositions about horse shows, rodeos, country fairs, markets, farms, jungles, dog shows, pets, zoos, and museums. Horses have inspired many happy explorations. For different age groups they may furnish the theme for one period or warrant further exploration resulting in an elaborate rodeo, impressions of the wild West days, or the escapades of Buffalo Bill. The following ideas about horses have been expressed by children:

Merry-go-round	Racers
Ponies	Shetlands
Bucking broncos	Cowboy
Police horses	Trucker
"Just ordinary"	Show horses
Jumpers	Farm horses
Stallions	Milkman's horse

Using such a simple device as "I say 'meow'—that's how I talk" can get a group to express ideas about animals, what they say, and how they move.

Circus animals furnish the idea for delightful studies and compositions. The circus song was composed as Nina watched a third grade working out their impression of a circus which had just come to town that morning. The song, "The Circus," served as accompaniment for their composition. Since that time it has served many circus purposes.

Birds and fish and sea life afford additional ideas for movement stimulation. Children may visit an aquarium or a bird sanctuary and be motivated to expression with such questions from the teacher as the following: "What did you see?" "How were they different?" "Which ones were big?" "How big?" "What is the difference between a robin and a hawk?" "How does a baby robin move?" Some bird studies and compositions have further motivated them to find out about bird calls and use some of these to accompany movement. A visit to an aquarium resulted in a fourth-grade composition called "The Bottom of the Sea." While at the aquarium, they saw swordfish, sea horses, dog fish, whales, octopuses, oysters, and starfish. The music teacher's assistance was solicited; this involved an exploration of sea chanties which became favorites of this fourth grade. A group of third-graders heard the singing of the sea chanties and asked if they could learn some of the songs. This was granted, and as they began to sing they also began to move their heads. The music teacher took this cue, and movement to sea chanties was explored. This experience caused many in the group to make up their own sea chanties to accompany movement studies. The composition by Parker Linton is a sample.

Toys have given ideas for toy shops, toy counters, toy frolic and fantasy, Santa Claus' toy

Ideas and Movement

THE CIRCUS

NINA COFFING

The cir - cus, the cir - cus, We're go - ing to the cir - cus, To

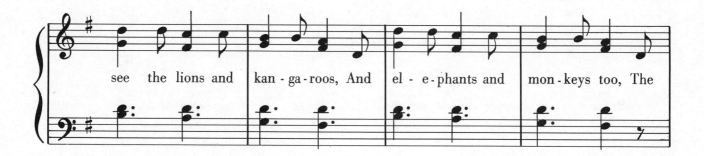

see the lions and kan - ga - roos, And el - e - phants and mon - keys too, The

cir - cus, the cir - cus, We're go - ing there to - day.

THE SAILING SAILORS

Words and Music by PARKER LINTON

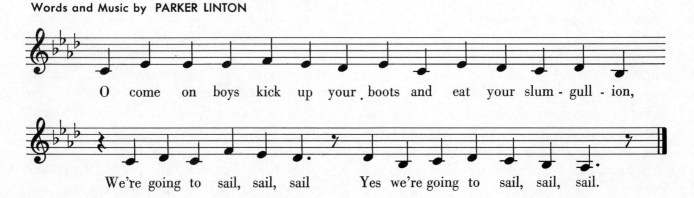

O come on boys kick up your boots and eat your slum - gull - ion,

We're going to sail, sail, sail Yes we're going to sail, sail, sail.

Ideas and Movement

town, toys that talk, toys that walk, toys that wind, and toys with keys and springs.

Sports furnish fine material for movement studies and compositions, particularly in the peer group, with impressions of football games, the World Series, donkey baseball, the Olympics, the Ice-Capades and Aquacades, kiting, television wrestling matches, and fishing and hunting.

Seasons project still other activities. In the summer there are picnics, vacation, swimming; in the winter, snowmen, coldness, Christmas; in the spring, flowers, roller skating, and baseball; and in the fall, color, leaves, school. Moving to ideas about fall caused Barbara to say (as she moved):

> The leaves are twisting as they fall,
> Say Fall!—why that's the reason
> When I see leaves turning brown
> I wonder what's the reason!

Work and occupational experiences are valuable for movement interpretations. Often these emanate from classroom interests. Folk songs, folk music, and percussion have been advantageously used as accompaniment. Movement interpretations have been developed from impressions of a super-market, department store, post office, coal mine and a ranch and some deep-sea divers, policemen, businessmen, bricklayers, and soda jerkers. Work songs of other lands may be meaningful to fifth- and sixth-graders when they are studying about countries and people. The United Nations and its concern about people and countries have many ramifications which can be utilized in creative rhythmic movement.

Holidays remind children of many things which we as adults are apt to overlook. Many of these ideas which are close to them take form in dance. Halloween has brought forth a variety of impressions and ideas in the form of ghosts, skeletons, haunted houses, witches, ducking for apples, and so on. Original poems, narratives, songs, and percussion effects have accompanied these studies and compositions. Young children's thoughts about Thanksgiving have been expressed in terms of the turkey, cranberry sauce, pumpkin pie, and other good things to eat. Older children's impressions of St. Patrick's Day have brought forth the following units for movements: shillelagh, parades, Blarney Stone, Mulligan and Irish Stew, "Who Threw the Overalls in Mrs. Murphy's Chowder," "Pat, the Cop on the Beat," "McNamara's Band," "Irish Washerwoman," and snakes. Many of these topics have been developed into compositions, using appropriate folk music. One, "St. Pat Takes a Trip," included original music and a script. Various other holi-

DIGGING TO CHINA

Teacher's Workshop

We're dig-ging to Chi-na We're dig-ging to Chi-na We're dig-ging to Chi-na to-day!__ We're dig-ging, We're dig-ging, We're dig-ging, We're dig-ging, We're dig-ging, to Chi-na to-day!__

Ideas and Movement

DUCKING FOR APPLES

With a splish and a splash, and a bob - bob - bob We'll

duck for ap - ples in a tub - tub - tub Try it once and

try it twice; You'll come up with some - thing nice!

days (Christmas, Chanukah, and Mavidad), and how they are celebrated in many lands, provide enjoyment, as well as appreciation and understanding of other cultures.

Field trips and children's visits provide subjects for movement interpretations. These are particularly meaningful when children have returned from a trip and are "full" of the experience. The following subjects have been used:

Farm	Post office
Dairy	Paper mill
Bakery	Airport
Water front	Grocery store
Apple orchard	Television studio
Book fair	United Nations

Sounds to which children react have been used for motivation of movement. Hearing the fire siren and the clatter of the fire engine pounding down the street was the reason for one class composing "Going to a Fire." (The ensuing discussion needed the leadership of the teacher to give everyone an opportunity to speak, and to keep the conversation from going too far afield about all the fires these children had seen, heard, or thought they had heard). The Fire composition developed by having first a telephone ring

awaken the "firemen," then getting dressed in fire-fighting clothes, jumping on the engine and hook and ladder, starting the siren, next fighting the fire, putting it out, and finally returning to the fire house to sleep. This was worked out in story form first, and then each of the thirty-four children carried out the idea in his own way, with a fire chief keeping the group together. To accompany their story, the music was recorded as it was improvised.

Sounds of certain *words* can be exciting, some samples of which are:

Bang	Pop
Crackle	Thunder
Smash	Fizz
Wind	Jingle
Zing	Popcorn
Crash	Bingady-bang
Plink	Splash
Clickity-clack	Plunk

The sound of the word "clickity-clack" made one group think of a light switch. In telling the class about their study, Sheila said:

The light switch sounds like "clickity-clack,"
Push it up, and pull it back.

GOING TO A FIRE

NINA COFFING

(Telephone)

(Fire siren)

(Getting dressed)

(Going to the fire)

R.

L.

(Fire - fast - loud)

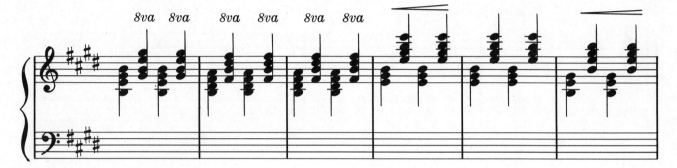

From one group working on "pop" where levels, jumps, and hops seemed to predominate, the following ditty resulted:

> Pop corn goes pop, pop.
> Pop corn goes pop, pop.
> Pop corn goes pop, pop, pop, pop, pop!

Sometimes words are used to bring forth an idea which in turn stimulates movement studies. The word "buzz" caused Velveta to think of "mosquito." She wanted to make up a song about Mr. Mosquito so she appealed to Joyce for help. This accompanied her movement study.

The word "water" brought forth these ideas:

Well	Bath
Rain	Sweat
Swimming	Boating
Fountain	Puddles
Fish	Birdbath
Water guns	Drink of water

To an older group the word "lawn" brought the following:

Statues	Croquet
Flowers	Football
Mowing	Weeds
"Keep Off" sign	Sprayer
Four leaf clover	Grass seed

Mr. MOSQUITO

Words and Music by Velveta

Arr. JOYCE ELDRIDGE

Mis-ter Mos-qui-to will soon be look-ing for me. Buzz, buzz, buzz! He thinks I'll taste good when he catch-es me! Buzz, buzz, slap!— Mis-ter Mos-qui-to will nev-er eat me! Buzz buzz!—

Sight affords another stimulus for movement interpretations. An older group developed a "spectrum" composition which was a simple abstraction that resulted from looking at the colors yellow, green, purple, blue, and red. Another older group wrote the following verse to accompany movement studies:

> Black is the cat.
> Black is the bat.
> Black is the night.
> How heavy is black?

"Color" music has been recorded. We see the difference in the way children respond in movement to "yellow" as contrasted with "red." This is evident in the music which has been improvised to accompany movement responses. At times, we look at a color, think about it, and then name the way it makes us feel. Other times, we try moving immediately in response to the color we see. (Large, colored poster paper is used effectively.) At some other times, we just use "color music" to help us relax.

COLOR MUSIC

NINA COFFING

Blue

Quietly

JOYCE ELDRIDGE

Green

Delicately

Red

With brilliance

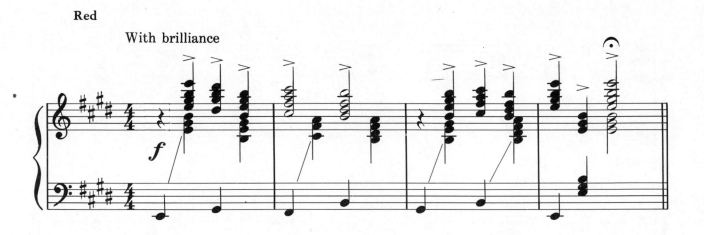

Pictures provide moods as well as ideas. Pictures, puppets, friezes, and models which children have created in art furnish impetus for movement. Finger paintings and chalks are excellent means of setting groups of children in motion. The sample of finger painting was produced by a fourth-grade art class, following a movement experience. The children were encouraged to try to express movement in their paintings. These products were used again in rhythms to stimulate further experiences. The sample included (before a Photostat was made) was of varying shades of red and white. When the children were asked to move the way it made them feel, they moved with intense, strong, swinging movements.

There is a close tie-up between rhythmic

Red finger-painting

Ideas and Movement

movement experiences and art, the two continually supplement each other. The more we use creations of the children to motivate our rhythmic movement experiences, the more meaningful they become. The art teacher or consultant, if there is one in the building, or any teacher talented in art, is a good friend to have.

Often younger children delight in responding to older children's creations. For example, Alice's elephant delighted a group of younger children; it stimulated them to different kinds of interpretations. Alice, a sixth-grader, benefited, too, from the appreciation of her creation and pride in her accomplishment. Alice's elephant resulted from a conversation which Miss Cannarsa, art consultant, initiated about animals and movement and the way many of the animals tried to dance.

Props have been used to motivate movement studies and compositions. As children become more and more adept in creating, they have interesting times with props. Children have been given a chance to select a prop from within the room which could motivate them in group expression. Props that have been used with a class responding, individually, in two's and three's, and in larger groups, have included shells, stones, boxes, chairs, feathers, balloons, and Halloween.

Stories and *poetry*, as mentioned before, provide another source of movement motivation. Because it is pertinent to this age, fifth- and sixth-graders have delighted in interpreting "Everybody Says" (from Blanche Thompson's *More Silver Pennies*), Paul Bunyan's tall tales, and others. Favorite stories often initiate movement responses and furnish the idea for compositions. Such favorites are "Chico," by Richard Crist; "Shapes" by Miriam Schlein; "Parade of the Animal Kingdom," by Robert Hegner; "Caboose," by Edith Hurd; "The Boats on the River," by Marjorie Flack; "Who Dreams of Cheese?" by Leonard Weisgard; "The Brave and Free," by Paul Witty; "Saturday Walk," by Ethel Wright; "Who Goes There?" by Dorothy Lathrop; "The Circus Baby," by Maud and Miska Petersham; "Cowboy Small," by Lois Lenski; "Rikki-Tikki-Ton," by Rudyard Kipling; "Make Way for Ducklings," by Robert McClosky; "Charlotte's Web," by E. B. White; and others.

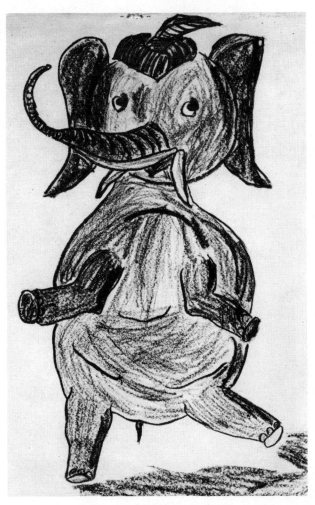

Alice's elephant

There are so many ideas surrounding us in our classrooms, in our homes, and in all things about us that their multiplicity means that only a few could be included here. Titles of dance compositions, resulting from some of these experiences, have been: "Indian Powwow," "Air Show," "Our City," "Boat Regatta," "Machine Age," "The Lone Cowboy," "Mr. Penny and His Animals," "The Ghost That Hated Halloween," "A Visit to the UN," "Our County Fair," "Poor Little Red Caboose," "Down Mexico Way," "Rockets from Mars." Studies and compositions are practically limitless when the teacher helps children develop the innumerable ideas they have.

IDEAS FOR RELAXATION

The strain of physical exertion, mental concentration, and everyday school organization makes it wise to have brief periods of relaxation. If Cre-

QUIET (Relaxation)

JOYCE ELDRIDGE

ative Rhythms is at a scheduled time, even in a class as short as twenty minutes, often relaxation is desirable and necessary. The period of relaxation provides a desirable break in a lesson (or in a day), because it gives the teacher an opportunity to "talk things over" with the group, or it acts as a starting point for a new activity. This method of getting a group quieted down may also be employed at the end of a Rhythms period, if children seem to be a bit overstimulated. We need to let loose, but we also need the feeling of leveling-off which follows a vigorous experience. Relaxation is necessary for older groups as well as for younger ones, but the approaches to it vary. With younger children the approach may be almost entirely *ideational*. These approaches are used primarily to help children gain relaxation of the entire body, and to get the group calmed down. Furthermore, these approaches help to bring a group together again after children have been off in corners exploring movement.

In using the ideational approach, the teacher sets the mood both by her voice and by her manner. In response to her words which are suggestive or descriptive, children react each in his own way. The tone of voice and tempo of speaking are as suggestive as the words themselves. Music accompaniments are not necessary.

The short period of relaxing involves body control and provides release of tension. Some of the ideas for relaxations, which have been found effective with the first three grades, include their "becoming" balloons slowly deflating, elastic bands shriveling up, faucets dripping, salt pouring from a shaker, icicles melting, bubbles getting smaller, flying saucers, merry-go-rounds stopping, soda fizzing, and ice cream cones melting. The tales of "Raggedy Ann and Andy" seem to be favorites, and often the children will ask for them again and again, and will join in with the motions of "flop." Some of these ideational approaches are developed as follows:

Ideas and Movement

Watching Raggedy Ann and Andy go "flop," "flop," "flop."

Raggedy Ann and Andy[1]

Poor old Raggedy Ann just couldn't hold up her head any longer and it went flop, flop, flop, flop. And poor old Andy couldn't hold up his shoulders and they went flop, flop, flop. Then poor old Raggedy Ann caved in at the hips and they went flop, flop, flop, flop. Pretty soon Raggedy Andy's knees gave way and they went flop, flop, flop, flop. And then poor old Raggedy Ann's ankles began to wobble and they went flop, flop, flop. Then poor old Raggedy Ann and poor old Raggedy Andy (and poor old first grade) just couldn't stand up any longer and so they all went F-l-o-p (onto the floor).

[1] Gladys Andrews and Marion Bozenhard, *Creative Rhythms for Children* (Master's thesis, University of Wisconsin), Mimeographed edition, copyright, 1939, by the authors.

Clothes on the Line

(The children sometimes choose the article of clothing they wish to be.)

I am a coat hanging on the line. There are two clothespins holding me up. The wind is blowing and it blows, and blows, and blows, and it tugs at the clothespins. All of a sudden one of my clothespins falls out (and one of my arms falls down) and there I am, left with just one clothespin. The wind blows, and blows, and blows some more until all of a sudden it pulls the other clothespin out, and then the wind blows me right down to the ground.

Ice Cream Cones

I am a big, big, big ice cream cone—strawberry. It is a very, very hot day. I begin to melt. And I melt and melt, and melt, and of course that makes me grow smaller and smaller and smaller and finally I just melt away into a little grease spot on the floor.

Poor old Raggedy Andy could not hold up his knees, so they went "flop."

Snowman

Ho, Ho, Ho, Hum, Hum, Hum.
You disappear by the minute.
There's one arm gone, now two arms gone.
And plop, there goes your head.
Your middle bends, your knees bend, too.
You're littler by the minute.
Ho, Ho, Ho, Hum, Hum, Hum.
Snowman's gone; all gone.
All but your funny hat.

As this experience becomes an accepted part of creative rhythmic movement, occasionally children suggest ideas for relaxing. When this happens, we try to follow the suggestions. Boys and girls should be encouraged to use ways of their own choosing.

Sheila suggested that we turn ourselves into faucets and drip away.

> The faucet drips and drips all day.
> If it doesn't stop it will drip away.

Now and then children and teacher discover something together which can serve this purpose. For example, after watching a beautiful snowfall and talking about different kinds of flakes and trying them out in movement, the "Snowflakes" poem just happened. Throughout that winter this particular group of children were eager to relax with *their* idea of the snowflakes.

Snowflakes

> From behind a cloud one wintry day
> Some little snowflakes came to play
> They floated high, high up in the air
> So high folks couldn't see them there.
> They drifted contentedly round and round
> 'Til Richard said, "Let's float on down."
> So first came Elspeth and then came Robin
> And Mia and Martha, gently bobbing.
> Then Norton and Helen and all the rest—
> The snowflakes floated their very best
> 'Til gently and quietly on the ground
> They finally settled without a sound.
> And when folks pass them by they say,
> "What a lovely snow we've had today."

Suggestions for Exploring Ideas

1. Take some noise associated with Halloween, such as a witch riding on a broomstick, a fence creaking, ghosts in a haunted house. Individually or in small groups work out movement suggested by the noise. Build a dance study which interprets the idea. Noise can be used as accompaniment. The study may be abstraction in movement, suggested by the noise which may be developed into a rhythmic pattern.

2. Have the group select a recent experience, such as a visit to a zoo, a visit to the post office, a picnic, a story. With the entire group recall the "things which happened," what they did, what they saw. Divide into small groups, according to the things enjoyed most. Have each child choose the group he would like to work with. Group should agree on the amount of time to be used to develop the idea. This may terminate with group studies or develop into a class composition.

3. Take an idea from the Indian (or another) culture. Develop the idea, using percussion as accompaniment. Use large groupings, part of the group playing the accompaniment and the other interpreting their idea through movement.

4. Discuss color with the group, asking such questions as "How does red make you feel?" "What does red make you think of?" A variety of colors may be used, or just one color. Cues from the response to one or several colors may be used for stimulation to studies or composition.

5. Use the idea of sports. Divide into groups of no less than two or no more than seven or nine. Each group should think of some sport or sport activity which they would like to translate or interpret in movement. Allow about ten minutes to develop the idea, which may range from a discus throw or a tennis serve to a football game. Have each group present its study or composition for the other groups. Select one which the entire class would like to try, and develop into a class composition.

6. Use the idea of Thanksgiving or Christmas. Through group discussion make a list of the work experiences involved, such as preparing the Thanksgiving dinner, going to the woods to cut down the Christmas tree, wrapping Christmas gifts, pulling in the Yule log, and so on. Divide into groups, each group choosing one of the ideas. Develop a chant, poem, or song which "talks out" the experience. Turn the experience into a dance, study, or composition, using the chant, poem, or song as accompaniment. (Refer to "Digging to China.")

7. Translate or re-interpret through movement some recent classroom experience. In social studies, the culture of the Middle Ages, the activities of the World Health Organization, or how people in other lands get food might be examples. In science, the study of water power or a study of constellations might be examples of areas used. (See Suggested Resources.) The following may happen in this type of activity. The group might decide to interpret the various mechanical ways water is harnessed for power through water pumps, windmills, and so on. Individually, or in small groups, this can be re-interpreted through movement. This activity may serve only for one class period, or for several. It can be an extensive project that interprets many experiences or ways in which water is converted into power.

"Promenade around the town!"

11. *Creativity in the School Program*

The school program has but one purpose—to serve children. It serves children when it provides meaningful experiences adapted to the varying needs and interests of boys and girls. These experiences are effective when they are extended *through the school day* and are not compartmentalized, pigeonholed, or confined to just the classroom, the music or art room, the gymnasium or play room, or the playfield. When there is common understanding concerning the extension of experiences and how they become a functioning part of the school program, the so-called "special areas"—art, music, physical education, science, dramatics—serve as resource areas to vitalize learning. These areas can intensify the interests which have emerged in the classroom. Similarly, interests which emerge in the "special area" can be stimulated and developed in the classroom.

When creative rhythmic movement is used in connection with other experiences which the children are having, it becomes an aid to learning. When it is considered as an integral part of the school program, movement can be used to vitalize learning, to develop and intensify interests, and to stimulate and express ideas. The wider and richer the school program, the greater are the possibilities for utilizing creative rhythmic movement to provide meaningful experiences for children. The accounts which follow are samples of the way in which rhythmic movement has been used as a vital part of the school program.

CLASSROOM ACTIVITIES

The following extensive experiences dealing with clocks occurred in a second grade. It was the kind of a day that "Seconds" occasionally have. Something had set them off. They were "all wound up" and needed the kind of calming down which would result from a healthful "letting go." The percussion instruments were readily available, so they used them to play out their feelings in terms of fast and slow and hard and soft gallops, galloping with their feet in place as they played the instruments. Next came a game of "Sounds." Listening for sounds provided a lull of some order and unity. It was spring, and there were many sounds that children were asked to listen for. When they had selected one, they were told to put their hands on top of their heads and wait in this position until several others had discovered sounds. Then the teacher closed her eyes and pointed blindly. (This kind of choosing children enjoy.) Tony was designated and asked to go and select an instrument which would best reproduce the sound which he had discovered. The other children tried to guess the sound as Tony reproduced it. When they guessed, the listening began again with *Tony selecting* the next child. (Because second-graders are apt to be "cagey" and change their idea when someone guesses it, they had to whisper their sounds to Nina [the accompanist] when they were selected to reproduce them.)

Clocks

With great care, Don chose the wood block and played such a perfect "tick-tock" that the class immediately chorused "our clock" (clock on the wall). Then all joined Don and played clock sounds, using percussion, hands, feet, mouths, and fingers. Just as the class was ready to "listen" for the next sound, Dorothy said she had found a different kind of clock. She bet the class could not guess. Dorothy played the temple bells, using the stick end of her beater to make it say "cuckoo." This was a cue for the teacher. A discussion of various types of clocks followed, and soon the group was calm enough to move on the floor. They moved first to the beat of the cuckoo clock, holding their step on the "cuckoo" part. Listening and moving to the big tom-tom "clock" and the contrasting little clackers which sounded like "Frank's Mickey Mouse wristwatch" fascinated the children. The game of "Sounds," now became the "Clock Game."

The following outline of the classroom unit which grew from the experience described above is reproduced as written and carried out by Miss Helen Besore, their classroom teacher.

A "Clock" Project

(Recorded by Miss Helen Besore, second-grade teacher; correlation between rhythm class and classroom work.)

1. Story Time
   (a) Stories concerning clocks were brought in by children to be read by the teacher.
   (b) Source books were used for discussion or presenting materials about historic clocks and methods used in telling time through the different ages.
2. Reading
   (a) Class work was based on the clock theme.
   (b) I lacked books to supply clock stories to a group of children as a reading class so I placed several such books on the library table. They read clock stories for their own enjoyment.
3. Spelling—Writing—Language
   (a) We learned to spell words pertaining to clocks.
   (b) We had several writing lessons using these spelling words in sentences and stories.

(c) Children wrote original clock stories.
4. Music
   (a) We learned clock songs. I had some and some of the songs were brought in by the children from their own magazines.
   (b) We composed our own clock song and set it to music. This song was used in rhythm class.
   (c) In Music Appreciation we had the Victrola record, "In A Clock Store."
5. Arithmetic
   (a) We learned to tell time and to write time.
   (b) We learned to make clocks tell time.
   (c) Some of us learned the Roman numerals.
6. Art—Free Activity (Choice Time)
   (a) We drew pictures interpreting our Victrola record, "In A Clock Store," and clocks as we created them in rhythm class.
   (b) The children collected the materials necessary to make the kind of clock they wished to make. This material included cracker or similar boxes, cardboard, Cellophane, scraps of colored paper, and various other things. Some of the children made alarm clocks, grandfather clocks, while others made wristwatches or electric clocks.

The clock story indicates how teachers and children can work together to determine goals, to make plans for further activity, and continually to evaluate accomplishment.

The clock game gave all an opportunity to learn to work together—children as well as teachers.

After the class had discovered a variety of clocks and learned more about them in the rhythms class, they divided into groups to "become" different kinds of clocks. There were alarm clocks, cuckoo clocks, electric clocks,

Just a regular clock

Creativity in the School Program

church clocks (the "Sunday morning" kind, included, because of an argument that the clock across the street was not like clocks on churches some of the children went to on Sunday—"Any way, it sounds different on Sunday," they claimed), wristwatch, and "just a regular clock." The children, accompanying the movement by percussion, moved as they thought their clock would move. The group working out movement and percussion patterns for the clock in the church across the street discovered that theirs said, "Boom, Boom, Boom, Boom, School is out . . . Boom, Boom, Boom, Boom." This initiated another project of getting the percussion patterns to *say* something. The groups with the electric clock could not find a percussion instrument which gave the desired effect, and therefore decided on a mouth and finger sound.

The exploration might have been discontinued at this point, or much sooner, but the children's interest was still high, and they formed a class composition to which they could play, sing, and move. The song to which Miss Besore referred was used as an introduction; the children wrote the rest according to what seemed to sound and fit best. Nina recorded the experience in music.

> My Clock.
>
> I am a cuckcoo clock.
> When the hand gets
> to 12 the little
> birdie comes out and
> says cuckcoo and jumps
> back in and waits
> till the next hour.
> By Dorothy
> Rosecrans

This report of experiences is more extensive than most; it is presented here to show to what extent interest may be developed when teachers

CLOCKS

NINA COFFING

Tick tock tick tock, Clocks, clocks eve-ry-where, Some run fast, Some run slow, Some say "Come," Some say "Go," Tick tock, tick tock, Lis-ten to the clocks.

Clocks (Cont.)

Tick tock, tick tock, brrrr

Alarm clock

Get up, get up, get up, get up, Get up you sleep-y head!

Church clock

Boom, boom, boom, boom, The

hour is four says the clock, School is out, time for play, Boom, boom, boom, boom.

Cuckoo clock

1. Cuck - oo   Cuck - oo
2. Cuck - oo   Cuck - oo

Clocks (Cont.)

Wake up in the morn-ing, Cuck - oo, Cuck - oo, Time to go to school.
Time to go and play.   Cuck - oo   Cuck - oo   Time to go to bed.

Electric clock

8va   faster

Church clock

8va

Come to church on Sun-day morn-ing, Come to church on Sun-day morn-ing.

Creativity in the School Program

Clocks (Cont.)

Tick tock tick tock tick tock tick tock

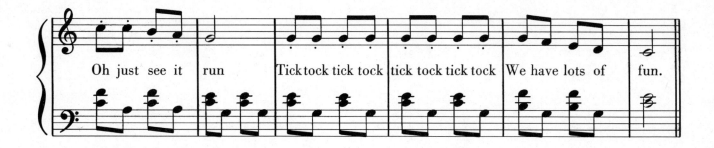

Oh just see it run Tick tock tick tock tick tock tick tock We have lots of fun.

Tick tock, tick tock, Time for break-fast,

Tick tock, tick tock, Time for din-ner, Tick tock, tick tock,

Creativity in the School Program

Clocks (Cont.)

Time for sup-per, Tick tock, tick tock, Time for bed.

Repeat first song and end here.

work together. Because of its extensiveness it may seem to the reader as though the experience was forced or overdone. This, however, was not the case, because the interest, enthusiasm, and spontaneity was maintained throughout. Several times during that spring the children would ask if they could do their Clock Story, and it became the "favorite" at choice time.

Air Show

Because several of their fathers were stationed at a nearby air base, one group of second-graders was particularly interested in airplanes. The constant roar overhead gave the opportunity to learn to identify some of the planes. They gained so much information that the children wanted to tell someone else about planes. They wanted to demonstrate through movement expression the different kinds of planes. Their "Air Show," with appropriate sound effects was shared first with a third and fourth grade and then with their parents. Bob's story was spontaneously written after one of the "shows."

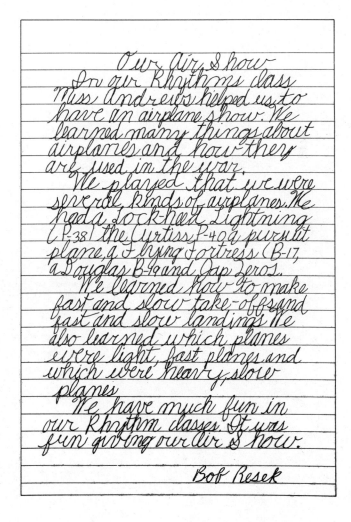

The Elephant.

I went to the Zoo last year and I saw the great big elephant he has a very big old trunk, I love to watch him walk, he is a very big funny thing he is as funny as can be.

The Elephant

Margaret Ann's story and illustration about the elephant was written during a second-grade unit exploration on animals. When she had finished her work, Margaret Ann showed her picture and

story and told about it. One can sense this child's love for movement in what she wrote and in the action she attributes to the clowns in her drawing. Margaret Ann's elephant was responsible for a class discussion about elephants and then about a zoo. This led to the members of the class turning into the animals of the zoo (monkeys, apes, zebras, and giraffes). The group talked about its "zoo" for weeks afterward. As children read about animals, talked of their customs and habitats, the experience was reinforced by opportunities for movement interpretations.

Halloween Sounds

The song the witches say, "Oo Oo," illustrated how the teacher can take advantage of experiences as they present themselves, because she is with the children when these events happen. This group of second-graders was excited about Halloween. Their planning time was about Halloween, and this turned into quite a discussion about the day for "dressed-up faces." Their discussion finally centered on sounds. Together, they listed the sounds they could think of which suggested Halloween, while the music teacher, Mary Robinson, recorded them on the board. Mary said we could make our very own song,

THE WITCHES SAY "OO-OO"

Arr. MARY ROBINSON

The wit - ches say "Oo - oo" The black cats say "Me - ow"

The gob - lins laugh "Ha - ha - ha" To - night is Hal - low - een.

starting with the witches saying "Oo Oo." Using as many of the sounds as possible, the class created a song. As they said the words and made the sounds, they caught a tune, which was also recorded. In their enthusiasm the experience was taken one step further; they decided that they would like to dance to their song (right there and then). This experience was enhanced by the movement interpretations which they had worked out together.

The four different kinds of experiences discussed above have been related to show the possibilities of using movement to intensify interest within one grade level.

Social Studies

Folk dancing is naturally incorporated as children's interests are caught by studies, stories, and units of other lands through social studies. When boys and girls understand the customs and traditions of peoples and know something about where they live, then folk dancing takes on definite meaning. A sixth-grade social studies unit on Mexico was enriched with folk dances, which included "La Jesucita," "Alas Altanitas," "La Raspa," "Jarabe Tapatio," "La Cucaracha," "Jesucita en Chihuahua," and "El Periquito."

Cultural patterns are often understood and appreciated through experiencing the dances of different people. The revival of the Israeli dances, simple and full of spirit, were excellent for use with another sixth-grade group. The "Hora,"

"Ari Ara," and "Harmonica" are favorites. They are most meaningful when presented by children of Israeli background, who can explain the meaning of the dances. Just such an experience with the "Hora" led Angie to remark that the dance was "like a dance that we do at weddings and on holidays." She was referring to the Greek dance "Hasopika." This aroused the curiosity of the group (though they were not studying about Greek culture at that time, it nevertheless worked in naturally), and Angie taught her dance.

The dance, the Ukranian two-step, worked in well with another unit on social studies. This was presented to the class by Helena, a girl of Slavic background, who had learned it from her grandfather. (On these occasions, when children are presenting material, it is often advisable that the teacher learn the dance from the child, or at least be somewhat familiar with the child's version so that she can be of assistance in the presentation.) This sharing of dances is an instance of children and teachers learning together.

American folk dances about the United States work in well with many of the fourth- through eighth-grade units. Trying to retrace "calls" which seems unique to American dancing becomes quite a game of finding out, and it adds interest to the study.

Stories about Indian culture have included singing, story play, percussion, and movement interpretations. Many of the Indian ceremonials have utilized the chants which Joyce has provided for accompaniment.

INDIAN CHANT No. 1

JOYCE ELDRIDGE

INDIAN CHANT No. 2

JOYCE ELDRIDGE

THE WAY THE INDIAN MADE HIS CLOTHES

Words and music by
DALE KULICK

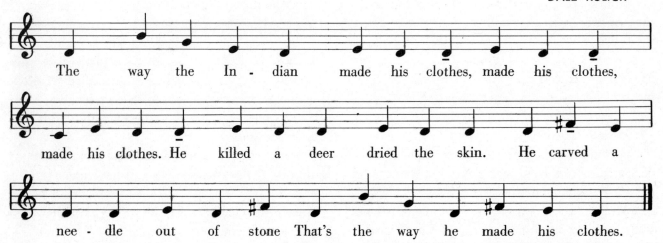

The way the In - dian made his clothes, made his clothes,

made his clothes. He killed a deer dried the skin. He carved a

nee - dle out of stone That's the way he made his clothes.

THERE ONCE WAS A BOY

Words and music by
DALE KULICK

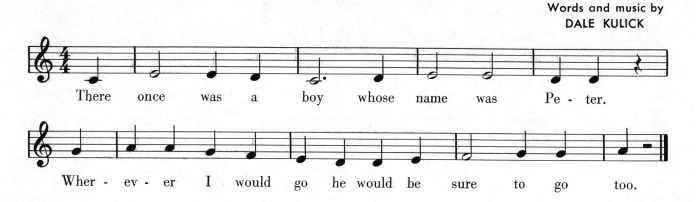

There once was a boy whose name was Pe - ter.

Wher - ev - er I would go he would be sure to go too.

Song

Dale, a third-grader, secured the assistance of Miss Ouellette, the music teacher, to help her "have music to her song." As the class studied about the life of the Indians, the children were divided into groups. Then they interpreted some of the Indian's activities through movements. Dale decided her group needed a song to accompany the movements. Her first effort was so rewarding to Dale that she said she couldn't stop, and another song just came. Both are included.

Susie, another third-grader in the same group as Dale, tells about her experience of writing a song. She went through the process of dictating this first to Miss Bowman, the classroom teacher, who recorded Susie's thoughts as she said them. Susie then rewrote her dictation in the present form. When Susie shared her song with the group, they clapped to it and moved to it. They talked about the kind of feeling that comes with new shoes—happy, bouncy, stiff, slippery—and, as Peter said, "Sometimes mine hurt." Susie's song was further interpreted in movement by the group, moving as new shoes might suggest. This experience immediately started others in the group to write songs.

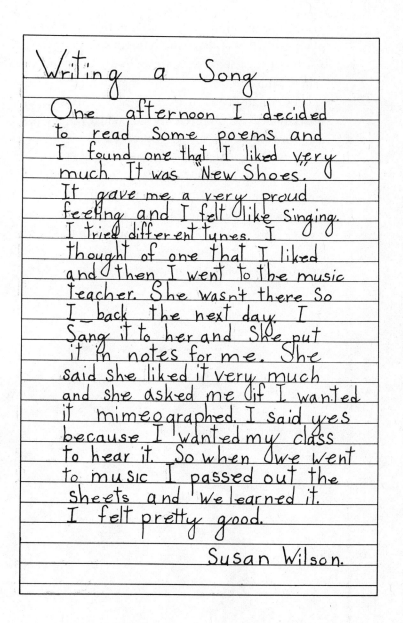

Writing a Song

One afternoon I decided to read some poems and I found one that I liked very much. It was "New Shoes." It gave me a very proud feeling and I felt like singing. I tried different tunes. I thought of one that I liked and then I went to the music teacher. She wasn't there so I _ back the next day. I sang it to her and she put it in notes for me. She said she liked it very much and she asked me if I wanted it mimeographed. I said yes because I wanted my class to hear it. So when we went to music I passed out the sheets and we learned it. I felt pretty good.

Susan Wilson.

NEW SHOES *

SUSAN WILSON

I have new shoes in Fall time and new ones in the Spring.—

When - ev - er I wear my new shoes I al - ways have to sing!

* From Alice Wilkins' poem, *The Golden Flute* (New York: John Day Publishing Company, 1932).

Art

Art and movement are similar in that they stimulate creative ability and encourage children's natural expression. Artistic activity is enriched when children learn to use their ideas and to express themselves on paper in free, rhythmical movements. As children are helped to move easily, they seem better to appreciate accomplishments in line, color, and design.

One group of fourth-graders liked to move as they painted. (Children enjoy translating their movement explorations into graphic representations.) This can be done at the board, on the floor with chalk, or on brown paper with chalk or crayons. Chalking and finger painting lend themselves readily to movement expression. A Miss Alcott had asked the children if they would like to express with finger paints some of the movements which they had just been working with in Creative Rhythms class. (Dorothy's finger painting seemed to say "swings and twist and turn.") The paintings decorated the room, and were used afterwards as a *stimulus* for movement. The children could easily determine the action depicted in the paintings.

A Miss Richter encouraged her classes to observe movement and to translate these experiences into sketches. She had them observe the movements of younger children, as well as their own. The sketches of the cartwheels and of the

Children in motion: cartwheels

two children skipping were done while Geitel and Hortense were observing a second grade in action. Elinor's sketch of the polka was done while her own group of sixth- and seventh-graders was trying to get more "lift" into the step pattern. These are illustrations of the way in which movement may be translated to paper.

Miss Cannarsa often discussed movement experiences with the children and frequently suggested that they begin to move freely (swinging, shaking, sliding, and doing the polka) *before* they began to paint, draw, or sketch. Joseph seemed to have a natural, secure feeling for movement and space. When given encouragement he often expressed his ideas about dancing. This is portrayed in his picture about square dancing in which even his flowers and animals are dancing. A feeling for movement is also depicted in Virginia's expression of folk dancing, and in Judy's translation of jitterbugging as a social dance form.

Folk dancing

Jitterbugging

ADDITIONAL SCHOOL EXPERIENCES

There is a logical reason for including in the school program certain kinds of dance experiences in early, middle, and later childhood. These experiences are in terms of what we know about children and not in terms of adult sequence of dance steps, techniques, or adult anxieties. When consideration is given to how children grow and the individual variations of maturity in the same chronological age group, dance experiences progress from basic fundamental movements and their use in folk, social, and other dance forms.

Dance Songs

Dance songs (action or movement songs) are appropriate to early childhood. This way of using movement children have termed "dance songs." They say, "We dance about what we sing," or "We sing about what we dance." Others have called this simple form of dance "action songs" or "movement games," and many teachers have called them "singing games."

During early childhood (the "I" period), children's thoughts and actions are largely centered on themselves as people. Dance songs have been composed to give children opportunities to say "*I* want to be," "*I* wish," "Follow *me*," "*I* can do," "When *I* grow up *I* want to be. . . ." This simple dance form provides an opportunity for children to think and express thoughts and feelings about themselves. It provides opportunity for all children, shy as well as aggressive, to assume a similar role and to help teachers and children dance together. Dance songs can be used in various situations in a small space: in a classroom (even with screwed-down seats) or in a large auditorium. They can be used for short periods of time as a change of activity, and lend themselves to circle, line, row, or informal formations.

These activities have been used in different ways with older children and adults. With this group they have been used as "ice breakers," "take-off's," means of starting a group of teachers exploring movement, and as camp and recreation "action songs." The following is a sample:

HERE COMES THE TRAIN

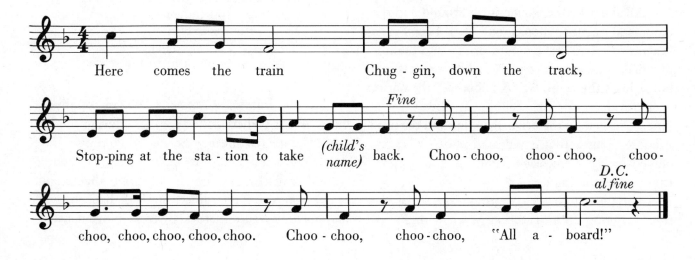

Here comes the train Chug - gin, down the track, Stop-ping at the sta - tion to take *(child's name)* back. Choo - choo, choo - choo, choo - choo, choo, choo, choo, choo. Choo - choo, choo - choo, "All a - board!"

"I want to be tall like the Empire State Building."

One person, or several, as "engines" can start chugging around the room, stopping before an individual or individuals whose name or names are sung in the song. Singing "Choo-Choo," the engine performs any movement he might think of. At "All aboard," the engine turns around and the individual named "hooks on" and becomes a "caboose." The train moves on to another individual. The song is repeated, and the new caboose joins the train. At "All aboard," the entire train reverses; the first caboose is now the engine, followed by the original engine and the new caboose. This action is repeated until all are included in the train, each having had an opportunity to be the engine.

A variation with a large group consists of the train breaking up into sections, each with an engine and caboose, as soon as a third individual has been added. This gets more children in action.

A modern version is:

> Here Comes the Plane
> Zooming through the air
> Stopping at the airport
> To take (*child's name*) aboard
> Z-z-z-z-ooooo-m-m-m-m-m-m-m-m.

In the following songs, a leader supplies a movement (where called for) and during the last line designates another person to continue. The words are repeated, with new movements, without losing the rhythm or changing the tempo. The songs are continued until all have had an opportunity to initiate a different movement.

THIS IS WHAT I CAN DO

Arr. JOYCE ELDRIDGE

This is what I can do. Ev-ry-bo-dy do it too.

Chorus

This is what I can do. Now I'll pass it on to you!
Now she'll pass it on to you!

YOU CAN

Arr. JOYCE ELDRIDGE

To the beat of the mu-sic you can (*movement*) To the

beat of the mu-sic you can (*movement*) To the

beat of the mu-sic you can (*movement*) - - - - - - !

Creativity in the School Program

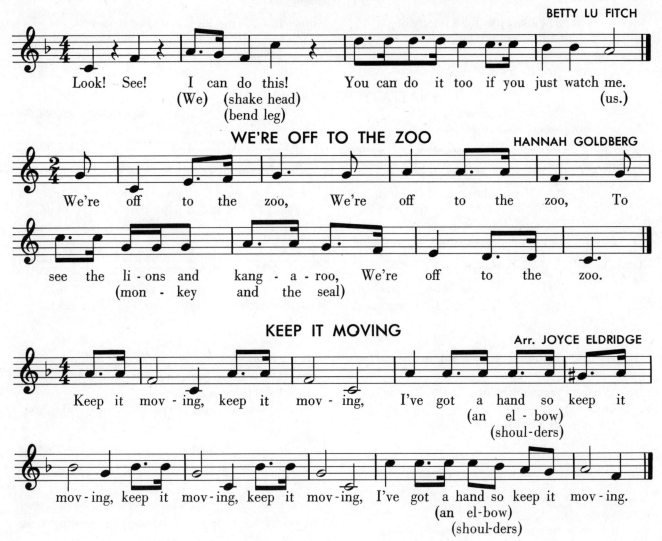

LOOK! SEE!

BETTY LU FITCH

Look! See! I can do this!
(We) (shake head)
(bend leg)
You can do it too if you just watch me.
(us.)

WE'RE OFF TO THE ZOO

HANNAH GOLDBERG

We're off to the zoo, We're off to the zoo, To
see the li-ons and kang-a-roo, We're off to the zoo.
(mon-key and the seal)

KEEP IT MOVING

Arr. JOYCE ELDRIDGE

Keep it mov-ing, keep it mov-ing, I've got a hand so keep it
(an el-bow)
(shoul-ders)
mov-ing, keep it mov-ing, keep it mov-ing, I've got a hand so keep it mov-ing.
(an el-bow)
(shoul-ders)

Action songs can be done with each child supply-ing a different movement. Emphasis is on "*I can do this*." The same action song may be used to bring out the "*We*," with groups of two or more children suggesting movements or ideas. "Keep It Moving" becomes "We have hands, keep them moving." In this instance, movement suggestions are often more organized and complex. Sometimes children enjoy another version of "Keep It Moving," adding one movement to another, until various parts of their bodies are moving at the same time.

Thoughts children have can often be used to stimulate movement songs. The singing and movement in these are continuous, such as "Look at Me." (See Chapter 8 for Music.)

Look at Me
IND.: Look at me, look at me, I'm a basketball

I bounce and bounce and bounce and bounce, just like a basketball.

ALL: (*Repeat*)

IND.: Look at me, look at me, I'm a black horse
I gallop and gallop and gallop away, just like a black horse.

ALL: (*Repeat*)

IND.: Look at me, look at me, I'm a kangaroo
I jump and jump and jump and jump, just like a kangaroo.

ALL: (*Repeat*)

IND.: Look at me, look at me, I'm an Easter bunny
I hop and hop and hop and hop, just like an Easter bunny.

ALL: (*Repeat*)

IND.: Look at me, look at me, I'm an airplane
I zoom and zoom and zoom all day, just like an airplane.

ALL: (*Repeat*)

IND.: Look at me, look at me, I'm a puppy dog
I wag my tail, l wag my tail, just like a puppy dog.

ALL: (*Repeat*)

IND.: Look at me, look at me, I am the end
I sit and sit and sit right down, just like the end.

ALL: (*Repeat*)

WHATTA YOU WANNA BE?

Arr. JOYCE ELDRIDGE

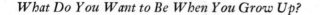

All: O what-ta you wan-na be when you grow up?
Ind.: I wan-na be a space ca-det and fly up high,

O what-ta you wan-na be when you grow up?
So I_____ can____ see what's in the sky!

What Do You Want to Be When You Grow Up?

ALL: What do you want to be when you grow up?
ALL: (*Repeat*)
IND.: I want to be a cowboy in the West.
So I can rope a steer
The very best
ALL: (*Repeat*)

ALL: What do you want to be when you grow up?
ALL: (*Repeat*)
IND.: I want to be a pilot in a plane
So I can beat the railroad train
ALL: (*Repeat*)

ALL: What do you want to be when you grow up?
ALL: (*Repeat*)
IND.: I want to be a fighter in the ring.
So I can hear the gong
Go bing, bing, bing!
ALL: (*Repeat*)

ALL: What do you want to be when you grow up?

ALL: (*Repeat*)
IND.: We want to be funny men
Like Jerry and Dean
So we can make the people scream and scream.

The above has many variations. Movement is continuous with group skipping and sliding, while they sing.

A dance song can be adapted into different meters. Many songs can be used in the same manner. Specific music is unnecessary.

These songs have been worked out with individuals or groups initiating the action. All can participate. The following example of "I Wish I Were" is shown in its adaptations to 2/4, 4/4, and 6/8 time. (Many verses can be made up.)

Example of "I Wish I were" to a folk tune (2/4, "*La Raspa*"):

I wish I were a fish A swim-min' to and fro. I

wish I were a fish and had some place to go!

Adapted to 4/4:

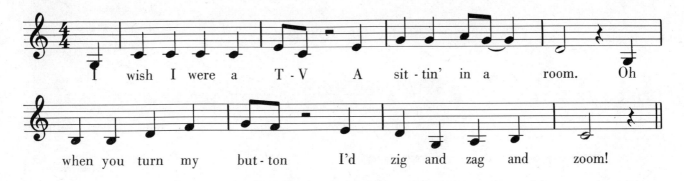

I wish I were a T - V A sit - tin' in a room. Oh

when you turn my but - ton I'd zig and zag and zoom!

Adapted to 6/8:

We wish we were a horse So we could gal - lop all day. We

wish we were a horse So we could gal - lop a - way.

Adapted to 2/4 jazz tempo (with older groups):

I wish I were a play - er with the Yanks!

I wish I were a play - er with the Yanks!

I bat and throw and catch, I bat and throw and

catch, If I were a play - er with the Yanks!

(Children use skip, slide, polka, moving together, until one child goes into the center to call out a movement which all follow.)

KEEPER OF THE ZOO

Arr. JOYCE ELDRIDGE

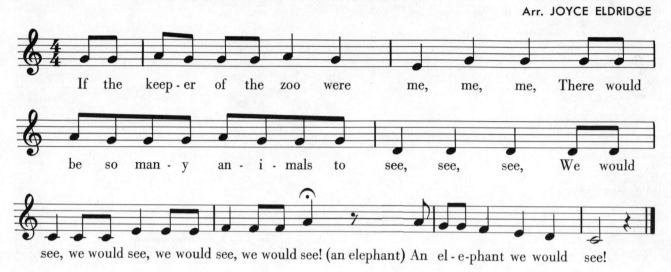

If the keep - er of the zoo were me, me, me, There would

be so man - y an - i - mals to see, see, see, We would

see, we would see, we would see, we would see! (an elephant) An el - e - phant we would see!

Dance songs can be adapted to popular music:

I'm going to kick those kinks right out of my legs
(*Repeat*)
(*Repeat*)
And send them on their way
(*Adapted to:* "I'm Gonna Wash That Man Right
Out of My Hair," from *South Pacific*)

or

I've got two arms
You've got two arms
We've got two arms
Who could wish for anything more
(*Adapted to:* "I've Got Rhythm," from *Girl Crazy*)

"Let's polka!"

Creativity in the School Program

Simple Folk Dancing

Simple dances, such as "Paw Paw Patch," "Pop Goes the Weasel," "Shoo-Fly," "Red River Gal," "Bingo," and "Hokie Kokie," have been particular favorites with middle childhood. These adapted forms of simple folk dances provide boys and girls with an opportunity to start moving at

HOKIE KOKIE

Arr. JOYCE ELDRIDGE

Put your one arm in Put your one arm out Put your one arm in and you shake it all a-bout, and you do the Ho-kie Ko-kie and you do it o-key do-key That's what it's all a-bout!

2. Put your other arm in . . .
4. Put your one leg in . . .

3. Put your head . . .
5. Put your whole self . . .

Doing the Hokie Kokie

once. Many of them can be used in a comparatively small space, and the children can carry the tune and provide their own accompaniment for the dancing.

"Hokie Kokie" is included here as a sample of the way in which these folk dances have been used. (This song has been called by various names in different parts of this country and abroad.) It is a good illustration of a spirited tune, with lively tempo that provides an opportunity for all to be active immediately and to create their own variations. The emphasis is placed on dancing and singing together as a group, rather than on just exactly what the words say. In this dance it does not matter which arm or foot is used. The important thing is that children participate, enjoy it, and ask for more. Variations have been worked out on the chorus of "Hokie Kokie" and have been used according to the interest and abilities of the different groups dancing it. Some of the variations are (*on the chorus*: "Cause you're doing the 'Hokie Kokie'. . . ."): all children clapping first to one side and then the other; shagging

around in individual circles; individually doing the lindy hop, *bleking* step, and so on; in couples, doing some movement pattern which they discover; one couple going into the center, with others following their movements; taking turns, with one couple and then another going in on each chorus; and going around the circle, following first the pattern of one couple, and then the next.

The "Hokie Kokie" is the kind of activity which has been used successfully, with children and adults dancing together.

Folk Dance Step Patterns

The schottische and polka steps have been used in a variety of ways by children as young as second-graders. These steps are particularly suited, however, to middle childhood when children have developed more coordination, a feeling for rhythm, and space. When boys and girls have had a background in movement these folk dance steps are developed easily, and children recognize them as a progression from the fundamental movements.

The schottische is what children recognize and analyze as a combination of locomotor movements—the walk and the hop. It is smooth and has an even rhythm.

Step pattern	walk	walk	walk	hop
Rhythmic pattern	4 ___	___	___	___
Underlying beat	___	___	___	___

The schottische is varied by changing tempo, changing partners, individually or in groups. In addition to using this step in folk dances, such as the Swedish schottische (which was appropriate when children had been studying about the Scandinavian countries, or when Olaf was a newcomer to the fourth grade), groups have composed a variety of schottisches to the music which has been recorded.

The polka seems to rate next highest to the skip in popularity with children. Often they will say, "Let's just polka." It is lively, space is necessary, and children need to have enough coordination to get them up into the air to do the polka (there

Creativity in the School Program

is nothing worse than a slow, deadly, down-to-floor polka). To most groups the polka means "Let's go!" They like the feeling of getting up in the air and seeing if they can keep themselves suspended.

Often, the polka is developed from exploring combinations of locomotor movements. However, when this has not been the case it has usually been developed in the following way:

The group sliding in a circle, all facing center all going around the circle the same way, continues sliding all facing out or away from the center; they continue in the same direction facing in and then out, changing after each slide; this pattern slide and change, facing first in and then out, becomes the polka. Children recognize it as a combination of locomotor movements—of the slide and walk hop (see next page):

SCHOTTISCHE

JOYCE ELDRIDGE

Step pattern		walk	leap	walk	hop

Rhythmic pattern and Underlying beat notation (2/4 time)

This step pattern is clapped, discussed, and analyzed as it is being done. Breaking away from the circle, and this time with partners, the polka is tried again. Partners start, facing each other (as though they were facing the center of the circle), and then turn away from each other. As they start to polka the children often say, "In and out," or "Face to face and back to back." Sometimes, it seems easier if two hands are joined while facing, and one hand is dropped on the turning out or away. The polka is tried another way with partners—first with hands both joined and then in

social dance position; this time it isn't a matter of turning in and out but rather of turning completely around on a polka. Watching, demonstrating, clapping the rhythm, changing directions, listening to the polka music, and changing partners frequently helps to establish the step.

As the polka becomes familiar, it is executed in various ways, depending upon the music and where the step is started. As it is developed above, in the circle, starting with the slide, the polka starts on the downbeat (the step pattern becomes a slide and walk, hop or actually a combination of the slide and skip). Children recognize *downbeat* and *upbeat*. Of the upbeat they say, "It is the sound which helps to get us up in the air—the lift," as they draw in their breath and pull up

POLKA
(With Downbeat)

JOYCE ELDRIDGE

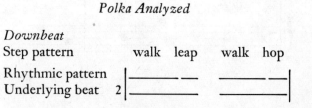

their shoulders. When polka music starts with an upbeat, the polka step starts with a hop, so the step pattern becomes a hop, gallop or slide, walk.

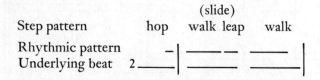

The polka becomes thoroughly familiar to groups of children, and is used in many folk

dances. There are different ways of doing the polka step. Most frequently children dance it to a 2- or 6-meter rhythm.

Polka Analyzed

Downbeat

Step pattern	walk	leap	walk	hop

Rhythmic pattern and Underlying beat notation (2)

Creativity in the School Program

POLKA
(With Upbeat)

NINA COFFING

Upbeat

Step pattern	hop	walk	leap	walk
Rhythmic pattern				
Underlying beat 2				

Downbeat

Step pattern	walk	walk	walk	hop
Rhythmic pattern				
Underlying beat 2				

Downbeat

Step pattern	walk	leap	walk	hop
Rhythmic pattern				
Underlying beat 6				

The polka is used as the basic step for many folk dances which children create. They have said as they were doing the polka:

We love to polka
To polka this way
We have such fun
We feel so gay

It makes us laugh
It makes us gay
Yi-pi-ai-ay!

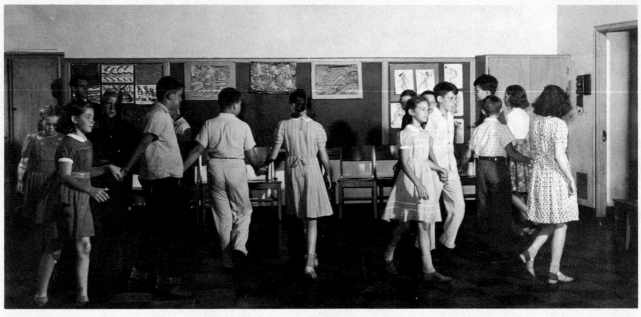

It's a serious business working out original calls

Folk Dancing

Folk dancing is a group activity. It fits into the developmental pattern of middle and later childhood. Its contribution begins as boys and girls desire to become associated with their own *group* and *gang*.

Folk dancing is meaningful and important when it is considered as a part of the school program. It can be used as an aid to learning, when boys and girls become interested in historical events and life in other lands, and when their interests extend from their immediate surroundings to the world outside their own. Folk dancing is a logical progression from experiences in fundamental movement. Boys and girls appreciate how much fun folk dancing can be when it is an outgrowth of movement fundamentals.

If children have acquired a fundamental movement vocabulary through a program in creative rhythmic movement, and if they enjoy movement, they will have experienced the basic folk dance elements—step patterns, space formations, phrasing, underlying beat, rhythmic pattern. Learning a particular folk dance with a schottische, polka, or walk will then simply mean a review, and it will be unnecessary to spend several periods teaching fundamentals. As children are able to associate directions, or "calls," and formations with what they already know, and have experienced, the time can be spent on

dancing together. They need to get the feel of the rhythm, which will start them moving and will give them the opportunity to have a pleasurable experience folk dancing. Length and involved descriptions, slow tempo, or practicing a set pattern over and over tends to kill any approach to folk dancing.

In the *beginning*, fun should be stressed. Mistakes can be overlooked, for it is the *spirit, tempo,* and *meaning* of the dancing that needs to be encouraged, rather than the style. If the emphasis is on *fun* and group activity, all the children can enter into the activity wholeheartedly, with limited embarrassment or self-consciousness. *Style and form are considered when children gain skill in dancing.* Patterns become automatic as they catch the spirit of dancing together and associate the dancing with something that is within their own experience. They become aware of style and spirit and of why the dance is danced in a particular manner. Gaining experience, they realize that the steps are basically similar, but that it is the *manner* in which they are danced and the *positions* that vary.

American Folk Dancing. It is important that all enjoy the very first American folk-dance experience. In beginning to learn about American folk dancing (including square dancing), it seems best to start with a *single circle.* This formation is familiar; it gives everyone a chance to participate actively at once, and to learn together a few simple "calls." At the outset, "calls" need to be *simple* and *repetitive* so that children may become readily familiar with them and follow them easily. As they experience dancing and calling they realize more and more that the "*call*" really gives them *direction* and tells them what to do. Children can figure out *key* "calls" from the very first time they dance them. The following is an example:

All *join* hands and *circle left*
And circle left, circle left
Yes, join hands and circle left
Circle left, circle left.

Into the *center* and *back again*
Back again, back again
Into the center and back again
And *listen to the call.*

This time *circle to the right*
To the right, to the right
This time circle to the right
And listen to the call.

Back to the left and don't get lost
Don't get lost, don't get lost
Circle left and don't get lost
That's all to the call.

Children figure out the key "calls" of *circle left*, *into the center*, and *circle right*. We try "calling" together as we move, giving the key "calls" emphasis. In the beginning, we are not too concerned with the positions children take to swing, or to promenade. Whether it is an elbow swing, two-hand swing, or social dance position is dependent upon their social maturity. The important thing is that they learn to listen to the "call," get moving, and swing in some manner. As they get the "feel" of the rhythm and become acquainted with "calls" and gain in experience, good swinging comes naturally.

We try to avoid boring children; therefore, we do not put emphasis in the beginning on such points as how to bow and curtsy. The latter is a difficult and an unnatural thing for many children, since this form of greeting is not usually a part of experiences of boys and girls. Instead of what might be considered wasting this time, we get them into action immediately. If they use their own form of greeting first, then, as they

understand more and more about folk dancing and its implications, the idea of formalized bowing and curtsying makes sense to them. In a like manner we handle the question of partners, taking for granted that this is a wholesome form of boy-girl relationship. If children have had happy, meaningful creative rhythmic movement experiences throughout the grades, there is little problem.

While figuring out the "calls," we talk about partners, because the "calls" ask for them. We decide we need couples of boys and girls and that in couple-dancing, the girl is on the boy's right. If we do not have enough boys or girls to go around, we pair up those remaining without making a point of it, or *without eliminating anyone.*

We start dancing together in a large, single circle, with the girls on the boys' right. We pick up the "call" as we dance. We talk about "the patter" or the *extra words,* which are called that help to keep the rhythm, but which is of no par-

"Stop in flight and promenade!"

ticular meaning to the main "call." As we experience these, we become familiar with what is meant by the "caller," "calls," why it is necessary to follow "calls," and what it is like to "call." At first, children "call" together as a group. When they have learned the essentials and are ready, they become the individual callers. As children experience saying what they are doing ("calling"), they find that the "call" really gives direction that tell them what to do:

> Swing, swing, everybody swing
> Swing a partner 'round and 'round
> And promenade the ring.

Children can figure out swing "calls." If they do not happen to know the term "promenade," we talk about it and decide it is like a walk around a ring or circle, going back to where we started. The swing and promenade are two of the most fundamental "calls" used.

A beginning "call," which can be given over and over again so children get used to "calling," listening, and responding, is:

> All jump up 'til you come down
> Swing your partner 'round and 'round
> 'Til that foot of yours
> Makes a sound on the floor
> And promenade your partner 'round.

Boys and girls pick out the key calls which tell them what to do, such as *jump up*, *swing partner*, and *promenade*, identifying the rest as "patter."

There are many calls which have been adapted, so that all children in the group can follow them readily. This has meant leaving off the "grand right and left," the "allemande," and other complicated beginning and ending "calls" and substituting for these, simple "swing" and promenades. Some "calls" which have been simplified and adapted to use in a single circle include "Little Old Log Cabin in the Lane," "O Suzanna," "Shoo Fly Swing," and "Dos-a-dos Your Corner."

Classes of boys and girls, when they are given the opportunity to call, do ingenious things in originating calls. Illustrations of some single circle formation calls are included:

> Gals into the center and back again
> Boys into the center and do the same
> Everybody home, let's swing your own
> And promenade, yes promenade.

> Everybody here, let's go
> Turn to your partner and do-sa-do
> Now to your corner and do the same
> Back to your partner and right promenade.

> All join hands and circle left
> Circle left around the floor
> Take your partner—give her a swing
> And promenade her around the room.

> Swing your sweetie
> 'Round 'n 'round
> 'Til she swings right off the ground
> Stamp your feet right on the floor
> Now start to swing, and swing some more.

> Whee, whee—watch 'er fly.
> Whee, whee—watch 'er fly.
> Whee, whee—that's enough
> Stop in flight and promenade.

When the children are familiar with a few of the basic "calls" and can respond readily to change in direction in tempo, and in phrasing, we figure out additional "calls" and use a double-circle formation. This helps to figure out many of the main "calls," with partners facing another couple. Many of the main "calls," in simplified and adapted form, have been worked out in this manner: Step Right Back and Watch Her Smile, Take A Little Peek, I'll Swing Your Gal, Star by the Right, Dive for the Oyster.

Dancing this way, everyone learns at once, and this avoids having children standing around waiting for their turn to dance. As children become familiar with a wide variety of "calls," they know the meaning of following a "call." Then they can take a faster tempo of music and are ready for dancing in a square dance. This is the time they also begin to acquire style, so that more complicated calls may be successfully given, such as, the allemandes and grand right and left. It is like any other learning experience within the school program, for as addition comes before long division, simple, repetitive "calls" come before the complicated grand rights and allemandes.

HOE DOWN

JOYCE ELDRIDGE

Folk dancing, of which American square danc-ing is one form, is a splendid activity for the middle grades and peer groups to participate in together; this includes the teachers and children.

Calling. Children enjoy writing and directing original calls. Many of these are composed to popular music or to songs which they have learned in music.

The teacher who includes singing within the day's program often suggests, "This song could make a good square-dance 'call.'" The period might find teacher and children working together to write a new kind of "call." A Miss Carrol and her group of fifth- and sixth-graders composed the "Hoe Down." The musical accompaniment Joyce supplied has served many young callers.

Creativity in the School Program

Circle to the left and away we go
Don't you step on my gal's toe
Move along with hands held tight
Now the other way, to the right.

Keep on going with a grin
Ready for the set that you'll be in
Swing your partner and swing some more
Swing her again and circle four.

(Swing the) gal on your left—small or big
And let's all go for the hoe down jig
Boys in the center and the gals all 'round
See the boys get a feather in their crown.

Boys step out to the left hand gal
Swing her around and swing like mad
Circle to the left and listen to the call
Of the hoe down jig, one and all.

Simple folk tunes and songs adapted to the individual group are good starting points for originating "calls." A wealth of other songs from music classes have been used for American folk dancing, including "The Drunken Sailor," "The Juniper Tree," "Jim Along Josie," "Home on the Range," "Can't You Dance the Polka?" "Blue-Tailed Fly," "Waltzing Matilda," "Twelve Days to Christmas," and "As the Sun Goes Down."

Lois' and Agnes' Call to "MacNamara's Band"

Oh, the head and foot go forward, and then go back to place
The side two couples do the same, and then go back to place.
Now swing your corner gal, swing her fast and strong.
Go back and swing your own, and don't you do it wrong.
Girls in the center, now back and face your gent.
Take him round the outside and make him glad he went.
Keep on promenading until you get him home.
Now swing your partner round and round, and don't let him go.

Social Dancing

Social dancing can assist in the "growing up" process. Later childhood is a logical time to initiate social dance experiences. It is the period when it is important for boys and girls to be together. When social dancing is considered an acceptable part of the school program, it contributes to the expanding social world of boys and girls by providing opportunities for them to be together in a

Learning together

Creativity in the School Program

social situation. It should not be considered as just another gymnasium period (once a week for eight times when boys and girls come together), but rather an experience they participate in as a class group—teacher, boys, and girls together.

Social dance experience is worth while for boys

FOX TROT

JOYCE ELDRIDGE

Creativity in the School Program

TWO - STEP

JOYCE ELDRIDGE

Creativity in the School Program

and girls. This experience need not be the responsibility of one teacher, but a joint effort on the part of several teachers. For instance, in one school the music teacher played the piano (assisted by an orchestra made up of boys and girls playing percussion instruments) while the classroom teacher (a man) and the physical education consultant took responsibility for the instruction. Occasionally, the principal and science teacher dropped in and joined the group. The attitude of teachers toward social dancing is important if boys and girls are to have a meaningful experience. Teachers' attitudes are reflected in their willingness to participate in making social dancing a social learning experience. Boys and girls will then feel it is an acceptable activity and will look forward to this period of school time—a time when they may participate in a social activity within their own class group, irrespective of social maturity.

The material, approach, procedure, and outcomes depend on the background of the group, social maturity, and situation. If boys and girls have had a background in fundamental movement and folk dancing, then social dancing is meaningful. If they have not had this background, then the first period of social dancing is extremely important. The social climate in which boys and girls feel secure and at ease must be established, at the outset, if social dancing experiences are to be successful.

Helpful Suggestions for Starting

Get the group into action fast, all moving around the room together—teacher, as well as boys and girls.

Have the group walk informally around the room, listen to a fox-trot rhythm, and try to adjust walk to the rhythm. Change the tempo of the fox-trot walk, going fast and slow.

Have the group walk, changing direction: forward, backward, and turning around. Combine fox-trot walks forward and backward, without losing a beat.

Start group moving and stopping with the phrasing of the music.

Suggest that boys and girls notice that when they walk slow their steps are longer and when they walk fast their steps are shorter. Make combinations of slow (long) and fast (short) walks.

It helps if the teacher calls out or talks out the steps as boys and girls are moving because it provides an opportunity to hear what they are trying to do—"slow, slow, fast, fast" or "long, long, short, short."

Give plenty of opportunity to the group to suggest combinations and create own patterns and variations. Change combinations often.

Encourage group to listen to music rather than count it. If the music is provided by a piano player, suggest that her music be well accented so as to help the group.

Make the partner situation an easy one: Realizing that this depends on the social maturity of the group, some will respond readily to partners, others in the same age group "wouldn't be caught dead with a girl" . . . not, at least, until it is made comfortable for them. The partner situation takes care of itself when boys and girls are not forced. The first partner situation can be an outgrowth of what the group is doing. For instance, if they are moving freely around the room and the boys are all bunched together, having the girls walking fast and the boys walking slow distributes the girls so that when getting partners is suggested there will be one close by. "Take the person nearest you" is a means of forming partners.

Use the open-dance position as the first couple position. This helps to make boys and girls feel secure. It helps boys and girls to see where they are going, and seems easier to adjust to each other's rhythm. In this position they can change direction and tempo without feeling they might step on one another's feet.

Start girls moving on the right foot and the boys moving on the left.

Provide opportunities within the school program so that boys and girls can use their social dancing in party situations.

Help make social dancing a fun experience by taking into consideration the great variance of maturation in any one group of boys and girls.

Illustration of a First Lesson

Fox-Trot Step Pattern

Start with the fox trot, 4/4 music, well-accented. Piano or Victrola.
clockwise together. Group encouraged to

Start moving around the room clockwise or counterlisten to the music as they move.

Partners in open position

Basic fox-trot step—walk in combinations
    Walking moderate tempo:
        forward; forward and backward; forward
        toward center of room and back out from
        center; forward toward center of room, turn-
        ing around and back out.
    Walking, fast tempo with short steps:
        forward; forward and backward; forward
        and turning around.
    Walking, slow tempo (half-time) with long steps:
        changing direction
    Walking, combining slow and fast walks (long
        and short): without losing the rhythm, alter-
        nating forward and backward.
    Walking, with combinations:
        4 slow and 4 fast (saying "slow, slow, slow,
          slow," and so on)
        4 slow and 8 fast (saying "slow, slow, slow,
          slow" and so on)
        4 slow and 8 fast turning
        2 slow and 4 fast turning
    Repeat any of the above patterns, changing di-
        rection:
        1 slow and 2 fast (saying "slow, fast, fast" or
          "long, short, short")
        2 slow and 2 fast and 1 slow
    Partners open position:
        girls and boys facing in the same direction

girl on boy's right, standing side by side
boy's right arm placed in back of girl's right
    shoulder
girl's left arm on top of boy's arm and lightly
    resting on left shoulder
girl's and boy's hands clasped in front
girl always starts moving with right foot
boy always starts moving with left foot
moving with any of the combinations as des-
    ignated above, such as 4 forward and 4
    backward.

A Progression to Social Dancing

There are several aspects of social dancing, all of which are interrelated. Progression of dance steps and positions is dependent upon the maturity level and experience of the group. There is no one way of teaching social dancing; there is no one progression of steps. However, the following sequence of steps and positions has been used successfully with peer age boys and girls:

Social Dance Steps
Fox Trot
Balance (or Hesitation)
Two-Step
Dip
Tango
Rhumba
Charleston or Jitterbug
Waltz
Samba
Mambo

Social Dance Positions
Open
Closed
Open Reverse

Social dancing contributes to social living, and should be offered as a part of school experiences for boys and girls of later childhood.

If it is presented as part of school experiences, it contributes, in a social way, to the growing up process of later childhood. The activity itself aids boys and girls to be together at the time when it is natural and important for them to *want* to be together. It helps to provide recognition of each other in a way which is fun and is right for them. Social dancing experiences also present a natural setting for the discussion and understanding of the common courtesies that boys and girls should be taught.

Experiences in social dancing can also help to make school parties more meaningful for the peer age. One of the traits of this period is the strong feeling of anticipation of a social affair. This can be satisfied by the extensive planning and important preparations which boys and girls make together in getting ready for their parties. Social dancing not only serves as a useful activity at the party, but it also provides for the solving of a social problem—where to have the dancing, when to have it, what kind of music, the arrangement of music and dance numbers, and the means of getting partners.

Social dancing can help boys and girls take a more active part in the important social experiences of their own age group when it takes into consideration the maturity level of the entire group. The children feel comfortable and secure when social dancing is considered fun.

Teachers can take advantage of opportunities as they present themselves to integrate creative rhythmic movement in the school program. Experiences in art, music, social studies, and others, in addition to creative rhythmic movement, offer many chances for teachers and children to explore, think, move, share, and laugh together. Integration provides enrichment and vitalization of learning experiences for children of elementary school age. (See Suggested Resources.)

Summary

Movement is a universal language of children. It expresses through action what they think, how they feel, and what they understand. Creative Rhythmic Movement is important in terms of how children grow. This form of expression becomes a meaningful part of the home, school, camp, or recreation experiences when it is offered in the light of individual needs and stages of development of *all* boys and girls.

There is a logical progression of creative rhythmic movement when it is in accord with the interests and experiences of boys and girls and when it is offered for their immediate use at their particular time of growing up. When children of early childhood are given the opportunity to discover movement and to create, express concepts, and solve problems, it is not only a means of learning, but it also provides a basis for a natural progression to folk and social and other forms of dancing. Children realize how enjoyable folk and social dancing can be when these forms are outgrowths of movement fundamentals. In middle and later childhood, folk dancing helps boys and girls in the "growing up" process. It helps them to adjust to the social group around them, giving them an active part in group relations. Social dancing, based upon a background in fundamental movement, goes hand in hand with the period of later childhood—that time when young teenage boys and girls think of themselves as social beings. It serves as an aid to learning and fits in with other daily experiences of art, music, social studies, and language arts.

In addition to the desire for a wide variety of meaningful experiences consistent with their varying levels of growth and development, boys and girls want the help of understanding grownups who will respect their individual rights as people and recognize their imperative need to be active. Children seek the help of grownups who, in a spirit of "togetherness," will participate in experiences, solve problems, and have fun with them. The home, classroom, playground, playroom, gymnasium, and camp recreation center may become a happier place for boys and girls. Indeed, living will be richer and fuller when grownups and children share creative experiences!

IT'S TIME TO GO

It's time to go now, it's time to leave. It's time to go now, We'll say so long. So long, so long, so long, we're glad you came. So long, so long, so long, so long, we're glad you came.

Suggested Resources
and Bibliography

SUGGESTED RESOURCES

Children and teachers are the most effectual resources for a program of creative rhythms. In addition to children and teachers and the experiences which continually surround them, there are other sources, which may prove helpful, that have been used in promoting experiences in Creative Rhythmic Movement. These resources are by no means the only ones or the best, but are listed here as suggestions and aids which have been used with teachers and children.

Teachers often ask these questions: "How can I tell when something is creative?" "How can the present topic in science be enhanced by movement?" "How can I relate movement to social studies?" "How can I find out more about music as it relates to movement, and are there any Victrola records available which can be used in rhythms?"

Here are a few sources which will help to answer these inquiries and to give the teacher security, assistance, and new ideas.

Art

Board of Education, City of New York, *Art in the Elementary Schools*. Curriculum Bulletin No. 2, 1947-1948.

Crane, Florence, *The Artist in Each of Us*. New York: Pantheon Books, Inc., 1951.

D'Amico, Victor, *Creative Teaching in Art*. Scranton: International Textbook Co., 1942.

Tomlinson, R. R., *Picture Making by Children*. New York: The Studio Publications, Inc., 1934.

Wilhelm, Viola, *Child Art and Franz Cizek*. New York: John Day Co., 1936.

Catalogues

Black Mountain Records, 4247 Walnut St., Long Beach, Calif.

Children's Record Guild, 27 Thompson St., New York City.

Folkways Records & Service Corp., 117 West 46th St., New York City.

Kismet Record Company, *Folk Dance Records, International Releases*, 227 East 14th St., New York City.

The Folk Dancer, P.O. Box 201, Flushing, L.I.

The Methodist Radio & Film Commission, *The World of Fun Series of Recreational Recordings*. Produced by Larry Eisenberg; Recording by RCA Victor. Audio-Visual Department, Division of Local Church General Board of Education, The Methodist Church.

Willis Music Co., *All Music of All Publishers*, Cincinnati, Ohio.

Dance—Rhythms

Herman, Michael, *Folk Dances for All*. New York: Barnes and Noble, Inc., 1947.

LaSalle, Dorothy, *Rhythms and Dance for Elementary Schools*, 2nd ed. New York: A. S. Barnes & Co., 1952.

Murray, Ruth L., *Dance in Elementary Education*. New York: Harper & Brothers, 1953.

Sanderson, Chris, *Hires Throws a Square Dance with Chris Sanderson*. Philadelphia: The Charles E. Hires Co., 1950.

Waterman, Elizabeth, *The Rhythm Book*. New York: A. S. Barnes & Co., 1936.

Dramatics

Burger, Isabel, *Creative Play Activity*. New York: A. S. Barnes & Co., 1950.

Ward, Winifred, *Creative Dramatics*. New York: Appleton-Century-Crofts, Inc., 1930.

———, *Playmaking with Children*. New York: Appleton-Century-Crofts, Inc., 1947.

General

Applegate, Mauree, *Everybody's Business—Our Children*. White Plains, N.Y.: Row Peterson Co., 1952.

Burrows, Alvina, *Teaching Children in the Middle Grades*. Boston: D. C. Heath, 1952.

Cole, Natalie, *The Arts in the Classroom*. New York: John Day Co., 1940.

Lowenfeld, Viktor, *Creative and Mental Growth*. New York: The Macmillan Company, 1947.

Mearns, Hughes, *Creative Youth*. New York: Doubleday Doran Co., 1925.

———, *The Creative Adult*. New York: Doubleday Doran Co., 1940.

Myers, Louise, *Teaching Children Music in the Elementary School*. New York: Prentice-Hall, Inc., 1950.

Raths, Louis, *Do's and Dont's of the Needs Theory*. Bronxville, N.Y.: Modern Educational Service, 1951.

Regan, William, *Modern Elementary Curriculum*. New York: Dryden Press, 1953.

Sheehy, Emma, *There's Music in Children*. New York: Henry Holt & Company, Inc., 1946.

Language Arts

Association for Childhood Education, Library Committee, *Sung Under the Silver Umbrella*. New York: The Macmillan Company, 1935.

Conkling, Hilda, *Poems by a Little Girl*. New York: Frederick A. Stokes Co., 1920.

Ferebee, J., D. Jackson, D. Saunders, and A. Treut Burrows, *They All Want to Write*. New York: Prentice-Hall, Inc., 1952.

Jackson, Katherine, *The Animals' Merry Christmas*. New York: Simon & Schuster, 1950.

Lindsay, Vachel, *Johnny Appleseed and Other Poems*. New York: The Macmillan Company, 1949.

Love, Katherine, *A Pocketful of Rhymes*. New York: Thomas Y. Crowell Company, 1946.

Sandburg, Carl, *Complete Poems*. New York: Harcourt, Brace & Company, Inc., 1950.

———, *Early Moon*. New York: Harcourt, Brace, & Company, Inc., 1939.

Strickland, Ruth, *The Language Art in the Elementary School*. Boston: D. C. Heath, 1951.

Thompson, Blanche Jennings, *More Silver Pennies*. New York: The Macmillan Company, 1938.

Wilkins, Alice, *The Golden Flute*. New York: John Day Publishing Company, 1932.

Wylie, Mrs. Elinor (Hoyt), *Collected Poems of Elinor Wylie*. New York: Alfred A. Knopf, Inc., 1921, 1932.

Music—Records—Percussion

Anderson, LeRoy, *Conducts His Own Compositions*, Decca Golden Label, Decca Album D 810.

Bartók Béla, *Piano Music for Children*, Vols. I & II, rev. ed. New York: Boosey and Hawkes, 1946.

———, *The Voice of the Arts*, Vox Album 625.

Boni, Margaret, and Norman Lloyd, *Fireside Book of Folk Songs*. New York: Simon & Schuster, Inc., 1947.

Coleman, Satis, *The Drum Book*. New York: John Day Co., 1931.

Faith, Percy, *Festival*, Columbia Record No. 39708.

Johnson, Hazel, *Music for Rhythms*, Vol. I (album) (128 West 13th St., New York City).

Luther, Frank, *Children's Corner*, Decca Album A 414.

Marias, Josef, *Songs of the African Veld*, Decca Album A 471, 113, 302.

Miller, Freda, *Music for Rhythms and Dance*, Album 4 (8 Tudor City Place, New York City).

Nelson, M. J., and Gladys Tipton, *Music for Early Childhood*. New York: Silver Burdett Co., 1952.

Pinto, Octavio, *Scenas Infantas* (Piano music). New York: G. Schirmer, Inc., 1932, 1934.

Pitts, L. B., M. Glenn, and L. E. Watters, *Our Singing World*. New York: Ginn and Company, 1951.

———, *Singing in Harmony*, Album 6 (Ginn and Company).

———, *Singing in Harmony*. New York: Ginn and Company, 1951.

———, *Singing Together*, Album 5 (Ginn and Company).

———, *Singing Together*. New York: Ginn and Company, 1951.

Prokofief, Serge, *Music for Children Opus 65*. New York: Leeds Music Corp., 1945.

Seeger, Ruth C., *American Folk Songs for Children*. Garden City, N.Y.: Doubleday & Company, Inc., 1948.

Tilles, Mae S., "Ever Made Rhythms Toys?" *Family Circle*, February, 1953, Vol. 42, No. 2, p. 78.

Tripp, Paul, and George Kleinsinger, *Tubby the Tuba*, Decca Record CU 106.

Walberg, B. J., *Dance-A-Long*, Folkways Records.

Williams, Tex, *A & E Rag*, Capitol Record 7-40203.

Science

Schlein, Miriam, and Leonard Kessler, *Fast Is Not a Ladybug*. New York: W. R. Scott, 1953.

Schneider, Herman, *Follow the Sunset*. New York: Doubleday & Company, Inc., 1952.

———, *How Big is Big?* New York: W. R. Scott, 1950.

———, *How Your Body Works*. New York: W. R. Scott, 1950.

———, *Let's Find Out*. New York: W. R. Scott, 1950.

———, *Now Try This*. New York: W. R. Scott, 1950.

Social Studies

Michaelis, John U., *Social Studies for Children in a Democracy*. New York: Prentice-Hall, Inc., 1950.

Preston, Ralph, *Teaching Social Studies in the Elementary School*. New York: Rinehart & Co., 1950.

BIBLIOGRAPHY

Adams, Fay, *Educating America's Children*. New York: Ronald Press Company, 1946.

Alschuler, Rose, and LaBerta Hattwick, *Painting and Personality*. Chicago: University of Chicago Press, 1947.

American Association for the Advancement of Science National Meeting, *Symposium on Meeting the Needs of School Children*. New York, December 27, 1949 (as reported in *The New York Times*, January 1, 1950).

American Association of Health, Physical Education, and Recreation, *Developing Democratic Human Relations*. Washington, D.C.: National Education Association, 1951 Yearbook.

American Council on Education, *Helping Teachers Understand Children* (Daniel Prescott, ed.). Washington, D.C.: Commission on Teacher Education, 1945.

Andrews, Gladys, and Marion Bozenhard, *Teaching Rhythms to Children*. Masters thesis, University of Wisconsin, 1939.

Applegate, Mauree, *Helping Children Write*. Scranton: International Text Book, 1949.

Association for Childhood Education, "About Children, How They Learn, Feel and Grow" (Reprint Service Bulletin of Childhood Education). Washington, D.C.: Association for Childhood Education, International, 1945.

———, *Working Together in Schools*. Washington, D.C.: Association for Childhood Education, International, 1952.

Association for Supervision and Curriculum Development, *Toward Better Teaching*. Washington, D.C.: National Education Association, 1949 Yearbook.

———, *Fostering Mental Health in Our Schools*. Washington, D.C.: National Education Association, 1950 Yearbook.

Bacmeister, Rhoda W., *Growing Together*. New York: Appleton-Century-Crofts, Inc., 1947.

Bailey, Nancy, and E. H. Jones, "The Berkeley Growth Study," *Child Development, No. 12*, 1941, pp. 167-173.

Baker, Harold, "Children's Contribution in Elementary School, General Discussion," *Child Development Monograph #29*, Teachers College Bureau of Publication, Columbia University, New York, 1942.

Baruch, Dorothy, "Helping Children Understand Why They Behave as They Do," *About Children*. Washington, D.C.: Reprint Service Bulletin Childhood Education, pp. 29-36.

Baxter, Bernice, Gertrude Lewis, and Gertrude Gross, *The Role of Elementary Education*. Boston: D. C. Heath and Company, 1952.

Bean, C. H., "An Unusual Opportunity to Investigate the Psychology of Language," *Journal of Genetic Psychology 40*, 1932, pp. 180-202.

Binet, Alfred, and Thomas Simon, *The Development of Intelligence in Children* (translated by E. S. Kite). Baltimore: The Williams and Wilkins Company, 1916.

Blair, Arthur W., and William Burton, *Growth and Development of the Pre-Adolescent*. New York: Appleton-Century-Crofts, Inc., 1951.

Boas, Franz, "Growth of Children," *Science*, Vol. XX, 1892, pp. 351-352.

Bossard, J. H. S., *The Sociology of Child Development*. New York: Harper & Brothers, 1948.

Breckenridge, Marian, and E. Vincent, *Child Development*, rev. ed. Philadelphia: Saunders Co., 1949.

Brown, Corinne, *Creative Drama in the Lower School*. New York: Appleton-Century-Crofts, Inc., 1929.

Burks, B. S., D. W. Jenson, and M. L. Terman, *The Promise of Youth*. Stanford, Calif.: Stanford University Press, 1930.

Cizek, Franz, "Child as Artist," *Independent*, No. 113, 1924.

Cole, Lawrence E., and William F. Bruce, *Educational Psychology*. Yonkers, N.Y.: World Book Co., 1950.

Coleman, Satis, *Creative Music for Children*. New York: G. P. Putnam's Sons, 1922.

Commonwealth of Pennsylvania, Department of

Public Instruction, *The Elementary Course of Study*, Bulletin 233, Harrisburg, Pa., 1949.

Curti, M. W., *Child Psychology*, New York: Longmans, Green and Company, 1938.

Davis, Allison, "Socialization and Adolescent Personality," *National Society for the Study of Education*, 43rd Yearbook, Chicago University, 1944, pp. 198-216.

Dearborn, W. F., and J. W. Rothney, "Predicting the Child's Development," *Science Art Publications*, Cambridge, Mass., 1941.

Department of Elementary School Principals, *Creative Schools*. Washington, D.C.: National Education Association, 23rd Yearbook, 1944.

Department of Supervisors and Directors of Instruction, *Supervision and the Creative Teacher*. New York: Bureau of Publications, Teachers College, Columbia University, National Education Association 5th Yearbook, 1932.

Deutsche, Jean Marquis, *The Development of Children's Concepts of Casual Relations*. Minneapolis: University of Minnesota Press, 1937.

Dewey, John, *Art as Experience*. New York: G. P. Putnam's Sons, 1934.

———, *Experience and Education*. New York: The Macmillan Company, 1938.

Dimnet, Ernest, *What We Live By*. New York: Simon & Schuster, 1932.

Driscoll, Gertrude, "How to Study the Behavior of Children," *Practical Suggestions for Teachers No. 2*. New York: Bureau of Publications, Teachers College, Columbia University, 1941.

Driver, Ann, *Music and Movement*. New York: Oxford University Press, 1936.

Elkisch, Paula, "Children's Drawings in a Projective Technique," *Psychological Monographs No. 1*, The American Psychological Association, Inc., 1945.

Fallis, Edwina, *The Child and Things*. Yonkers, N.Y.: World Book Company, 1940.

Fenley, Malcolm, "The Developmental Aspects of the Latency Period Significant for Education," *American Journal of Orthopsychiatry*, 1943, pp. 271-275.

Fierfey, Paul F., *The Growing Boys*. New York: The Macmillan Company, 1930.

Fletcher, John, *Psychology in Education, with Emphasis on Creative Thinking*. New York: Doubleday Doran Company, Inc., 1934.

Fox, Mrs. Lillian, and Thomas Hopkins, *Creative School Music*. New York: Silver Burdett Company, 1936.

Frank, Lawrence K., "The Fundamental Needs of the Child" (New York Committee on Mental Hygiene of the State Charities Aid Association). Reprint from *Mental Hygiene*, Vol. 22, July, 1938, pp. 353-379.

———, "The Projective Methods for the Study of Personality," *Journal of Psychology*, Vol. 8, 1939, pp. 389-413.

Gans, Roma, "A Study of Critical Reading Comprehension in the Intermediate Grades," Contribution to Education No. 811. New York: Teachers College, Columbia University, Bureau of Publications, 1940.

Gesell, Arnold, *The Child from Five to Ten*. New York: Harper & Brothers, 1946.

Goodenough, Florence, *Developmental Psychology*. New York: Appleton-Century-Crofts, Inc., 1945.

Gruenberg, Sidone, "Half Way Up the Stairs," *Child Study*, New York, 1934.

Guilford, J. P., "Creativity," *The American Psychologist*, Vol. V, No. 9, 1950.

Hartman, Gertrude, and Ann Shumaker (editor), *Creative Expression*. Milwaukee: E. M. Hale & Co., 1939.

Havighurst, Robert, *Developmental Tasks and Education*. Chicago: The University of Chicago Press, 1948.

Hawkins, Alma, *The Role of Modern Dance in Higher Education*, Ed.D. final document, Columbia University, 1952.

H'Doubler, Margaret, *Dance—A Creative Art Experience*. New York: Appleton-Century-Croft, Inc., 1940.

Hetherington, Clark W., *The Demonstration Play School of 1913*. Berkeley, Calif.: University of California Publication, Vol. V, No. 2, July, 1914.

———, *The School Program in Physical Education*. Yonkers, N.Y.: World Book Company, 1922.

Hildreth, Gertrude, *Child Growth Through Education*. New York: Ronald Press, 1948.

Hopkins, L. Thomas, *Creative Development for World Citizenship*, Reprint, Eastern Arts Association Yearbook, 1946.

———, *Interaction: The Democratic Process*. Boston: D. C. Heath Company, 1941.

Horn, Ernest, *Methods of Instruction in Social Studies* (Report of the Commission on Social Studies, American Historical Association). New York: Charles Scribner's Sons Company, 1937.

Horrall, Albion, *Let's Go to School* (An Integrative Experience in Public Elementary Schools). New York: McGraw-Hill Book Company, Inc., 1938.

Hurlock, Elizabeth B., *Child Development*. New York: McGraw-Hill Book Company, Inc., 1942.

Hymes, James, *Understanding Your Child*. New York: Prentice-Hall, Inc., 1952, pp. 3-188.

———, *Teacher Listen, the Children Speak*. New York Committee in Mental Health of the State Charities Aid Association, 1949.

Isaac, Susan, *Social Development in Young Children*.

London: Routledge & Company, 1933.

———, *Recent Advances in the Study of Child Development*, Yearbook of Education No. 4. Psychological Aspects of Child Development, The University of London Institute of Education: Evans Brothers, 1935.

Jenkins, Gladys, Helen Shacter, and Williams Bauer, *These Are Your Children*. New York: Scott Foresman and Company, 1949.

Jennings, Helen Hall, *Sociometry in Group Relations*. Washington, D.C.: American Council on Education, 1948.

———, *Leadership and Isolation*, 2nd ed. New York: Longmans, Green & Company, 1950.

Jersild, Arthur, and associates, *Child Development and the Curriculum*. New York: Bureau of Publications, Teachers College, Columbia University, 1946.

Kearney, Nolan, *Elementary School Objectives*. Russell Sage Foundation, 1953.

Keliher, Alice, *Life and Growth*. New York: Appleton-Century-Crofts, Inc., 1938.

Kilpatrick, W. H., "The Education We Need," *Childhood Education*, Vol. 23, 1946, pp. 5-8.

———, "Modern Education and Better Human Relations," *Freedom Pamphlets*, Anti-Defamation League of B'nai B'rith, 1949.

———, *Philosophy of Education*. New York: The Macmillan Company, 1951.

Koch, Helen, "A Study of Some Factors Conditioning the Social Distance Between the Sexes," *Journal of Social Psychology*, 20, 1944, pp. 79-107.

Koenig, Frances, "Classroom Teachers Guidance in Relation to Learning Activities," *Understanding the Child*, Vol. 2, 1951, pp. 41-42.

Lane, Howard A., "Shall Children, Too, Be Free," *Freedom Pamphlets*, Anti-Defamation League of B'nai B'rith, 1949.

Lee, J. Murray, *The Child and His Curriculum*. New York: Appleton-Century-Crofts, Inc., 1950.

Lehman, H., and P. A. Witty, *The Psychology of Play Activity*. New York: A. S. Barnes, 1927.

Levy, D. M., "On the Problem of Movement Restraint, Ties, Stereotyped Movements, Hyperactivity," *American Journal of Orthopsychiatry*, No. 14, 1944, pp. 644-670.

Lewin, Kurt, "Experiments on Autocratic Atmospheres," *Social Frontier*, Vol. IV, 1938.

Lippett, R., and R. K. White, "Social Climate of Children's Groups," *Child Behavior and Development* (Baker, Kounin and Wright, eds.). New York: McGraw-Hill Book Company, 1943.

Loomis, Arthur, "The Internal Organization of a Local School System," *American Education in the Post War Period*. Chicago: University of Chicago Press, 44th Yearbook, National Society for the Study of Education, 1945.

Meir, N. C., *The Graphic and Allied Arts in Child Development and the Curriculum*. Bloomington, Ill.: Public School Publishing Company, 1939.

Merrill, John, and Martha Fleming, *Play-making and Plays*. New York: The Macmillan Company, 1930.

Meyer, Adolph, *The Development of Education in the Twentieth Century*. New York: Prentice-Hall, Inc., 1949.

Mitchell, Lucy Sprague, *Our Children and Our Schools*. New York: Simon and Schuster, 1950.

Moore, K. C., "The Mental Development of a Child," *Monograph Supplements of the Psychology Review*, Vol. I, No. 3, 1896, p. 150.

Morgan, Hazel (ed.), *Music Education Source Book*. Chicago: Music Educators' National Conference, 1947.

Morgan, John, *Child Psychology*. New York: Rinehart & Company, 1942.

Morrison, J. Cayce, *New York Society for Experiment of Study of Education*, 1943 Yearbook.

Munro, Thomas, "Creativity in Art," *Public School Publication*, Bloomington, Ill., 1941.

Murphy, Gardner, *Personality*. New York: Harper & Brothers, 1947.

Murray, Josephine, and Effie Bathurst, *Creative Ways for Children's Programs*. New York: Silver Burdett Company, 1938.

National Research Council, White House Conference on Child Health and Protection, *Growth and Development of the Child*. New York: Appleton-Century-Crofts, 1932, 1933, pp. 377 and 629.

Nesbitt, Marion, *A Public School for Tomorrow*. New York: Harper & Brothers, 1953.

Newgarten, Bernice, "Social Class and Friendship Among School Children," *American Journal of Sociology* No. 51, 1946, pp. 305-313.

Olson, Willard, "The Meaning of Growth," *Child Growth in an Era of Conflict*. Lansing: Michigan Education Association, Department of Elementary School Principals, Fifteenth Yearbook, 1944, pp. 1-9.

———, "Growth of the Child as a Whole," in *Child Behavior and Development* (R. B. Barker, J. S. Kounin, and H. F. Wright, eds.). New York: McGraw-Hill Book Company, 1943, pp. 199-208.

———, *Child Development*. Boston: D. C. Heath Company, 1949.

———, *The Concept of the Organism as a Whole*. Ann Arbor: Bureau of Educational Reference and Research, University of Michigan, 1937.

Piaget, Jean, *The Child's Conception of the World*. New York: Harcourt Brace, 1929.

———, *Language and Thought of the Child*. New York: Harcourt Brace, 1926.

Pistor, F., "How Time Concepts Are Acquired by Children," *Educational Methods*, Vol. 20, 1920, pp. 107-112.

Pratt, Caroline, *I Learn from Children*. New York: Simon and Schuster, 1948.

Prescott, Daniel A., *Emotion and the Educative Process*. Washington, D.C.: The American Council on Education, 1938.

Pryor, Helen, *As the Child Grows*. New York: Silver Burdett Company, 1943.

Read, Herbert, *Education Through Art*. London: Faber & Faber, 1943.

Redl, Fritz, "Preadolescents, What Makes Them Tick?" *Child Study*, Winter, 1944, pp. 44-48.

———, *What Should We Know About a Child?* Lansing: The Michigan Cooperative Teachers Education Study, 1945.

Rees, Helen E., *A Psychology of Artistic Creation*. New York: Bureau of Publications, Teachers College, Columbia University, 1942.

Rice, Rebecca, *Creative Activities with Patterns and Illustrations*. Boston: Pilgrim Press, 1947.

Riedman, Sarah, *The Physiology of Work and Play*. New York: Dryden Press, 1950.

Rugg, Harold, *Foundations for American Education*. Yonkers, N.Y.: World Book Company, 1947.

Russell, D. H., "Interclass Grouping for Reading Instruction in the Intermediate Grades," *Journal of Educational Research*, 39, 1946, pp. 462-470.

Sanford, R. Nevitt, *et al.*, "Physique, Personality and Scholarship," *Society for Research in Child Development Monographs*, VIII, No. 1. Washington, D.C.: National Research Council, 1943.

Seegers, R. Conrad, and Robert Seashore, "How Large Are Children's Vocabularies?" *Educational English*, No. 26, April, 1949, pp. 181-194.

Sehon, Elizabeth, *Rhythms in Elementary Education*. New York: A. S. Barnes and Company, 1951.

Shuttleworth, F. K., *The Physical and Mental Growth of Girls and Boys Age Six to Nineteen in Relation to Age at Maximum Growth*. Washington, D.C.: Society for Research in Child Development, Vol. IV, 1939.

Smith, Stevenson, "Age and Sex Differences in Children's Opinion Concerning 34 Differences," *Journal of Genetic Psychology*, No. 54, 1939, pp. 17-25.

Sontag, L. W., *The Fels Research Institute for the Study of Human Development*. Yellow Springs, Ohio: Antioch College, 1940.

Spiesman, Mildred, *Creative Dance in American Life and Education*, Ed.D. final document. New York: Teachers College, Columbia University, 1949.

Stratemeyer, Florence B., Hamlen Forkner, and Margaret McKim, *Developing a Curriculum for Modern Living*. New York: Bureau of Publications, Teachers College, Columbia University, 1947.

Struck, Ferdinand, *Creative Teaching: Industrial Arts and Vocational Education*. New York: J. Wiley and Son, 1938.

Stuart, H. C., *et al.*, "The Center, the Group Under Observation, Sources of Information, and Studies in Progress" (Harvard University, The Center for Research in Child Health and Development, School of Public Health). *Society for Research in Child Development Monographs*, Vol. 4, No. 1, 1929.

Thorpe, L. P., *Child Psychology and Development*. New York: Ronald Press, 1946.

Thrasher, F. M., *The Gang*. Chicago: University of Chicago Press, 1936.

Thyng, Franc, "They All Like to Read," *Association for Arts in Childhood*, 1943, pp. 28-31.

Trow, William C., "Conflicting Codes of Morality in the Life of the Child," *Childhood Education*, Feb. 1, 1942, pp. 256-263.

Van Hagen, W., G. Dexter, and J. F. Williams, *Physical Education in the Elementary Schools*. California State Department of Education, 1951.

Veatch, Jeannette, "An Experimental Study of the Relation of a Program of Specific Creative Activities to Group Acceptance, Emotional Needs and Academic Achievement," Ph.D. final document, New York University, 1953.

Waterman, Elizabeth, *The Rhythm Books*. New York: A. S. Barnes, 1936.

Whitley, Mary, "Children's Interests in Collecting," *Journal of Educational Psychology*, April 1929, pp. 26-28.

Winslow, L. I., *The Integrated School Art Program*. New York: McGraw-Hill Book Company, 1949.

Witty, Paul, "Encouraging Growth and Development Through Language Arts," *Arts in Childhood*, Series VI, Bulletin 3, October, 1951, pp. 14-18.

———, and Harvey Lehman, "Further Studies of Children's Interest in Collecting," *The Journal of Educational Psychology*, February, 1930, pp. 112-127.

———, *Reading in Modern Education*. Boston: D. C. Heath & Co., 1949.

Young, T. Campbell, *The Making of Musical Instruments*. London: Oxford University Press, 1939.

Zachary, Caroline, "Understanding the Child During Latency Period," *Educational Methods*, 1938, pp. 162-165.

———, and Lighty M., *Emotion and Conduct in Adolescence*. New York: Appleton-Century-Crofts, Inc., 1940.